T o every thing there is a season,
and a time to every purpose under the heaven . . .
a time to break down, and a time to build up . . .
a time to cast away stones, and a time to gather
stones together . . . a time to keep silence, and . . .

a time to speak

Ecclesiastes 3:1–7

a time to

Herbert C. Kelman

HARVARD UNIVERSITY

speak: ON HUMAN VALUES AND SOCIAL RESEARCH

Jossey-Bass Inc., Publishers
615 Montgomery Street • San Francisco • 1968

THE JOSSEY-BASS BEHAVIORAL SCIENCE SERIES

General Editors

WILLIAM E. HENRY, *University of Chicago*
NEVITT SANFORD, *Stanford University and Wright Institute, Berkeley*

To my parents,
who taught me to reflect on values
and to value reflection

Preface

I was fortunate, in the course of my professional training and my early career, to be exposed to men who combined a commitment to high scientific standards with a concern for social issues and the problems of the "real world." They both encouraged my own gropings in these directions and served as ideal role models for me. I cannot list all the names that come to mind, but there are five men in particular whose influence I value and want to acknowledge.

During my undergraduate days at Brooklyn College, Daniel Katz introduced me to the potential of a social psychology that both uses rigorous methods and addresses itself to significant societal problems. His advanced course in social psychology—which was unique in combining training in the techniques of survey research with such readings as Floyd Allport's *Institutional Behavior* and Franz Oppenheimer's *The State*—was one of the major influences on my decision to enter that field. Throughout the years, he continued to be an ever-reliable source of support and inspiration. Many years later, when I came to the University of Michigan in 1962, I was able not only to deepen my friendship with him, but also to initiate a collaborative research program on national roles and political ideology which I hope will continue for some time to come. I have been amazed at how much

I have learned from this collaboration about a truly relevant social-psychological analysis of societal processes.

My major professor in the course of my graduate training at Yale University was the late Carl Hovland. Though he was by no means indifferent to social issues (I remember very vividly, for example, his great pleasure in turning down a visiting professorship at the University of California because of the California Regents' violation of academic freedom in the loyalty oath controversy), he was not especially identified with a "social issues" orientation to social psychology. He did, however, have the habit of defining his research problems in terms of practical, "real world" concerns and he demonstrated that, at the hands of a master, such problems can be subjected to the most elegant and sophisticated conceptual and experimental analysis. He also was a man who treated the individual orientations of his students and colleagues with profound respect. Thus, while exposing me to his high standards, he encouraged me to develop my own thinking in directions suited to my personal style and preoccupations.

In my post-doctoral experiences, I continued to find support and role models for my concern with the interplay between value questions and social research. In 1951 I came to the Johns Hopkins University to work with Jerome Frank on his psychotherapy research project. Both in his clinical, theoretical, and experimental work on psychotherapy and, more recently, in his untiring efforts on behalf of international sanity, he has combined a dedication to human values with the rational, empirically-based analysis of the social scientist. In 1955 I came to the Laboratory of Psychology at the National Institute of Mental Health, then under the direction of David Shakow. Himself an active researcher and scholar who has constantly concerned himself with the professional, philosophical, and social issues that surround the discipline of psychology, he warmly supported my own efforts in similar directions. Between 1957 and 1962, as a member of the Harvard Department of Social Relations, I greatly valued my personal contacts with its elder statesman in social psychology, the late Gordon Allport. His life-long efforts to provide a scientific basis to the study of racial prejudice, religious values, and international understanding, and to develop a psychology that accounts for the mature and creative aspects of human personality, have served to encourage and inspire me in my work.

This volume was written entirely during my tenure at the University of Michigan. I want to take this occasion, therefore, to express my profound appreciation to my colleagues and students in the Department of Psychology, the Doctoral Program in Social Psychology, and the Center for Research on Conflict Resolution, for providing an environment that has always been both intellectually challenging and personally supportive. I found the atmosphere at Michigan—the richness and diversity of research activities and approaches, my colleagues' respect for and openness to different points of view, and my students' intellectual competence and social concern—maximally conducive to my own thinking and development. Beyond my specific professional involvements, I have greatly valued my participation in the teach-in movement at the University of Michigan and in various other expressions of a social activism that has been both thoughtful and passionate.

A major part of the editorial work and some of the writing on this volume were done during the spring and summer of 1967, while I was a Fellow at the Center for Advanced Study in the Behavioral Sciences. As one of the first group of Fellows at the Center in 1954–55, I felt especially privileged to be able to return for another half-year's stay. I am very grateful to Ralph Tyler, Preston Cutler, Jane Kielsmeier, and the other members of the Center staff for providing the perfect setting and facilities for thinking and writing. Julie Raventos did an excellent job in typing the bulk of my manuscript. Several of my colleagues at the Center, particularly Maurice Meisner and Hilde Himmelweit, read a number of the chapters and I greatly appreciate their helpful and constructive comments.

For many years, the National Institute of Mental Health has generously supported my research in a variety of ways, particularly through a series of grants for a research program on social influence and behavior change. The present volume cannot be viewed as a direct product of this research program, since it is concerned with some broader implications and applications of social research and not with a presentation of theoretical and empirical work per se. Nevertheless, at least parts of the volume are specifically linked to NIMH-supported activities: Chapter One raises ethical questions that grow directly out of the substantive problems to which my research on social influence has addressed itself; Chapter Eight raises ethical and methodological questions about the experimental procedures that have been used in my research; Chapter Three presents some of the thinking that instigated the International Conference on Social-Psychological Research in Developing Countries held at the University of Ibadan in December 1966 to January 1967, with major financial support from NIMH; and Chapter Six is based on a paper written while I was on the NIMH staff. More generally, I am indebted to NIMH for the freedom it has given me to pursue a broad research program under conditions that have allowed me to reflect on its long-range meanings and its potential uses.

Finally, I thank my secretary, Elizabeth Musgrave, for the faithful way in which she has carried out the numerous chores connected with the preparation of the manuscript; my friend, Thomas Pettigrew, for his especially detailed and helpful comments on the original draft of Chapter Nine; and my wife, Rose, who has read and commented on all of the chapters in this book and then read them again and again through the various stages of proofreading, and who has borne with me during the often painful and hectic process of developing my ideas and writing them down.

I have dedicated this book to my parents. Unfortunately, my father died last April, without seeing the book and its dedication in print. I have always seen my own thinking and writing as a continuation, under more favorable circumstances, of my father's concerns. Perhaps the greatest tribute I can pay my father is in the extent to which, in a volume devoted to a call for change, I stress the importance of continuity—in human values, in social institutions, and in scientific endeavors.

HERBERT C. KELMAN

Ann Arbor, Michigan
September 1968

Contents

a time to speak

Prologue

Questions about the value implications of social research are being raised with increasing frequency and urgency, both within the profession and outside. These questions cover a wide range of issues. They concern the ethical problems in the use of human subjects for research, and the social consequences of producing knowledge about the control of human behavior; the potential contributions of social research to social action and social change, and the ambiguities inherent in the involvement of the social scientist in the policy process; the models of man and the definitions of the scientist's task with which the social researcher works, and the problems of scientific objectivity as they arise in the study of man and society. This book is an attempt by one social psychologist to speak on some of these questions.

1

Six of the eleven essays in this book are based entirely on earlier papers, prepared for different occasions. The remaining five were prepared specifically for the book, but they draw in part on various pieces written for earlier occasions. Moreover, most of the earlier papers that entered into all eleven essays were originally prepared for oral presentation. Thus, each of them represented my conviction that it was, literally, a time to speak on some specific issue at the intersection between human values and social research. In bringing these essays together in this book, I am expressing the further conviction that now, with the increased sensitivity to the value implications of social research both within and outside of the profession, it is a time to speak on these various issues in a broader context and to a wider audience.

Though the chapters of this book are based on papers prepared for different occasions and over a number of years, there is considerable unity and continuity as they appear here. All but two of the chapters were written, in their original or final form, during the past three years and in direct relationship to one another. The remaining two were written in 1963 and 1964, respectively. Furthermore, I have prepared introductory and interstitial comments in order to point up the relationships between the different chapters and to weld them into an integrated product.

The book is divided into three parts, each focusing on a different role in which the social scientist often finds himself. Part One is primarily concerned with the social scientist as a producer of social forces—as someone who, via his research and scientific work, contributes to a reshaping of the social order. Part Two is primarily concerned with the social scientist as experimenter and social thinker—with his relationships, in the course of his regular professional activities, to his subject matter and to other people (particularly subjects and students). Part Three dwells on the social scientist as a participant in social action—a role defined in nonprofessional terms, but to which his standing and knowledge as a social scientist have obvious relevance.

Cutting across these three roles, there are three value domains to which the book addresses itself: values that refer to human relationships, those referring to societal processes, and those referring to the scientific study of man. Within the first domain of values, I am concerned with the ethical implications of the standard procedures used in social research for the investigator's relationship to his subjects or clients—whether they be individuals, organizations, or societies; and with the relationship the social scientist establishes with colleagues and students in his professional work, and with allies and adversaries in social action. Within the domain of values that refer to societal processes, I am concerned, on the one hand, with the possible uses of social research for the spread of manipulation and dehumanizing forces in society and for the blocking of social change; and, on the other hand, with the potential contributions of social research to the questioning of basic assumptions, to critical thinking about social institutions, and to the promotion of constructive social change and of humanizing forces. Finally, within the domain of values that refer to the scientific study of man, I am concerned with the appropriateness of the social scientist's observational techniques, of his assumptions about scientific methodology, and of his models of man to the nature of the task before him.

How one approaches these different value issues and, indeed, whether one raises them at all, depends to a considerable degree on his view of scientific objectivity in social science. Those who assume, for example, that—while it may be more difficult for the social scientist to achieve scientific objectivity than for the natural scientist—it is possible for him to do so, as long as he has the proper attitudes, uses the proper methods, and collects the proper data, are likely to react to such value questions with impatience and suspicion. They may feel that ethical questions about the social scientist's relationship to the individuals and groups he studies are irrelevant, since these are not personal relationships but the external relationships of an investigator to his subject matter. Moreover, they may even regard such questions as illegitimate, as reflecting an attitude that is dangerous from a scientific point of view. With regard to societal values, they may feel that the potentially negative consequences of social research are not the scientist's business, since the knowledge he produces is neutral and the decision about the uses to which this knowledge is put are out of his hands. Research that is deliberately oriented to social change may have some uses as applied research, in their view, but is by definition unobjective because it allows the intrusion of non-scientific considerations. Within the domain of values relating to the scientific study of man, they are very much concerned with data quality and the improvement of research methods, but they are likely to be suspicious of attempts to redefine the investigator-subject relationship, of the use of qualitative methods, and of an excessive reliance on reflection. Moreover, they are likely to prefer a mechanistic model of man since such a model lends itself more readily to the application of scientific method.

My own approach to the value questions I have mentioned starts with the assumption that, to achieve scientific objectivity in social research, it is neither necessary nor sufficient to avoid value-laden problems, to treat the subjects of research in a completely impersonal way, to rely entirely on experimental and quantitative techniques, and to adopt simple mechanistic models. Social research, in my view, must be based on the recognition that neither the social researcher as a person, nor the process of social research can be entirely value-free; that the observations of the social scientist cannot be carried out from a wholly external vantage-point; and that the findings of social research cannot stand by themselves as scientifically validated facts about nature. A total separation of the role of scientist from the role of valuing man, of the definition of the research problem from the investigator's value preferences, of the investigator from his human subjects and subject matter, and of research findings from ideas about these findings and about the world into which they fit cannot be achieved and, what is more, the effort to achieve such separation leads to an impoverished social science. What is necessary, however, for the enhancement of scientific objectivity, is that the investigator deliberately take his values, attitudes, and expectations into account and systematically analyze their effects on the definition of the research problem, the observations obtained, and the interpretations placed on these observations. We can never eliminate the effects of values and subjective factors, but we must push against the limits to scientific objectivity that inevitably govern our efforts. In my view, the tension between the investigator's values and a recalcitrant reality world, and the constant—though never wholly successful—effort to disentangle the two, are central and constructive features of the scientific study of man.

This view of scientific objectivity has several implications for the task of the social researcher:

(1) Since the role of scientist cannot be totally separated from that of human being, of citizen, and of participant in social action, I see no objection to the broadening of the social scientist's repertoire and to his enactment of a variety of roles. As I point out in Chapter Seven, a social scientist who engages in action research, applied research, or social engineering is making as valid a use of his scientific training as one engaged in "pure" research. It is essential, however, that the social scientist be perfectly clear, both to himself and to others, about the context in which he is operating and the role he is taking at any given time, and that he make a deliberate effort to assess the effect that his personal involvement has on his observations and conclusions.

(2) Since the purposes of the research and the definition of the research problem cannot be totally separated from the investigator's value preferences, I see no reason to avoid value-laden research. There is no way of assuring objectivity by the type of problem or method we select and there is no reason, therefore, to consider any problem scientifically taboo. Those who make a sharp distinction between proper and improper research in terms of the nature of the problem and method are usually unaware of the possibility that their own research may be far from value-free. One can easily fail to notice the role of value preferences when he works within the frame of reference of the status quo, since its value assumptions are so much second nature to members of the society that they perceive them as part of objective reality. Similarly, one may miss the intrusion of value preferences when he uses experimental or quantitative methods, which give an often deceptive appearance of objectivity. Thus, the issue is not how we can keep out intrusive values by virtue of the problems we study and the methods we use, but how we can take systematic account of the values and subjective considerations that inevitably enter into our research. (In Chapter Three I propose a series of steps that can contribute to this essential process.) As long as we are actively aware of the possible effects of our values, there are many advantages to research that is avowedly based on value preferences. Because of his involvement in the problem, the investi-

gator may be able to bring to the research a level of motivation and a depth of insight that are conducive to an especially creative effort.

(3) Since the investigator cannot be totally separated from his human subjects and subject matter, I see a need for new approaches to social research that include the relationship of the investigator to the individuals and societies he is studying as a salient dimension. We have to reassess the methodological assumption that a completely impersonal relationship can be achieved in social research and explore new methodologies that call for different patterns of relationship. In Chapter Eight, for example, I discuss as one possible model a more participatory type of relationship, which attempts, not to bypass the motivations the subject brings to the research situation, but to mobilize them in support of the research enterprise. I do consider it important to maintain the separation of the investigator from his subject matter; this is, after all, one of the major differences between social science and other ways of studying man. Efforts at such separation, however, must be based on a realistic conception of the degree of "outsideness" that a social researcher is able to achieve.

(4) Since research findings cannot be totally separated from ideas about these findings, I regard empirical investigations primarily as sources of new inputs into our thinking about social behavior, rather than as verifications of the laws of such behavior. The scientific study of man is, indeed, concerned with developing general propositions, but I do not feel that our experiments and observations can in any sense "establish" these propositions as proven. The gap between the observations we are able to make and the reality to which we wish to generalize is too great for that. As I point out, especially in Chapter Six, I see the basic task of the social researcher as systematic thinking about social behavior, fed and tempered by empirical evidence. Empirical research, in this view, is thus essentially an aid to thinking—albeit one that is especially and uniquely valuable and that constitutes one of the central contributions of a scientific approach to the study of man.

This book is addressed both to professional social scientists and to readers with other backgrounds who are concerned with the status of human values and the role of social science in modern society. To my fellow social scientists I have tried to convey the importance of examining, within the profession, the value implications of social research—of its products, its processes, and its place in society. To those outside the profession I have tried to present a balanced view of both the dangers and potentialities of social research and, in doing so, to illustrate the way in which at least one social scientist sees the world and the place of his discipline within it. My perspective throughout is that of an active, committed social scientist who speaks from within the profession, who believes in the potential of social research as a significant source of insights about man and society and of contributions to human welfare, and who is concerned with maintaining an atmosphere conducive to the free conduct of such research. At the same time, however, I try to challenge some of the assumptions that occasionally surround the scientific study of man and to push for a broad conception of scientific work in the social sciences. I regard the scientific approach as a uniquely valuable way of studying man, but by no means the only way; and as an intellectual tool rather than an ideology and a basic source of values. Thus, I consider it essential to view social science within the context of humanistic values and societal needs.

PART **I**

꣠꣠꣠꣠꣠꣠꣠꣠꣠꣠꣠꣠꣠꣠꣠꣠꣠꣠꣠꣠꣠꣠꣠꣠꣠꣠꣠

*S*ocial research, at least in some of its manifestations, has become an increasingly important factor in our social and political life. The contributions of opinion polling to election politics, of sensitivity training to industrial management, and of achievement testing to educational policy are among the more obvious examples of procedures and products of social research that play major roles in our societal processes. As social research becomes more extensive, more sophisticated, and more widely accepted, its potential inputs into social policy and practice are likely to expand considerably.

The social scientist is, therefore, confronted ever more sharply with the question of what kind of social force his research represents. What is the nature of the social processes that it is

THE SOCIAL SCIENTIST AS PRODUCER OF SOCIAL FORCES

helping to foster, the quality of the social values that it is helping to promote? The *procedures* of social research—the approaches that we take to the study of man—have important value implications in themselves. Insofar as they reflect certain assumptions about the nature of man, and represent certain patterns of human relationship, they contribute to social forces favorable to some values and inimical to others. Of perhaps even greater importance are the value implications of the *products* of social research—of the nature of the knowledge that our studies produce. On the one hand, there is the danger that the findings of social research may be used for the suppression of human freedom and the dehumanization of social life. On the other hand, there is the potential that social science knowledge may contribute to the advancement of human welfare, the rationality of social decisions, and the achievement of constructive social change.

In the first set of chapters, value questions relating to the procedures and approaches of social research are raised at times, but these questions are more central to Part Two of the volume. Part One is primarily concerned with the products of social research and their value implications. The four essays included in this section address themselves, in one way or another, to the necessity and possibility of mitigating the "negative" consequences and enhancing the "positive" consequences of the knowledge we produce—where "positive" and "negative" are defined in terms of an essentially humanistic value framework. They examine the implications of social research for such values as freedom of choice, social participation, and the universality of human welfare. They are based on the further assumption that the methods and approaches of social science—despite some of their dangers—are significant sources of new insights about man and society, which can contribute to improving the conditions of human life the world over. These four essays were written for separate occasions, but represent a sequence. Each attempts to build on the preceding one and to develop a continuing argument.

CHAPTER 1

INTRODUCTION

The first chapter takes up what I regard as one of the negative consequences of social research: the danger that the products of such research will be used for more extensive and more pervasive manipulation of human behavior. This problem has disturbed me ever since I became interested in social psychology. The study of personal and social change was always a major focus of my interest, but along with enthusiasm for this line of research came concern about the social uses to which its findings are likely to be put.

One of my earliest exposures to social-psychological research, while I was in college, was a lecture by Kurt Lewin on his group decision studies. I was immediately attracted to these studies, but at the same time distressed by their manipulative im-

11

plications. During my graduate training, this concern was aroused again and again: in 1948, when I spent the summer at the National Training Laboratory for Group Development; in 1949, when I spent the summer at the Survey Research Center, University of Michigan, working on a study of human relations in industry; and throughout my graduate studies at Yale, in connection with my work on Carl Hovland's attitude change project. In fact, I first presented the ideas contained in the essay that follows early in 1951, when Arthur Gladstone and I spoke at a Yale Psychology Colloquium on the social implications of psychological research.

Subsequent experiences reinforced my concern with the problem. Among these was my participation in research on psychotherapy and my continuing experimental work on social influence and attitude change. Over the years, I have raised the problem in my graduate classes and on a number of other public occasions. The essay in its present form was prepared for a symposium on "Social responsibilities of the psychologist," held at the meetings of the American Psychological Association in Philadelphia, on August 30,1963. The paper was published in The Journal of Social Issues, *1965, 21 (2), 31–46, and is reprinted here with the permission of the editor.*

The term "manipulation," used in the title and throughout the paper, is often a source of controversy. It implies, and is intended to imply, that there is something questionable about the actions to which it refers. And yet I include in its purview attempts at influence that most of us would regard as necessary and even socially desirable. It might be wiser, perhaps, to use a more neutral term, but I feel that this modest degree of provocativeness helps to underline a general point that several of the essays in this volume attempt to make: The fact that a piece of social research may contribute to scientific knowledge—and even to human welfare—does not make it unambiguously good, as some social scientists would like to believe. Conversely, the fact that a piece of social research may, in its purpose, method, or style, treat man as an object, shorn of his individuality, does not automatically damn it, as some humanists are prone to assume.

Manipulation of Human Behavior: An Ethical Dilemma

The social scientist today—and particularly the practitioner and investigator of behavior change—finds himself in a situation that has many parallels to that of the nuclear physicist. The knowledge about the control and manipulation of human behavior that he is producing or applying is beset with enormous ethical ambiguities, and he must accept responsibility for its social consequences. Even the pure researcher cannot withdraw into the comforting assurance that knowledge is ethically neutral. While this is true as far as it goes, he must concern himself with the question of how this knowledge is *likely* to be used, given the particular historical context of the society in which it is produced. Nor can the practitioner find ultimate comfort in the assurance that he is helping others and doing good. For, not only is the goodness of doing good in itself a matter of ethical ambiguity—a point to which I shall return shortly—but he also confronts the question of the wider social context in which a given action is taken. The production of change may meet the momentary needs of the client—whether it be an individual, an organization, or a community—yet its long-range consequences and its effects on other units of the system of which this client is a part may be less clearly constructive.

There are several reasons why the ethical problems surrounding the study of behavior change are of increasing concern. First, our knowledge about the control of human behavior is increasing steadily and systematically. Relevant information is being developed in various areas within psychology—clinical, social, and experimental—as well as in sociology and anthropology. There is reason to question whether the dangers from that direction are imminent. I have the feeling that the power and sensitivity of scientifically based techniques for controlling and shaping complex human behaviors are often exaggerated. Nevertheless, we are constantly working toward a systematization of this knowledge and we must at least anticipate the day when it will have developed to a point where the conditions necessary for producing a particular change in behavior can be specified with relative precision. Second, there is an increasing readiness and eagerness within our society to use whatever systematic information (or misinformation) about the control of human behavior can be made available. This readiness can be found in different quarters and in response to different motivations. It can be found among therapists and pedagogues, among idealists and agitators, among hucksters and image-makers. Third, social scientists are becoming increasingly respectable, and many agencies within government, industry, the military, and the fields of public health and social welfare are becoming interested in our potential contributions. Here too there is no imminent danger. We still have a long way to go before becoming truly influential and we may find the road rather bumpy. Nevertheless, we must anticipate the possibility that social scientists will meet with a serious interest in their ideas about behavior control and have an opportunity to put them to the test on a large scale.

For all of these reasons, concern about the implications of our knowledge of behavior control is less and less a matter of hypothetical philosophical speculation. The possibilities are quite real that this knowledge will be used to control human behavior—with varying degrees of legitimacy, effectiveness, and scope. Moreover, this knowledge is being produced in a socio-historical context in which its use on a large scale, for the control of vast populations, is particularly likely. Ours is an age of mass societies, in which the requirements of urbanization and industrialization, together with the availability of powerful media of communication, provide all the necessary conditions for extensive manipulation and control of the behavior of masses. An interest in controlling the behavior of its population is, of course, a characteristic of every society and by no means unique to our age. What *is* unique is that this is done on a mass scale, in a systematic way, and under the aegis of specialized institutions deliberately assigned to this task. Like the nuclear physicist, then, the social scientist is responsible for knowledge that, in the light of the world situation in which it is being produced, has decided explosive possibilities. It behooves us, therefore, to be concerned with the nature of the product that we are creating and the social process to which we are contributing.

≥ *THE SOCIAL SCIENTIST'S DILEMMA* ≤

In their attempts to come to grips with this problem, it seems to me, the practitioner and investigator of behavior change are confronted with a basic dilemma. On the one hand, for those of us who hold the enhancement of man's freedom of choice to be a fundamental value, any manipulation of the behavior of others constitutes a violation of their essential humanity. This would be true regradless of the form the manipulation takes— whether, for example, it be based on threat of punishment or positive reinforcement. Moreover, it would be true regardless of the "goodness" of the cause that this manipulation is designed to serve. Thus, an ethical problem arises not simply from the ends for which behavior control is being used (although this, too, is a major problem in its own right), but from the very fact that we are using it. On the other hand, effective behavior change inevitably involves some degree of manipulation and control, and at least an implicit imposition of the change agent's values on the client or the person he is influencing. There are many situations in which all of us—depending on our particular values—would consider behavior change desirable: for example, childhood socialization, education, psychotherapy, racial integration, and so on. The two horns of the dilemma, then, are represented by the view that any manipulation of human behavior inherently violates a fundamental value, but that there exists no formula for so structuring an effective change situation that such manipulation is totally absent.

In calling attention to the inevitability of behavior control whenever influence is being exerted, I am not suggesting that we should avoid influence under all circumstances. This is not only impossible if there is to be any social life, but it is also undesirable from the point of view of many important social values. Nor am I suggesting that we need not worry about the manipulation inherent in all influence attempts, simply because it is inevitable. The view that we can forget about this problem, because there is nothing we can do about it anyway, ignores the fact that there are important differences in degree and kind of manipulation and that there are ways of mitigating the manipulative effect of various influence attempts even if the effect cannot be eliminated entirely.

This leads me to another very crucial qualification with respect to the first horn of the dilemma that I have presented. In stating that all manipulation of behavior, regardless of its form or of the purpose it is designed to serve, is a violation of the person's essential humanity, I am not suggesting that differences between different types of manipulation are ethically insignificant. The extent to which the influence attempt, despite its manipulative component, allows for or even enhances the person's freedom of choice, the extent to which the relationship between influencer and influencee is reciprocal, the extent to which the situation is oriented toward the welfare of the influencee rather than the welfare of the influencing agent—all of these are matters of great moment from an ethical point of view. In fact, these differences are the major concern of the present analysis. But I consider it essential, as a prophylactic measure, to keep in mind that even under the most favorable conditions manipulation of the behavior of others is an ethically ambiguous act.

It is this first horn of the dilemma that Skinner seems to ignore, as can be seen from his debate with Rogers, several years ago, on issues concerning the control of human behavior (Rogers and Skinner, 1956). Rogers, on the other hand, tends to minimize the second horn of the dilemma.

Skinner is well aware of the inevitability of control in human affairs, and argues for a type of control that is based on intelligent planning and positive reinforcement and is not "exercised for the selfish purposes of the controller" (p. 1057). He makes a number of telling points in responding to his critics. For example, he reminds us that, while we object to external controls, we often ignore psychological constraints that limit freedom of choice to the same or an even greater extent. He asks why a state of affairs that would otherwise seem admirable becomes objectionable simply because someone planned it that way. He points out that control based on the threat and exercise of punishment, which is built into our political and legal institutions, is fully accepted, but that use of positive reinforcement by government is regarded with suspicion. I find these and other points useful because they help us to focus on forms of control that often remain unrecognized and to consider forms of control that may be ethically superior to current ones but that we tend to reject because of their unorthodox nature. But Skinner fails to see the basis of many of the criticisms directed at him, because he is concerned about the control of human behavior only when that control is aversive, and when it is misused, that is, when it is used for the benefit of the controller and to the detriment of the controllee. He seems unable to see any problem in the mere *use* of control, regardless of technique or purpose. This inability is consistent with his value position, which does not recognize the exercise of choice as a good per se.[1]

My own statement of the first horn of the dilemma is predicated on the assumption that the freedom and opportunity to choose is a fundamental value. To be fully human means to choose. Complete freedom of choice is, of course, a meaningless concept. But the purpose of education and of the arrangement of the social order, as I see it, is to enable men to live in society while at the same time enhancing their freedom to choose and widening their areas of choice. I therefore regard as ethically ambiguous any action that limits freedom of choice, whether it be through punishment or reward or even through so perfect an arrangement of society that people do not care to choose. I cannot defend this value because it is not logically derived from anything else. I can, of course, offer supporting arguments for it. First, I can try to show that the desire to choose represents a universal human need, which manifests itself under different historical circumstances (not only under conditions of oppression). Second, I can point out that freedom of choice is an inescapable component of other valued states, such as love, creativity, mastery over the

---

[1] This in turn is related to a point stressed by Rogers, namely Skinner's underestimation of the role of value choices in human affairs in general and in the application of science to social problems in particular.

environment, or maximization of one's capacities. Third, I can try to argue that valuing free individual choice is a vital protection against tyranny: Quite aside from the notion that power corrupts its user, even the well-motivated, unselfish controlling agent will be tempted to ignore human variability and to do what *he* thinks is good for others rather than what they think is good for themselves—and thus in essence become tyrannical—if he is unhampered by the right to choose as a basic human value. While I can offer these supporting arguments, I recognize that freedom of choice is, in the final analysis, a rock-bottom value for me. Skinner is not concerned with the dilemma presented here because apparently he does not share this fundamental value, even though he is strongly committed to certain other related values, such as the rejection of aversive control and selfish exploitation (albeit without recognizing their status as values).

With Rogers on the other hand, I feel a complete affinity at the value level. He values "man as a self-actualizing process of becoming" and in general proposes that "we select a set of values that focuses on fluid elements of process rather than static attributes" (p. 1063). He favors a society "where individuals carry responsibility for personal decisions" (p. 1064). He regards "responsible personal choice" as "the most essential element in being a person" (p. 1064). But, as I have pointed out, Rogers tends to minimize the second horn of the dilemma presented here: the inevitability of some degree of manipulation in any influence attempt. He makes what appears to me the unrealistic assumption that by choosing the proper goals and the proper techniques in an influence situation one can completely sidestep the problem of manipulation and control. He seems to argue that, when an influencing agent is dedicated to the value of man as a self-actualizing process and selects techniques that are designed to promote this value, he can abrogate his power over the influencee and maintain a relationship untainted by behavior control. This ignores, in my opinion, the dynamics of the influence situation itself. I fully agree that influence attempts designed to enhance the client's freedom of choice and techniques that are consistent with this goal are ethically superior, and that we should continue to push and explore in this direction. But we must remain aware that the nature of the relationship between influencing agent and influencee is such that inevitably, even in these influence situations, a certain degree of control will be exercised. The assumption that we can set up an influence situation in which the problem of manipulation of behavior is removed, because of the stated purpose and formal structure of the situation, is a dangerous one. It makes us blind to the continuities between all types of influence situations and to the subtle ways in which others can be manipulated. It lulls us into the reassuring certainty that what we are doing is, by definition, good. I would regard it as more in keeping with both the realities of behavior change, and the ethical requirements of minimizing manipulation, to accept the inevitability of a certain amount of control as part of our dilemma and to find a *modus vivendi* in the face of the ethical ambiguities thus created.

⤳ MANIPULATIVE USES OF KNOWLEDGE ⤶

Let me proceed to examine briefly the implications of this general dilemma for each of three roles involving social science knowledge about behavior change: the practitioner, as exemplified by the psychotherapist and the group leader or group process trainer; the applied researcher, such as the social scientist in industry or the public opinion pollster; and the basic researcher, such as the investigator of attitude change. These roles are, of course, highly overlapping, but separating them may help us focus on different nuances of the general dilemma.

The practitioner. The practitioner must remain alert to the possibility that he is imposing his own values on the client; that in the course of helping the client he is actually shaping his behavior in directions that he, the practitioner, has set for him. Thus, psychotherapy, even though it is devoted to what I would consider a highly valuable end—enabling the patient to live more comfortably and achieve his own goals more effectively—is definitely open to the possibility of manipulation. Psychotherapy (at least "good" psychotherapy) is markedly different from brainwashing: the client enters into the relationship voluntarily; the therapist is concerned with helping the patient, rather than with furthering his own ends or the ends of some institution that he represents; influence techniques are designed to free the patient, to enhance his ability to make choices, rather than to narrow his scope. Yet there are some striking similarities between the methods of therapy and those of brainwashing to which the therapist must always remain alert, lest he overstep what is sometimes a rather thin line. The therapist cannot avoid introducing his own values into the therapeutic process. He cannot be helpful to the patient unless he deliberately tries to influence him in the direction of abandoning some behaviors and trying out others. But in doing so he must beware of two types of dangers. One is the failure to recognize that he is engaged in the control of the client's behavior. The other is intoxication with the goodness of what he is doing for and to the client, which in turn leads to a failure to recognize the ambiguity of the control that he exercises. Only if he recognizes these two conditions is he able to take steps to counteract them.

Similar considerations hold for the group leader. Some of the principles of group leadership developed by social psychologists and variously called applied group dynamics, human relations skills, or group process sensitivity are highly congenial to democratic values. They are designed to involve the group in the decision-making process and to foster self-expression on the part of the individual member. Yet the possibilities for manipulation abound. A skillful group leader may be able not only to manipulate the group into making the decision that he desires, but also to create the feeling that this decision reflects the will of the group discovered through the workings of the democratic process. This need not involve a deliberate Machiavellian deception on the part of the group leader; the leader himself may share the illusion that a group product has emerged over which he has exercised no influence. It is essential, therefore, to be fully aware of the leader's control implicit in these techniques. Some of their proponents argue that, by their very nature, these techniques can be used only for democratic ends. I would question this assumption and, in fact, consider it dangerous because it exempts the group leader from asking those questions that any practitioner of behavior change should keep before his eyes: What am I doing in my relationship to the client? Am I creating a situation in which he can make choices in line with his own values, or am I structuring the situation so that my values dominate?

When the group leader is involved in training others in human relations skills or sensitivity to group process, he is confronted with a further problem. Typically, the trainee is a member of some organization—industrial, governmental, military, educational, religious—in which he will apply the skills he is now learning. The human relations trainer is, thus, in a sense improving the trainee's ability to manipulate others in the service of the organization that he represents. Of course, this is not the goal of the training effort, and trainers always try to communicate the value of the democratic process in group life. But the fact remains that they are training a wide variety of people who will be using these skills for a wide variety of ends. It can certainly be argued that the widespread introduction of human relations skills is likely to have more positive than negative effects from the point of view of a democratic ideology. Perhaps this is true. But it is dangerous to assume that these skills carry their own built-in protection. There is no substitute for a continued attention, on the trainer's part, to questions such as these: Whom am I training? To what uses will they put the skills that I am placing at their disposal? What are the organizational processes in which I am now becoming a partner?

The applied researcher. It is essentially these same questions to which the applied social researcher in the broad field of behavior change must address himself. I am here thinking specifically of applied research in the sense that it is done for a client. While the researcher is merely gathering facts, he is nonetheless participating quite directly in the operations of the organization that employs him. If his work is successful, then his findings will be applied to the formulation and execution of the organization's policies. There is thus the real possibility that the investigator is directly helping the organization in its attempts to manipulate the behavior of others—workers in an industry, consumers, or the voting public.

Let us take, for example, the industrial social scientist who studies factors affecting worker morale. On the basis of his recommendations, and often with his direct assistance, management may become more aware of human relations aspects of industrial work and introduce methods designed to improve morale. Ideally, these methods would consist of increased involvement and participation of workers in decisions relating to their jobs. Critics of this type of approach argue that the social scientist is working for management, providing them with information and introducing procedures that are designed to increase productivity at the worker's expense. The assumption in this criticism, to which I think there is some validity, is that the worker is being manipulated so that he experiences a sense of participation and involvement which is not reflected in the reality of his position within the industrial organization. In response to this criticism it can be argued that, considering the over-all lack of satisfaction in industrial work, it is a net good to give the worker some sense of participation and involvement in the work situation, to give him at least a limited opportunity to make choices and thus find some meaning in the job. To be sure, management is interested in these innovations because they expect the changes to increase productivity, but does that necessarily vitiate the advantages from the worker's point of view? This is a rather convincing defense, but in evaluating the pros and cons we must also take into account the social context in which these changes are introduced. What effect does the human relations approach have on unions, which represent the only source of independent power of the industrial worker? Does it sidestep them, and will it eventually weaken them? What are the general implications of helping the worker adjust to a situation in which he has no real freedom of choice, in any ultimate sense? These questions are not easy to answer, and every social scientist has to decide for himself whether his work in industry is doing more good than harm. In deciding whether or not, and in what way, to do applied social research in industry or elsewhere, the social scientist must ask himself: Whom am I doing this work for? How are my findings likely to be used? Will they increase or decrease the freedom of choice of the people whose behavior will be influenced? What are the social processes, both short-run and long-run, in which I am participating through my research?

Another example of applied social research that raises questions about manipulation of the population is public opinion polling, when used in connection with political campaigns or the political process in general. For instance, in a recent presidential election, computer simulation was used—based on data derived from numerous opinion polls—to predict the responses of various segments of the population to different campaign issues. Information generated by this process was made available to one of the political parties. This type of social research has some troubling implications. It raises the possibility that a candidate might use this information to manipulate the voters by presenting a desirable image, that is, saying what the public presumably wants to hear. In defense against such criticisms, the originators of this technique have pointed out that it represents a systematic way of providing the candidate with relevant information about the interests and concerns of the public, or of particular publics. He can then address himself to those issues with which the public is deeply concerned, thus making his campaign more relevant and meaningful and enhancing the democratic political process. They point out further that this is what candidates try to do anyway—and properly so; all the social scientist does is to help them base their campaigns on more adequate information, rather than on the usually unreliable estimates of politicians. Of course, what assurance do we have that opinion polls and computer simulations based on them will, in fact, be used in this ideal manner to bolster the democratic process, rather than to short-circuit it? The information can be used both to widen and to restrict the citizen's freedom of choice. But, as long as it is information that can help political organizations to manipulate the public more effectively, the researcher must concern himself actively with the question of how it is going to be used and to what kind of process it is going to contribute.

The basic researcher. For the man engaged in "basic" research on one or another aspect of behavior change—in contrast to the man who does research for a specific client—it is much easier to take the position that the knowledge he produces is neutral. Yet, since there is a possibility that his product will be used by others for purposes of manipulation, he cannot be completely absolved from responsibility. He must consider the relative probabilities, given the existing socio-historical context, that this knowledge will be used to enhance or to restrict people's freedom of choice. These considerations must enter into his decision whether or not to carry out a given piece of research, and how to proceed with it.

Take, for example, the area of attitude change, with which I myself am strongly identified. Much of the research in this area is clearly dedicated to the discovery of general principles, which can presumably be applied to many situations with differing goals. Yet, because of the nature of the principles and the experimental settings from which they are derived, they can probably be applied most readily, most directly, and most systematically to mass communications. And, because of the nature of our social order, they are particularly likely to be used for purposes of advertising, public relations, and propaganda, forms of mass communication that are least oriented toward enhancing the listener's freedom of choice. There are, of course, many reasons for continuing this line of research, despite the probability that its findings will be used for manipulative purposes. First, one can argue that extending our general knowledge about processes of attitude change and increasing our understanding of the nature of influence are in themselves liberating forces whose value outweighs the possibility that this knowledge will be used for undesirable ends. Second, such research may not only increase the knowledge of the potential manipulator, but also help in finding ways to counteract manipulative forces, by providing the information needed for effective resistance to manipulation, or by developing knowledge about forms of influence that enhance freedom of choice. Third, one might argue that information about attitude change, despite its potential for manipulative uses, is important for the achievement of certain socially desirable goals, such as racial integration or international understanding.

I obviously find these arguments convincing enough to continue this line of research. But the nagging thought remains that the knowledge I am producing, if it has any scientific merit, may come to be used for ever more effective manipulation of human behavior. Thus, even the basic researcher in the domain of behavior change must always ask himself: Given the realites of our present society, what are the probable uses to which the products of my research are going to be put? What are the social processes to which I am contributing by the knowledge that I feed into them?

☙ MITIGATING THE MANIPULATIVE ASPECTS OF BEHAVIOR CHANGE ❧

The very fact that I have presented my position in the form of a dilemma should make it clear that I do not see an ultimate "solution," a way of completely avoiding the ethical ambiguity with which practitioners and researchers in the field of behavior change are confronted. I do feel, however, that there are ways of mitigating the dehumanizing effects of new developments in the field of behavior change. I would like to propose three steps designed to contribute to this end. Stated in their most general form, they would involve: (1) increasing our own and others' active awareness of the manipulative aspects of our work and the ethical ambiguities inherent therein; (2) deliberately building protection against manipulation or resistance to it into the processes we use or study; and (3) setting the enhancement of freedom of choice as a central positive goal for our practice and research. To spell out in somewhat greater detail what these three steps might imply, I would like to examine them from the point of view of each of the three separate (though overlapping) roles that have already been differentiated: the role of the practitioner, of the applied researcher, and of the "basic" researcher in the field of behavior change. The argument that follows is summarized in Table 1.

The practitioner. I have already stressed how essential it is for the practitioner of behavior change to be aware of the fact that he is controlling the client, that he is introducing his own values both in the definition of the situation and in the setting of standards. Thus, in the therapeutic situation, it is not only inevitable but also useful for the therapist to have certain values about what needs to be done in the situation itself and what are desirable directions in which the patient might move, and to communicate these values to the patient. But he must be clear in his own mind that he is bringing these values into the relationship, and he must label them properly for the patient. By recognizing himself that he is engaged in a certain degree of control—and that this is an ethically ambiguous act, even though his role as therapist requires it—and by making the patient aware of this fact, he provides some safeguards against this control. Among other things,

TABLE 1

Steps Designed to Mitigate the Manipulative Aspects of
Behavior Change in Each of Three Social Science Roles

Desirable Steps	Practitioner	Applied Researcher	Basic Researcher
(1) Increasing awareness of manipulation	Labeling own values to self and clients; allowing client to "talk back"	Evaluating organization that will use findings; considering how, on whom, and in what context they will be used	Predicting probabilities of different uses of research product, given existing socio-historical context
(2) Building protection against or resistance to manipulation into the process	Minimizing own values and maximizing client's values as dominant criteria for change	Helping target group to protect its interests and resist encroachments on its freedom	Studying processes of resistance to control, and communicating findings to the public
(3) Setting enhancement of freedom of choice as a positive goal	Using professional skills and relationship to increase client's range of choices and ability to choose	Promoting opportunities for increased choice on part of target group as integral features of the planned change	Studying conditions for enhancement of freedom of choice and maximization of individual values

such a recognition would allow the patient, to a limited extent, to "talk back" to the therapist, to argue about the appropriateness of the values that the therapist is introducing. A therapeutic situation is, of course, not a mutual influence situation in the true sense of the word. By definition, it is designed to examine only the patient's values and not those of the therapist. But, from the point of view of reducing the manipulativeness of the situation, it would be important to encourage mutuality at least to the extent of acknowledging that what the therapist introduces into the situation is not entirely based on objective reality, but on an alternative set of values which are open to question. There may be particular therapeutic relationships in which a therapist finds it difficult to acknowledge the values that he brings to them, because his own motivations have become too deeply involved. There may also be institutional settings in which the therapist is required to present the institutional values as the "right" ones, in contrast to the patient's own "wrong" values. These are danger signals, and the therapist may well consider refraining from entering a therapeutic relationship or working in an institutional setting in which he is not free to acknowledge the contribution of his own values.

Second, in addition to increasing awareness of the manipulative aspects of the situation, it is important to build into the change process itself procedures that will provide protection and resistance against manipulation. For the practitioner of behavior change this means structuring the influence situation in such a way that the client will be encouraged to explore his own values and to relate new learnings and new behavioral possibilities to his own value system. At the same time, it is important that the practitioner, be he therapist or group leader, keep to a minimum the direct and indirect constraints that he sets on the influencee. Constraints are, of course, necessary to varying degrees, both for the protection of clients and for keeping the process moving in useful directions. Insofar as possible, however, the situation should be so structured that the influencee determines the direction of the process to a maximal extent. It should be noted that what I am suggesting here is not the same as the use of nondirective techniques. In and of themselves these merely represent a set of formal techniques which may or may not have the desired effect. The crucial point is that the client's own values should be at the center of attention when change is under consideration and should be readily available as criteria against which any induced behavior can be measured. To the extent to which this is true, the patient or the group will be in a better position to resist manipulation in the service of alien values. Often, however, this will require much more than noninterference on the part of the practitioner. It may require active efforts on his part to encourage the client to bring his values to the fore and measure the induced changes against them.

Third, it is important to go beyond providing protection and resistance against manipulation that would encroach on the client's freedom of choice. The actual *enhancement* of freedom of choice should, ideally, be one of the positive goals of any influence attempt. Thus, the therapist should use his professional skills and his relationship to the patient to provide him with new experiences that enhance his ability to choose (and thus to maximize his own values) and with new information that widens his range of choices. Similarly, the group leader should attempt to bring the group to a point where members can make more effective and creative choices, conducive to the achievement of individual and group goals. The enhancement of freedom and creativity as the positive value toward which behavior change should be directed has been discussed most eloquently by Rogers (for example, Rogers and Skinner, 1956).

Needless to say, it would be essential to include in the training of practitioners of behavior change and in their professional standards some consideration of these three desiderata for mitigating the manipulative aspects of their activities. If they learn to acknowledge the role of their own values in the situation, to make active efforts at keeping the client's values in the foreground, and to regard increased freedom of choice as a primary goal, they are less likely to make full use, either unwittingly or by design, of the potential for manipulation that they possess.

The applied researcher. In deciding whether to take on a particular piece of research, the applied researcher must keep in mind that the information he is being asked to supply may be used for the manipulation of others, for example, workers in an industry for whom he is doing a morale survey or the voting public if he is working with poll data. The question of *who* is employing him becomes crucial, therefore. He must evaluate the organizations that will be using his findings, and consider how they are likely to use them, whose behavior they will attempt to influence, and in what context this influence will occur. He must consider the probable uses of these findings not only in the short run but also in the long run. Thus, for example, he cannot simply rely on the fact that his contact man in an organization is someone he trusts. If this man is in a peripheral position within the organization, and if the organization is generally undemocratic and exploitative in its orientation, then the long-run prospects are not too reassuring. There is, of course, the possibility that the research itself will have a liberalizing effect on the organization; the probability that this will, in fact, happen must also be estimated. In the final analysis, there can be no foolproof guarantees, but the investigator must at least feel reasonably certain that the net effect of his research will not be a reduction in the freedom of choice of a segment of the population. Each investigator has to draw his own line, with respect to both the probability and the amount of manipulation that he is willing to tolerate. If they are likely to go beyond this line, then he must consider turning down the assignment. Once a researcher has decided to take on an assignment, he must continue to keep the manipulative potential of his findings in mind, and try to counteract it by the way he communicates his findings and the recommendations he bases on them. If his research is, indeed, to have a liberalizing effect on the organization, then he will have to take active steps in this direction.

In order to build some protection against manipulation into the change procedures based on his findings, the researcher should make it a rule to communicate directly with the target group—the group that is to be influenced—and to involve it in the research, and in the change process insofar as he has charge of it. Thus, an industrial social scientist employed by management might insist on informing the workers in detail about the purposes and findings of the research and the attempted changes that are likely to result from it. In giving them this information, he would try to help them protect their interests against undue attempts at manipulation and to offer them specific recommendations for resisting encroachments on their freedom of choice. Furthermore, in order to promote freedom of choice as a positive goal, he should make a concerted effort to influence the planned change that will be based on his research so that it will actually leave the target group with greater choice than it had before. In submitting his findings and recommendations to the organization that contracted for the research, he should actively seek and point up opportunities for enhancing freedom of choice on the part of the target group that can be integrated into the planned change.

The two last points both imply a rather active role for the researcher in the planning of change based on his research. I would not want to say that the researcher must always participate directly in the change process itself; there are many times when this would be impossible or inappropriate. But since he is providing information that will, at least in principle, be directly translated into action, it is his responsibility to take some stand with respect to this action. The uses to which the information is put are not only the problem of the contracting organization, but also very much the problem of the man who supplied the information. The researcher should be clear about this, and he should have the support of his profession when he takes an active part in expressing his point of view.

The basic researcher. Let me finally, and more briefly, turn to the basic researcher. I have already stated my position that, even though the products of pure research are in a sense neutral, the investigator cannot escape responsibility for their probable consequences. The student of attitude change, for example, must keep in mind that his findings can be used for the systematic manipulation of the population, in ways and for purposes that would produce a net constriction in freedom of choice. In deciding whether or not to proceed with his research, he must try to make some estimate of the probabilities of different uses of his research product, in the light of existing social forces. If he expects restrictive uses to outweigh constructive ones, he would be bound to refrain from engaging in this research. If, on balance, he decides to undertake the research—and there are, of course, many good reasons for doing so—then he must continue to remain alert to its manipulative potential, and must constantly review his decision, particularly as his research emphases shift or as social conditions change.

Researchers in this area also have a special responsibility to be actively concerned with the ways in which the knowledge they produce is used by various agencies in their society. Eternal vigilance to the possibilities of manipulation is, of course, the duty of every citizen. But, as producers of knowledge about manipulation, social scientists are in a position similar to that of the many nuclear physicists who feel a *special* sense of responsibility for the ways in which their knowledge is being used.

Earlier, I suggested that research on attitude change may not only increase the knowledge of the potential manipulator, but also help in finding ways to counteract manipulative forces. So far, research along these lines has been rather limited. If investigators of attitude change and related problems are to mitigate the manipulative potential of their research, they will have to focus more deliberately and more actively on this other line of work. Thus, in order to build some protection against manipulation into the social structure, we will have to extend our research on processes of resistance to control and make a special effort to communicate relevant findings to the public. Such an emphasis will contribute to the development of antidotes against manipulation at the same time that research is contributing to the development of knowledge about manipulation itself. From a scientific point of view, such work will be highly germane to the study of attitude change, since it represents an exploration of its limiting conditions.

In order to promote the enhancement of freedom of choice as a positive goal, research will have to focus on the conditions favoring a person's ability to exercise choice and to maximize his individual values. Admittedly, this is a rather value-laden way of stating a problem for basic research. However, if we want our science to contribute to the liberation of man rather than to his dehumanization, this is the kind of problem to which we will have to turn our attention.

CHAPTER 2

❧❦❧❦❧❦❧❦❧❦❧❦❧❦❧❦❧❦❧❦❧❦❧❦

INTRODUCTION

The next chapter continues the discussion of potentially negative consequences of social research, but places it in a somewhat broader context than Chapter One. It points to the ambiguous social implications of the involvement of social scientists in policy-related activities and the possibility that social science approaches might be misused or used in the support of policies that have dehumanizing consequences. Beyond that, it raises questions about the general role of social science in modern society, expressing the fear that social research may, by its very nature, reinforce the tendencies toward dehumanization rampant in our society. In calling attention to these potentially negative consequences, I do not abandon my conviction that social science ought to contribute

32

to the policy process and that it is basically a constructive and liberating force in society.

The main thrust of this essay is the proposition that social science must counteract its potential role in the dehumanization of society by taking an active role in the humanization *of society. I speak in this connection of the need for radical thinking about societal processes. In many respects this is synonymous with the application of scientific method to the study of man and society, although it includes an explicit value component, the assumption that institutions and policies must be evaluated in terms of their consonance with human needs. I shall argue more fully in Chapter Three that it is impossible to exclude value considerations from social research, particularly when it relates to significant social issues; and that it is actually unnecessary to do so, provided certain precautions are taken. One of these, of course, is to state one's values clearly and explicitly. My own values, I am sure, will become quite clear to the reader as he proceeds through this volume.*

The following essay constituted my Presidential Address for the Society for the Psychological Study of Social Issues (Division 9 of the American Psychological Association). It was delivered on September 4, 1965, in the course of the meetings of the American Psychological Association in Chicago, Illinois. The Society (abbreviated SPSSI, which is affectionately pronounced "spissy") has been a natural home for me throughout my professional career. As I mention at the beginning, I joined SPSSI even before I started my graduate training. (Membership requirements were more casual in those days.) I continue to be active in SPSSI and to pursue many of my interests within its framework.

The Presidential Address was first published in the SPSSI quarterly, The Journal of Social Issues, *1965, 21 (3), 21–40. An essay entitled "Social research and the triple revolution" and based on parts of the address received a second award in the National Study of the Triple Revolution Report, an essay contest sponsored by* FOCUS/Midwest *magazine and Teamsters Local 688 (St. Louis). That essay was published in* FOCUS/Midwest, *1967, 5 (37), 14–18. Material taken from these two articles is reprinted here by permission of the editors of both publications.*

The Social Consequences of Social Research

My initial interest in psychology grew out of a concern with social change—out of the dual conviction that we must construct a social order more suited to human needs, and that we must find means for doing so that would be congruent with our ends. I decided that one way to work toward these goals was the effort to gain greater understanding of man and society through the study of social psychology. Given this orientation, I was naturally attracted to the Society for the Psychological Study of Social Issues when I first heard about it toward the end of 1946. I was invited to join by Daniel Katz, who was chairman of the Psychology Department at Brooklyn College at the time and whom I had come to consult about possibilities for graduate training. And so it came to be that, before I even entered graduate school, before I was clearly committed to a career as a psychologist or even had a good idea of what such a career might entail, I was already a member of SPSSI.

I share with other members of SPSSI the conviction that psychology, and social science in general, can be instruments for the liberation of man that can help to counteract the massive forces toward dehumanization with which our world is confronted. Through analysis and understanding of the human dimensions of our social institutions we hope to increase the likelihood that they will serve human purposes. Through systematic application of social-psychological concepts and methods we hope to contribute to the rational solution of social problems, consistent with fundamental human needs for security, dignity, and personal fulfillment.

In line with the view that this kind of contribution is part of the potential and part of the task of psychology, SPSSI has stressed, over the years, the importance of conducting research that would be relevant to questions of social policy, and of bringing social-psychological thinking and the products of social-psychological research to bear on policy issues. We have assumed that, as such thinking is fed into the policy process, it becomes more likely that humane policies will emerge. We have tended, therefore, to make the further assumption that involvement of psychologists in policy-related activities is in and of itself a positive good.

These latter assumptions, it seems to me, are open to question. I am as convinced as ever that it is legitimate and important for us to engage in policy-related activities, but we cannot assume that such activities necessarily have a humanizing influence on the social order. I have become increasingly concerned about the possibility that policy-related activities, and social research in general, may have negative social consequences, that they may contribute to rather than counteract the powerful forces toward dehumanization. It is to the implications of this possibility that I shall address myself.

Specifically, I shall try to show: (1) that there is reason to be concerned about the human implications of some of our policy-related activities; (2) that this concern relates not only to certain abuses of social and psychological research or to certain of the auspices under which it is carried out, but also to some of its inherent features and thus to the general role of the social scientist in society; and (3) that this concern must ultimately be met by commitment of the social scientist to an active role in the humanization of society.

☙ SOCIAL IMPLICATIONS OF POLICY-RELATED ACTIVITIES ❧

In the early days of SPSSI, involvement of psychologists in policy-related activities was hardly known. It was important, therefore, to emphasize the principle that the psychologist does have potentially relevant contributions to make to the policy process and to promote it as a value in its own right. Over the years, the picture has changed considerably. To be sure, research of direct relevance to social issues is still quite underdeveloped, and there are many areas of public policy in which the potential contributions of social science remain largely unrecognized. Yet there is an increasing readiness within the profession to engage in policy-oriented research, and within public agencies to make use of the products of such research.

We can distinguish, very roughly, between two types of involvement in policy-related activities. On the one hand, there is the involvement of those social scientists who, in the SPSSI tradition, are concerned with social issues. Their primary orientation is toward social change or toward the resolution of social problems in accordance with humane values. They engage in policy-related research because, ultimately, they hope to influence policy in a direction that would promote their values, because they hope to induce the system to respond to new inputs based on their research. If they are good social scientists, of course, their research will conform to certain standards of objectivity and their findings will stand by themselves, regardless of the values that initially prompted the research. Nevertheless, they enter into the research because they feel that it can contribute to the promotion of their values. On the other hand, there is the involvement of those social scientists who possess special skills relevant to the execution of certain policies and who have, therefore, been drawn into the process by officials in charge of it. Unlike the social scientists oriented toward social issues, they are not trying to change the system but rather are responding to the demands of the system by making their technical skills available to it. A good example is the psychologist who uses psychological instruments for the selection of personnel or the evaluation of procedures within a particular agency.

It would be a mistake to draw an overly sharp line between these two types of involvement, since they often overlap. A psychologist may, for example, undertake to work in a certain agency —such as the Arms Control and Disarmament Agency, or the Agency for International Development, or the Office for Economic Opportunity—because he sees it as having potential for furthering social change in a direction that he values. Many of the tasks that he performs may be set by the demands of the agency, but through his participation in this agency he is able to contribute to the promotion of policies that he favors within the larger system. A good case in point is the involvement of many psychologists in the Peace Corps selection process. They were specifically brought in because they possessed technical skills required for the execution of Peace Corps policy, but they responded to the call enthusiastically because they are committed to the values that this agency is promoting.

A different kind of overlap between the two types of involvement occurs when a social scientist uses his position within an agency to promote certain humane values. A psychologist working within the military, for example, may be in a position to influence personnel policies or training procedures in a direction more consistent with the needs of the individuals involved.

In short, social scientists participating in the work of ongoing agencies may very well contribute to desirable social change, depending on their own roles within the agency and on the role of the agency within the larger system. I am stressing the distinction between the two types of involvement, however, because the involvement of social scientists in research and other activities related to the *execution* of policy—in contrast to the *formulation* of policy—brings into focus more readily the kinds of concerns that I wish to voice.

A social-issues-oriented psychologist cannot help but feel some degree of ambivalence about the increasing use of psychological knowledge and methods in agencies charged with the execution of public policy. On the one hand, he is gratified that the relevance of psychological approaches is increasingly recognized and sees in this recognition a promise that policies may move in a direction more congruent with human needs. On the other hand, he is painfully aware that the use of psychological approaches is not an unmixed blessing. A great deal depends on the particular ways in which these methods are used and the particular purposes they are designed to serve. There is often reason to be concerned whether, on balance, the use of these approaches in fact contributes more to humanizing than to dehumanizing tendencies.

Let me draw some illustrations from the use of psychological tests for purposes of selection or prediction, which has become a matter of increasing public concern.

A rather straightforward example occurred several years ago when the New York City Youth Board issued a report claiming it had established the validity of an instrument for predicting delinquency early in life, and suggesting that the technique be used more extensively. A review of this report by a subcommittee of SPSSI Council revealed that the claims were premature and highly questionable. SPSSI Council was particularly concerned about the danger that this instrument, with all of its inaccuracies, would be used to "identify" children as probable future delinquents and to treat them in ways that would only constitute a self-fulfilling prophecy. These and other concerns were voiced in a statement released by SPSSI Council, which ended with the following paragraph: "As psychologists interested in the constructive application of psychological knowledge to the solution of social problems, we are necessarily alert to the possible abuses or destructive use of psychological concepts, methods, and data. As these psychological approaches play an increasing role in our daily lives, it becomes more imperative that the public be protected from distorted and extravagant claims made in the name of scientific validity" (SPSSI, 1960, p. 2). The statement from SPSSI Council, incidentally, probably had some bearing on the decision not to extend the use of this instrument to the New York City public schools.

This is a straightforward example because it involved a misinterpretation of statistical findings and exaggerated claims on the basis of these. But even if the instrument were highly valid, its extensive use would still raise numerous questions. Can the instrument (which requires home interviews) be applied reliably on a mass basis? What are the possible effects of wrong classifications, which are bound to arise both from unreliability in application of the instrument and from its imperfect predictive power? Even when a potential delinquent is correctly identified, what are the chances that this information will be used in a constructive way, to give the child the kind of special help that he needs, rather than in a destructive way, to place the child under a cloud of suspicion and thus exacerbate his antisocial potentials? This example illustrates the ambiguities involved in the use of psychological methods in the execution of public policies, in this case policies relating to the identification and treatment of potential delinquents. Since the policy involves differential treatment of individuals as a function of their classification, we must immediately ask about the probability that psychological methods will be used in a way that permits accurate classification, and the probability that the treatment of individuals who fall in the designated class will enhance rather than threaten their dignity and freedom. The very fact that an individual is being classified on the basis of a score makes abuse and dehumanization at least a likely possibility. It is interesting that SPSSI's role in this case was not to support, but to view with alarm the use of psychological methods in a policy context.

During the past few years, there have been numerous criticisms of psychological testing in general, and the social implications of testing have become a lively public issue. Many of these criticisms are totally unreasonable and based on a lack of understanding of the nature and purposes of psychological tests. Yet there are some real issues behind these criticisms that those of us who are concerned with the human implications of psychological methods cannot ignore. On the basis of a Russell Sage Foundation study of the social consequences of standardized ability tests, Orville Brim (1965) listed five issues that are involved in most of the criticisms of intelligence tests: (1) the inaccessibility of test data to the respondent; (2) the invasion of the respondent's privacy, often without justification; (3) rigid use of test scores, such that a person's life chances may be affected by his early performance; (4) the denial of opportunity to persons with talents other than intelligence that may be highly valuable, such as creativity, honesty, or the like; and (5) unfairness of tests to persons from culturally deprived backgrounds who may give spuriously inferior performances on the tests and thus be screened out from opportunities for advancement. These are serious issues concerning the nature of the human relationship between tester and respondent, and the consequences of tests for the individual and for society, issues that must concern even those of us who recognize the potential personal and social usefulness of psychological assessment.

Some of these criticisms, Brim points out, can be met by the proper use of tests and by more careful training and supervision of those responsible for their use. This presupposes, of course, active efforts on the part of psychologists to provide the necessary guidance and background information to the many nonspecialists who will inevitably make use of tests. One important effort of this kind, designed to deal with the dangers of inappropriate and unfair interpretation of test results of deprived children, was undertaken by a SPSSI work-group under the chairmanship of Joshua Fishman. The "Guidelines for testing minority group children" (Deutsch *et al.*, 1964) prepared by this group have constituted a very constructive response to at least one of the issues raised by the use of psychological tests. Other issues, however, such as "the invasion of privacy, the inaccessibility of records, and the kinds of talent that psychologists want to nurture . . . are not matters of educating others, or of technical improvements in tests, but of a carefully reasoned legal, moral, and scientific position which the American psychologist chooses to take" (Brim, 1965, pp. 127–128). Ultimately we must ask ourselves whether, from a human point of view, the positive contributions of tests outweigh their negative contributions.

The use of personality tests raises some questions similar to those raised by intelligence tests, and some different questions as well. Public criticism of the use of personality tests focuses primarily on the issue of invasion of privacy with special reference to items of the MMPI variety that deal with religion, sex, and family relations. Much of this criticism, again, is based on a lack of understanding of the nature of these tests, and some of it, no doubt, reflects the anti-intraception characteristic of authoritarian personalities. But I find it very difficult to dismiss, for example, an article that appeared in the *New Republic* (Ridgeway, 1964), in which personality tests are part of the target of an attack on "snooping" in federal personnel procedures. It is disturbing to find psychological instruments listed, along with interrogation procedures and security checks dating from the McCarthy era, as threats to the civil liberties and human rights of employees or potential employees. To be sure, many of the criticisms are based on cases in which personality test data are misused by unqualified persons. Nevertheless, these are psychological methods and we as psychologists must ultimately be concerned about the way in which they will be used—and the likelihood that they will be misused. Moreover, even when personality tests are used properly, by trained psychologists, they may still represent an unjustified invasion of privacy, inconsistent with the dignity of the individual.

The ambiguities with which this issue confronts us become particularly apparent when we consider the use of personality tests in the selection process for the Peace Corps, or the Department of Labor's Youth Opportunity Program (see Gordon, 1965). Selection of participants in terms of certain personality characteristics is clearly important to the success of these innovative programs. Moreover, the selection process is conducted by qualified psychologists who are sensitive to the welfare and dignity of the individual applicant. Yet the broader implications of using personality tests for purposes of selection—the possibility of abuse, the invasion of privacy—must be kept in mind even under these favorable circumstances.

I have dwelt on the issue of psychological testing because it illustrates quite clearly various ways in which psychological approaches may contribute to the forces toward dehumanization present in our society, often because of misuse by unqualified and irresponsible agents, but sometimes because of the very nature of the context in which they are employed. Moreover, this issue has aroused concern both in the public and within the profession, and has provided the occasion for SPSSI actions designed to counteract potentially negative social consequences of psychological procedures. This issue, however, is by no means the only one that creates concern about the social consequences of our activities as social scientists.

Similar concerns, though with different ramifications, arise in connection with policy-related *research*. Take for example, research carried out within the framework of certain foreign-policy assumptions—research, let us say, on ways of increasing the credibility of military threats, or of preventing insurgency in developing nations, or of persuading the public of the value of fallout shelters. Such research uses the tools of social science, not for the purpose of critical evaluation of policies from the point of view of their human meaning, nor for the purpose of formulating policies that are in keeping with human needs, but rather in the implementation of policies that are, in my opinion, based on unrealistic assumptions and inconsistent with the goal of enhancing human welfare. One's view of these policies is, of course, a matter of judgment, but the point I wish to make is that social research does not necessarily humanize the policies whose execution it is designed to facilitate. Thus, if these policies, on balance, have a dehumanizing effect, the social consequences of the research enterprise represent a contribution to the dehumanization process.

The point of my argument so far is quite simple. Participation of the social scientist in a policy context cannot be viewed as a positive value in its own right. There are many reasons to be concerned about the human implications of various kinds of policy-related activities, particularly when these are connected with the execution of policies set by public agencies. We must remain alert, therefore, to the possibility that psychological approaches may be abused and channeled in destructive directions, and we must find ways to counteract such possibilities. Furthermore, we must examine carefully the nature of the policies to whose execution we are asked to contribute, and decide whether our participation is indeed more likely to have humanizing rather than dehumanizing consequences.

My concern about the consequences of social research, however, is not merely a concern about the possibility that social science approaches might be misused, or that they might be applied in the support of policies that are inconsistent with fundamental human needs. My concern goes deeper than that. It is a concern about the place that social science occupies within our social structure, about its basic relationship to those forces in our society that tend toward dehumanization. I have already expressed my conviction that, in its efforts to study man and society systematically and understand them rationally, social science represents an inherently liberating force. But I am also struck by the possibility that certain dehumanizing tendencies may be equally inherent in the methods and orientations of social science. I worry lest these tendencies become the ones to dominate the uses of social science in policy contexts, and lest the primary role of the social scientist in society become that of an agent for dehumanization. I do not propose this as a likely outcome because, unlike many humanists who voice similar concerns, I am fully cognizant of the constructive and liberating implications of social research. But it is a danger that we must recognize; if we fail to do so, and if we fail to confront it actively, it may turn into a reality.

➥ DEHUMANIZING FORCES AND THE
SOCIAL SCIENTIST ⬿

Before discussing the role of the social scientist in relation to dehumanizing forces, let me comment on the nature of these dehumanizing forces as I see them.

I do not take the position that everything in our world is going badly and that we are on a steady downward drift as compared to some golden age of the past. There is no question that our generation has experienced horrors and faces dangers that are as extreme as any known to man. There is no question that the mass society that we have spawned threatens our very humanity. But there are also many hopeful signs on the horizon. The "triple revolution" (Ad Hoc Committee, 1964) that is taking place today holds the promise of a world more suitable for human occupancy. The "cybernation revolution," by extending productive capacity to an almost unlimited degree, makes possible the total elimination of poverty; the "weaponry revolution," by introducing weapons "which can obliterate civilization," makes possible the elimination of war as an instrument for resolving international conflicts; the "human rights revolution," both within the United States and all over the world, promises "the establishment of social and political regimes in which every individual will feel valued and none will feel rejected on account of his race" (p. 9).

There are many indications that some of our political leaders are aware of the significance of these revolutions, although they are often unable to draw the full implications from them and to reorganize their thinking accordingly. Serious efforts to combat the problem of poverty are being made, even though they fail to go to the roots. The necessity of avoiding nuclear war and creating some sort of international security community seems to be recognized, even though much of our foreign policy fails to reflect this recognition. There has been genuine progress in the establishment of human rights, even though we have not accepted the idea that the human rights revolution calls for a basic restructuring of our national and international systems.

The cautious optimism that I am expressing here does not diminish my feeling that the current *threats* to human values are of serious proportions. This feeling is based on two considerations.

(1) While it is true that the triple revolution holds great promise for a more humane society, it has also created a situation of extremely high risk. If we face up to the implications of these revolutions, we may come closer to a society built on peace, human welfare, and social justice. Failure to grasp the implications of these revolutions, however, and to re-examine our values and institutions in the face of the new conditions they are creating, is likely to lead to disaster. Failure to adapt to the weaponry revolution may lead to nuclear war and to the brutalization that is bound to come in its wake. Failure to adapt to the cybernation revolution may lead to the establishment of a permanent class of the poor, living restlessly within our affluent society but excluded from it and deprived of the opportunity to gain entry into it. Secretary of Labor Willard Wirtz has spoken, in this connection, of "the development of a separate nation of the poor, the unskilled, the jobless, living within another nation of the well-off, the trained and the employed" (quoted in Ad Hoc Committee, 1964, p. 12). Failure to adapt to the human rights revolution may lead to a world dangerously divided along racial lines, with our nation as the chief protagonist of the rich and arrogant white world. So, while the triple revolution holds great promise, it also confronts us with enormously threatening possibilities.

(2) While there are indications that some of our political leaders are aware of the significance of these revolutions, we cannot be at all certain that they will have the insight and courage to take the radical steps that are necessary, or that they will be allowed to do so. The emergence of a vociferous right-wing movement and its capture of the Republican Party in 1964 suggest, despite Goldwater's decisive defeat, that the political forces arrayed against a constructive and realistic response to the triple revolution are likely to be quite powerful. The Johnson policy in Vietnam and in the Dominican Republican suggests that, even where there is awareness of changing conditions, it is likely to be uneven and to be preempted, at critical moments, by irrelevant and antiquated approaches.

Whether these revolutions will fulfill their promise or lead to disaster depends, to a considerable extent, on the response of the American people and particularly of the opinion-making elites—on their readiness to give active support to innovative policies conducive to the abolition of poverty, the elimination of war, and the universal extension of human rights, and to resist policies destructive of these ends, be they the products of limited vision or of a desire to perpetuate special privilege. A public likely to respond in this way must have acquired the habits of caring enough to embrace policies for the simple reason that they extend human welfare, of participating actively in the debate of basic issues, and of resisting the manipulations of those who count on old fears, hatreds, and patterns of thought in their own quest for power.

The prospects for this kind of public response in our mass society are not very reassuring. In the huge urban and bureaucratic centers, the feeling of alienation and the loss of the sense of community are often so widespread that active commitment to the welfare of others cannot be readily generated. In the small towns and rural areas, the sense of isolation from the centers of power is often so desperate that it leads to a desire to return to a simpler life, at the expense of those who have been neglected by society. Everywhere, the vastness and complexity of the system is such that individuals feel unable to give it direction or even to control their own destinies within it. They are willing to go along with the demands made upon them, even at the expense of their own values.

At the same time, elements ready to take advantage of the public's manipulability are ever-present, as I have already noted in Chapter One. The centralized nature of modern society and the availability of powerful mass media create opportunities for large-scale manipulation of the behavior of masses. Such manipulation is often carried out in systematic fashion by specialized agencies expressly set up for this purpose. In its extreme form, it consists in the effort by the state to achieve total control over the environment of entire populations, characteristic of totalitarian systems. The Nazi regime in Germany and the public reactions in the face of it are not just accidents that happened, but very much products of the modern world, the meaning and implications of which we have yet to fathom. In less extreme form, large-scale manipulation consists in the systematic control of information necessary for public opinion-making and the consequent engineering of consent.

Only to the extent that we can overcome this degree of dehumanization that already characterizes our society, and move toward creative and humane responses to the revolutionary forces in the world, will we be able to prevent the more drastic dehumanization that may otherwise be in store for us.

And this brings me back to the question of the role of social science in relation to the forces toward dehumanization in our society. The reason for my deep concern is that the products, procedures, and orientations of social research inherently reflect these forces in the sense that they treat man as an object rather than as an active, choosing, responsible agent. There is thus a danger that the widespread use of social science approaches—of psychological tests, interviews, experiments, and observations—may in itself contribute to people's sense of alienation and helplessness, to the feeling that their destinies are entirely controlled by external forces; and that, furthermore, these approaches may lend themselves most readily to the purposes of those agencies who are concerned with manipulating and controlling the behavior of individuals, with or without the consultation or the active involvement of the social scientist himself. To the extent that this danger becomes a reality, the social scientist becomes an agent and mediator of dehumanizing forces. It is even conceivable that a caricatured and perverted version of social science principles and techniques may serve as the operational code for an efficient dehumanized society.

Let me expand somewhat on my statement that, by treating man as an object, the products, procedures, and orientations of social research inherently reflect dehumanizing forces. As for the products of social research, I can briefly recapitulate the argument of Chapter One. A great deal of social research is designed to provide information on the social conditions under which one or another type of behavior is likely to be manifested, or—to put it in other terms—on the variables that control various kinds of responses. The knowledge produced by this kind of research, assuming that the findings are relatively stable and valid, can readily be translated into attempts to manipulate human behavior.

By creating the necessary social conditions, one ought to be able to produce any desired response. I am not proposing that all such uses of social science knowledge are necessarily objectionable. While I regard any manipulation of the behavior of others as an ethically ambiguous act, I also feel that such manipulation is often socially useful and even necessary. Certainly I would not argue that this kind of knowledge is in itself dangerous. But there is the danger that it will be used for purposes of systematic and large-scale manipulation inconsistent with the welfare of the person being manipulated and with his rights as a fully choosing individual.

As for the procedures of social science research, they typically involve at least some degree of invasion of privacy, and frequently also some form of deception. I shall not go into detail on these points, particularly since I have already touched on the issue of invasion of privacy in connection with psychological tests, and I shall deal in Chapter Eight with the problem of deception with special reference to social-psychological experiments. Though I am troubled by these features of our research procedures, I am also aware of the fact that they are often essential to the execution of a piece of research. If we regard this research as significant, we are thus confronted with a genuine conflict of values. For present purposes, however, the main point about the use of deception and the invasion of privacy is that they mimic procedures used extensively in totalitarian settings and frequently by public agencies in any mass society. Thus, in his very procedures, the social scientist may contribute to the denial of personal dignity and the deprivation of decent human relationships that the individual already experiences elsewhere in his life.

Finally, in its orientation to man, social research deprives him of his wholeness and his unique individuality. We are interested in him as part of a group, to whose mean score he contributes. We try to wash out the random error generated by his idiosyncrasies. We categorize him, classify him, and typologize him. We isolate dimensions and parts of him that we investigate outside of the context of his total personality. I do not deplore this, because the task of the social scientist, unlike that of the novelist, is not to capture the richness of an individual's existence but to develop general propositions, and his orientation to man is completely consistent with that task (see Chapter Five). Nevertheless, by taking this orientation, for perfectly valid intellectual reasons, are we not contributing to those forces in our society that tend to transform man into a depersonalized object?

The treatment of man as an object is actually inherent in the very foundation of the scientific study of behavior. What the social scientist tries to do is to gain some distance from man and from society, to place them outside of himself—in short, to objectify them—so that he can analyze them systematically. I consider this approach highly valuable as a means of gaining understanding and rational control of social forces (just as I consider the splitting of the ego in psychotherapy a valuable tool for gaining self-understanding and control of one's own behavior). The treatment of man as an object is socially useful as long as it remains an analytic means. It becomes dangerous when it is turned into a social end, when it defines the image of man around which society is organized. (I might point out, in passing, that those right-wing critics of social research who complain about invasion of privacy and manipulation of the mind take precisely the opposite position. They are concerned about the treatment of man as an object when it is used as an analytic means, but are more than willing to endorse it as a social end—as they do in their readiness to deprive fellow human beings of their freedom because they hold deviant views, or of their dignity because they are black or poor.)

The reason for my concern about the consequences of social research is that it is often so difficult to draw the line between means and ends. In a society suffused with pressures toward dehumanization, there is always the danger that the products, procedures, and orientations of social research will be applied, by others, if not by ourselves, to the creation of a social order in which man is treated as an object, deprived of his individuality, and manipulated for purposes outside of himself. Unless we concern ourselves with this danger, we may be contributing to the very forces that we hope to arrest, and we may be taking upon ourselves an active role in the dehumanization of society.

How can we respond to these dangers? We can keep ourselves constantly aware of them. We can try to communicate them to our students, to the agencies who use the knowledge we produce, and to the public at large. Increased active awareness of the problem is in itself an important part of the solution. We can maintain our vigilance toward clear abuses of social science approaches, both within the profession and outside of it. We can make deliberate attempts to build protections against manipulation or resistances to it into the processes we use or study (see Chapter One). We can explore new methods of investigation that permit a greater degree of true participation of our respondents in the research process (see Chapter Eight). These are all meaningful answers to which I subscribe wholeheartedly. But it seems to me that we must go beyond them. I have argued that there is a danger that we may be taking an active role in the dehumanization of society. At least part of our response to this danger must be a deliberate commitment to an opposite role, to an active role in the humanization of society.

THE NEED FOR RADICAL THINKING

What I am proposing is that we—and I mean we as a discipline—ought to devote at least part of our energies to carving out a role for the social scientist in the effort to define a social order that is more consonant with human needs. This, in turn, implies that the social scientist must contribute to radical thinking about societal processes. The kind of radical thinking I have in mind is captured very nicely in the title of Dwight Macdonald's essay, "The Root Is Man" (1946). While this essay is a fundamental critique of Marxism, its title is derived from a quotation by Karl Marx: "To be radical is to grasp the matter by its root. Now the root for mankind is man himself."

There are two components to the radical thinking that I am advocating. The first is that, in analyzing societal processes, it searches for causes and attempts to specify the conditions that define a given state of affairs. Thus, it views any particular social arrangement or policy as one of many possible ones and helps us escape the trap of thinking that what is must therefore be. It throws into question the assumptions on which current arrangements and policies are based, and tests out alternative assumptions. By specifying the conditions that have made the present situation necessary, it readily guides us to thinking about those conditions that would make alternative situations possible. In short, both in the analysis of the present state of affairs and in the search for alternatives, it goes to the roots.

But the root is man—and this is the second component of the radical thinking that I am advocating. It tries to get away from abstractions, from thinking about institutions as if they had a life of their own apart from the men who have created them and who are served by them. In analyzing social arrangements and policies, it asks what they mean to concrete human beings. In seeking solutions to pressing social problems, it asks what institutions and what courses of action are most likely to meet the needs and enhance the dignity and self-fulfillment of individuals.

I hope it is clear that what I mean by radical thinking is not the advocacy of extreme actions or of social upheavals. It is, rather, the willingness to view any societal arrangement, not as necessary or inevitable, but as one of many alternative possibilities, man-made and dedicated to the purposes of men, and therefore open to change if it no longer fulfills these purposes adequately. What is sometimes called radicalism—whether of the left or right variety—is really a perversion of the kind of radical thinking that I am speaking of, for it merely substitutes one set of dogmas and clichés for another. The reorganization of society that it calls for is not based on an analysis that goes to the roots and on an open examination of a wide range of alternatives in terms of their human dimensions, but on a total acceptance of a series of preconceived solutions derived from an all-encompassing ideological system.

The radical thinking that I am proposing is not a distraction from the task of the social scientist, but one way of carrying it out. It is directly continuous with the approach of the social scientist, and particularly with that of the social psychologist. It is continuous methodologically, since a social-psychological analysis is concerned with propositions about the conditions under which different kinds of effects occur, and thus naturally tends to view any particular historical situation as only one of a range of possibilities, subject to change with changing conditions. It is continuous in terms of subject matter, since social psychology is concerned with the intersection between individual behavior and societal processes. It represents, in short, a genuine social-psycho-

logical contribution to the policy process—a participation by social scientists, within their roles of social scientists, not in the
execution of policies, but in their formulation.

Let me illustrate what I have in mind by coming back to
the triple revolution I touched on earlier. What are some of the
ways in which a social scientist, who is willing to go to the roots,
can contribute to the development of appropriate responses to
the revolution in weapons systems, the revolution in our system
of production, and the revolution in human rights that characterize our present situation?

The weaponry revolution. To think radically in response
to the dangers posed, as well as the promise held, by the weaponry revolution means to start with the proposition that there are
alternative ways of organizing the international system, alternative
goals that a nation can pursue within that system, and alternative
means that can be employed in the pursuit of these goals. Social
science analysis can address itself to delineation of these alternatives and identification of the conditions presupposed by each.

Thus, there is no reason to assume that the sovereign
nation-state represents the only principle by which the international system can be organized. A comparative perspective would
soon make it apparent that the nation-state was not always and
is not everywhere the basic political unit, that it represents only
one of a range of possible systems. If, therefore, it ceases to be an
adequate arrangement for meeting human needs, we have every
reason to seek for alternatives. Clearly, given the nature of modern
weapons, the nation-state can no longer provide security for its
members. Ought we not, therefore, to look for other mechanisms
to provide security, along the lines, for example, of a proposal for
internationalizing military force that I made a few years ago (Kelman, 1962c)? This proposal did not call for an abandonment of
the national state, but for breaking the link between the nation-
state and military force, a link that is by no means inevitable. I
might add that there are already many indications of fundamental
changes within the international system that point toward a gradual deterioration of the sovereign nation-state as we have known
it. What I am proposing then may seem more radical in relation
to the current rhetoric than it does in relation to current realities.

Many of our actions within the international system are

predicated on a hierarchy of goals that gives primacy, for example, to the containment of Communism everywhere and at all costs, and to the maintenance of our status as the greatest world power. Our foreign policy is entirely dominated by these goals, often at a great sacrifice in other values, especially in our relations with the developing nations. Our entrapment in the Cold War framework as the only basis for foreign policy choices has led us, for example, into postures in Vietnam that are antithetical to the needs and desires of the population of that country and carry the risk of ultimate escalation. It is necessary and possible to question the whole set of assumptions that has led us into such predicaments, and to extricate ourselves from these assumptions. Solutions may emerge more readily if we re-examine the hierarchy of goals that govern our policy, and entertain the possibilty that maintaining our great power status and a dominating presence in all parts of the globe may be less important than responding to the human needs of weaker nations.

In the pursuit of national goals we have also assumed that certain means are inevitable. Thus, for example, we are committed to a strategy of deterrence that is based, in part, on questionable psychological assumptions and sometimes on faulty historical analysis. As social scientists, we can question these assumptions; instead of accepting a commitment to an established strategy, we can ask what goal a given strategy is designed to achieve and then search for an alternative most suited to the achievement of that goal. Out of such an analysis, radically different strategies might emerge. A strategy of nonviolence, for example, which seems unthinkable in terms of our current assumptions about the relationships between nations, may turn out to be eminently realistic in the light of the human purposes that we hope to achieve and the human costs that various alternatives entail.

The cybernation revolution. In response to the revolution in our system of production, the document on the triple revolution (Ad Hoc Committee, 1964) starts out with the proposition that the traditional assumptions about the distribution of resources, which are based on ideas of scarcity, are inappropriate to a cybernated system, in which "potentially unlimited output can be achieved by . . . machines which will require little cooperation from human beings" (p. 10). If we continue on the assumption that income obtained through contributions to production is "the only major mechanism for distributing effective demand—for granting the right to consume" (p. 11), then we are not only failing to take advantage of the potential for human welfare of a cybernated productive system, but also creating a permanent class of the poor in the midst of general abundance. The *sine qua non,* then, for developing alternatives is to break the traditional link between jobs and incomes, to entertain the possibility of a distribution system in which the legitimate right to economic security is not based entirely on a productive job. The document goes on to urge "that society, through its appropriate legal and governmental institutions, undertake an unqualified commitment to provide every individual and every family with an adequate income as a matter of right" (p. 13). Whatever we may think of this particular recommendation, it demonstrates the possibilities of radical thinking, of a readiness to view any given institutional arrangement as but one of many alternative possibilities.

In our society, a conventionally productive job is not only the basis for economic security, but also the basis for true participation in national life. A more general way, therefore, to approach the problem of poverty is to ask how we can offer meaningful roles to the poor and the jobless within the social system. There are some indications that federal agencies recognize that creating jobs and providing financial assistance are not enough, but that there is also a need to integrate those who have been effectively excluded from the life of our nation into full participation in the system. The emphasis on education, which is the key to participation in the modern world, and on involvement of the poor in decision-making in antipoverty programs, are signs of this awareness.

I might add in passing that the problem of meaningful participation in the system does not only arise among the underprivileged. Thus, for example, I would guess that one of the sources of right-wing protest is the feeling, among individuals who are often highly privileged in terms of income and status, of exclusion from the centers of power in a vast bureaucratic system. Student unrest is no doubt related, at least in part, to a sense of lacking community and participation within a mass institution. The social scientist must thus concern himself with the larger question about the ways in which society fails to meet the needs of various of its members by excluding them from satisfying participation in its central undertakings. The situation of the chronically poor, however, is uniquely poignant, because they suffer not simply from insufficient participation in the larger society, but, to all intents and purposes, from total exclusion from it.

One other set of assumptions that is brought into focus by the cybernation revolution relates to our attitude toward social planning. While private planning in the interest of personal or corporate profit is fully accepted in our society, public planning in the interest of human welfare is regarded with suspicion. Our thinking seems to be bound by too narrow a range of planning models, in all of which planning is synonymous with control by some individuals, whether they be corporation management or a centralized bureaucracy, over the fate of others. We are properly concerned that plans imposed by the few on the many are undemocratic, but we fail to note that planlessness imposed by the few on the many is equally undemocratic. Social scientists can contribute to the development of alternative models of planning that are genuinely democratic, that call for planning *by* individual citizens rather than *for* them. Such models can have ramifications for the acceptability of planning, not only in the economic sphere, but also in urban renewal, conservation of natural resources, and even population control.

The human rights revolution. An adequate response to the human rights revolution, both in the United States and worldwide, may require us to question the implicit assumption that groups that have been disadvantaged, exploited, and excluded for generations can now be allowed to enter the system without the system itself undergoing some fundamental changes.

Within the United States, there has been enormous progress in civil rights. I would not want to underemphasize the amount that has been and is being accomplished. But increased access to public facilities, greater opportunities for jobs, equal protection under the law (at least in the formal sense), and extension of the right to vote, vital though these steps are, may not be enough to bring the entire Negro community, with its history of total exclusion, into full participation in the larger society. The extension of rights and opportunities provides openings for the few and assures that color as such will no longer be a basis for exclusion. It does not change the fact, however, that the masses of American Negroes are caught in a self-perpetuating system that makes it impossible for them to take advantage of the rights and opportunities that have become available—at least not within a future that they can foresee. The resulting hopelessness may help to explain the continued unrest in the face of what, to outside observers, may appear to be steady progress. Perhaps we can gain a better understanding of the nature of the Negro revolution if we recognize that it calls not merely for a removal of barriers so that individual Negroes can advance within the system, but for a restructuring of the system so that the Negro community as a whole can become an integral part of it. Social scientists might devote some thought to the delineation of institutional arrangements that would come closer to meeting this requirement.

Such efforts ought to include an analysis of the help-giving process, with the aim of finding patterns of assistance that would decrease rather than increase the dependence of the recipient. Help and opportunities that are given to Negroes in a spirit of self-righteous or even guilt-based generosity may improve, to some extent, the welfare of the Negro community, but not its sense of participation, by right, in meaningful roles within the larger society. The amount of assistance given may turn out to be less important than the patterns of participation that an assistance program sets into motion.

When we examine rioting and civil disobedience from the point of view of the restructuring of the system that may be required, it soon becomes clear that the issue is not how to increase respect for law and order, but how to provide a meaningful basis for legitimacy. The laws of a society that does not provide an integral role for an individual and does not meet his basic needs are irrelevant to him, particularly when they are part of a history of legal structures that discriminate against him and enforcement agencies that fail to protect him. The problem then is to find ways of creating legitimacy for the system by assuring individuals a part in it, with all of the reciprocal obligations this entails.

Similar considerations arise in our relations with the developing world, which are the major concern of the next chapter. The social revolutions in disadvantaged countries can only be understood if we realize that their populations are no longer willing to be excluded from the international system because of race, color, and history of servitude. They call for a restructuring of the system so that it would provide full participation, not only for the privileged Westernized few, but for the populations at large. An adequate response to these revolutions presupposes the development of models for foreign aid and economic development that encourage wide participation rather than grateful dependence, and of models for new political systems that emphasize bases for legitimacy rather than conditions for stability.

Conclusion. Let me close with two qualifications. First, I do not regard as unimportant the various attempts at ameliorating the conditions of the American Negro and the developing world that are taking place within the existing institutional framework. While we must ultimately go to the roots, in response to all three of the revolutions that I have been discussing, I reject the position that anything less than a complete restructuring of our institutions is useless. Moreover, the complexities and contradictions of our system are such that there are already many activities under way, some of them sponsored by the federal government, that reflect the kind of radical thinking for which I am calling. Often, therefore, our problem is not to work against the system, but to support those forces within it that move in the direction of rational thinking for human welfare.

Secondly, I am not proposing that all social scientists devote all of their time to active participation in policy formulation, based on a radical analysis of institutional patterns. I am dedicated to the proposition that social scientists should feel free to pursue theoretical problems that arouse their interest, regardless of the social significance that such research might have. Similarly, I see great value in the participation of social scientists in activities related to the execution of certain policies by existing agencies. I personally engage in both of these types of activities, and intend to continue doing so. There are many ways of being a responsible and effective social scientist, and each individual must work within his own style and establish his own balance. What I am asking for is merely that our field as a whole provide a significant place on its agenda for radical thinking about our social institutions, that activities deliberately directed toward the humanization of society be recognized as a legitimate part of the social scientist's role.

CHAPTER 3

※※※※※※※※※※※※※※※※※※※※※

INTRODUCTION

One problem area to which social science thinking of the kind advocated in the preceding chapter can contribute is that of social change—or the revolution of human rights, as it is described in Chapter Two. It is to this problem—more specifically, to the possibilities of social-psychological research on this problem—that this next chapter is devoted. I am primarily concerned here with social change in the context of developing countries.

After arguing that social-psychological research can and ought to make contributions in this area, I turn to two sets of questions that refer, respectively, to the scientific and to the ethical implications of this kind of effort. Each set brings some unique value considerations into focus.

The first set of questions relates to the scientific value and to the scientific objectivity of this type of "social-issues" research. I try to point out that one cannot make a simple dichotomy between the social significance and the theoretical significance of research, and that indeed there is an array of theoretical problems that can be studied most effectively through research on social change. Furthermore, I maintain that scientific objectivity depends not on the absence of value commitments, but on the way in which these are taken into account. In general, I take the position that the model of value-free research is inapplicable at least to large portions of social science and that a new model for scientific work in value-laden areas must be forged.

The ethical questions discussed in this essay relate to the fact that much of the research in developing countries is carried out by social scientists from industrialized nations, who readily fall or appear to fall into a neo-colonialist pattern. I draw some of my examples in this discussion (and even more so in Chapter Four) from Project Camelot, which was a cause célèbre at the time the piece was written. These examples were particularly germane since the paper was originally presented at a conference in Latin America.

For those readers who are not familiar with Project Camelot, let me review its complex history very briefly. (For more detail, see Horowitz, 1965; Lowe, 1966; Silvert, 1965; and Vallance, 1966.) Project Camelot was designed to be a large-scale multidisciplinary study of the conditions conducive to internal conflict and insurgency in developing nations and of ways of preventing or coping with such disturbances. The initiative for the study and its funds came from the U.S. Army Research and Development Office. The design and conduct of the research were in the hands of the Special Operations Research Office, an agency set up at American University (Washington, D.C.) to carry out various contract research projects for the Army. A sum of three to six million dollars, spread over a three-to-four year period, was made available to SORO for what was essentially a "feasibility study," designed to see to what extent behavioral science research can help predict and influence social forces leading to internal war. An interdisciplinary staff, assisted by a variety of consultants, began to develop the research plan in the fall of 1964. The plan involved both a series of historical case studies and a series of

*empirical studies (using surveys and other field methods) of a
number of developing countries, mostly in Latin America.*

*The Army's interest in Project Camelot was related to the
growing concern of American foreign policy with guerrilla warfare and "wars of national liberation" and the new emphasis on
the role of the military in counterinsurgency and civic action. It
seems quite clear, however, that the Project was designed as a
basic research effort rather than as a cover for espionage or as a
source of information directly applicable to counterinsurgency
operations. The social scientists who participated in Camelot were
generally attracted by the opportunity to do large-scale, well-funded
research on basic processes of social change, to engage in detailed
analyses of total contemporary societies, and to provide an input
into decision-making on vital issues of the day. The attractiveness
of Camelot is quite understandable in view of the growing interest
among social scientists in cross-national comparisons and in the
study of modernization, economic development, and social revolution, and in view of the difficulty of obtaining financial support
for such research from nonmilitary sources. Despite the apparent
commitment of both sponsors and investigators to Project Camelot
as a basic research program on social change, its conception and
presentation reflected its "counterinsurgency" origins. Thus, the
Army Research Office justified the Project to skeptics in terms of
its usefulness for dealing with wars of national liberation; and
the social scientists, in their own documents, combined sociological analysis with the language and rationale of counterinsurgency.*

*Project Camelot came to an abrupt end in July, 1965, be-
fore data collection had even begun. The precipitating event took
place in Chile, where a consultant to Camelot—a U.S. social
scientist born in Chile—was exploring, with local colleagues, the
possibility of conducting one of the Camelot studies in Chile,
which, incidentally, was not on the original list of countries to be
included in the research. In contrast to the official Camelot documents, in which the source of funds and the links to the counterinsurgency approach were openly acknowledged, he omitted all
references to Army funding and misrepresented the Project's sponsorship. The truth leaked out very soon, however, and created an
uproar in the Chilean press, Senate, and academic circles. Project
Camelot was held up as an espionage mission, as a threat to*

Chilean sovereignty, and as a betrayal and subversion by North American social scientists of their Latin American colleagues. Camelot quickly became a symbolic focal point for the suspicion and resentment of U.S. social researchers in the developing world, particularly in Latin America, though the causes of these reactions go much deeper and are of longer standing. The memory of Camelot still lingers on and, together with the more recent disclosure of the Central Intelligence Agency's involvement with U.S. universities, has greatly increased the difficulties confronting U.S. social scientists in foreign areas.

When Project Camelot came under public attack in Chile, the U.S. ambassador there denied any prior knowledge of it and sent an urgent cable to the State Department asking for an explanation and requesting that the Project be discontinued. Soon Camelot became as lively an issue in Washington as it had been in Santiago. It became the subject of Congressional hearings and criticisms. Above all, it became a focus for the continuing conflict between the Departments of State and Defense about the latter's role in the foreign policy process and particularly about jurisdiction over counterinsurgency matters. Under the pressures generated by these various criticisms, the Defense Department, on July 8, 1965, canceled Project Camelot completely. Subsequently, the State Department, in accordance with a Presidential directive, set up procedures for clearance of all social research in foreign areas and on foreign policy sponsored by operating agencies of the federal government. In addition to these official reactions, Project Camelot stimulated long-overdue discussions among social scientists about the relationships between government and the universities in foreign area research (to which Chapter Four is devoted) and about ethical problems arising in such research (which are part of the concern of the present chapter).

The discussion of the ethical problems that arise in foreign area research brings us back again to the potentially negative consequences of social research with which this volume began. While social research in developing countries is a potentially positive force contributing to constructive social change, it is subject to many thoughtless and ethically questionable acts on the part of the intruding investigator—which, incidentally, also reduce the quality and effectiveness of his work. Much depends on the as-

sumptions behind the research, the auspices under which it is undertaken, the manner in which it is carried out, and the kinds of relationships that the investigator establishes in the host society. Even an investigator with good will and scientific integrity may do more harm than good if he fails to take into account the goals, values, and interests of the society he enters and of his colleagues there.

This essay is based on an address presented at the Tenth Interamerican Congress of Psychology in Lima, Peru, on April 5, 1966. A somewhat briefer version was published in the International Journal of Psychology, *1967, 2, 301–313. It is reprinted here by permission of the International Union of Psychological Science and DUNOD, 92 rue Bonaparte, Paris VIᵉ.*

Psychological Research on Social Change

The world community is faced with the necessity of finding creative responses to the powerful forces of social change that are nudging the old order everywhere. These forces are most pronounced and most obvious in the so-called developing parts of the world, where demands for political independence, economic development, and social reform are producing a pattern of change that is too rapid at some points, too slow at others. The forces toward social change, however, are by no means restricted to the developing countries. They manifest themselves wherever there are populations that have been excluded from effective participation in the political process, from a share in the benefits of the national economy, and from meaningful roles within the social structure. Thus, for example, the civil rights struggle and the renewed awareness of the problem of poverty in the United States are part of this worldwide revolution of human rights.

What can be done to meet the challenge posed by this revolution—to facilitate social change and to increase the likelihood that it will move in constructive directions? What kinds of institutional arrangements can be fashioned that would improve the conditions of the masses of the population, that would be consistent with their fundamental human needs for security and dignity, and that would bring ever wider segments of the population into full participation in their societies, polities, and economies? What institutions and values might increase, within the population of a developing country, the sense of the legitimacy of its political regime, the feeling of national identity, the readiness for involvement in citizenship responsibilities, in economic enterprises, in population-control programs, in other forms of social planning? What techniques of change can be developed that would minimize the use of violence, the brutalization of the active and passive participants in the change process, and the predisposition to govern by coercion and repression? How can change be introduced without destroying the existing culture patterns and values that provide meaning and stability to a people, while at the same time helping to build the new patterns and values that an urbanizing, industrializing, and ever-changing society requires if it is to remain human?

Any attempt to answer these questions requires the input of new ideas and new data, often, in fact, of entirely new perspectives and ways of thinking. Social psychology is clearly a relevant source of such new inputs, for all of the questions I posed have distinctly psychological components. Thus, the challenge presented by the forces toward social change is also a challenge to us. Can social-psychological research meet this challenge—can it contribute to the systematic analysis, to the understanding, and to the rational solution of the problems of social change? That it cannot do so alone and that it cannot produce a grand and all-inclusive design for answering the questions goes without saying. But we do have concepts and methods that ought to be applicable and, in my view, we should be able to play a significant role in a many-sided effort to deal with these problems.

Without attempting to be either comprehensive or systematic, let me list a number of research questions that are clearly relevant to the problems of social change in developing countries and that are directly continuous with the current activities of social psychologists. How effective are different techniques of inducing attitude and behavior change and what are their long-run consequences? What is the role of the schools in the process of social change? The role of the mass media? What are some of the sources of resistance to change in individuals, particularly under conditions of rapid social change, and how can these be overcome? What are some of the sources of resistance in groups and communities, and what conditions are conducive to innovation and diffusion within a social system? To take a specific important example, what are some of the major resistances, within the individual and within the system, to population control, and how can an effective program in this area be mounted? What ideological orientations create a readiness for social change in general, for economic development, and for acceptance of political legitimacy in individuals, and how are these related to the prerequisites for change, development, and legitimacy at the level of social institutions? How do national awareness, national loyalties, and national role definitions develop, and what is the relationship of these processes to nation-building?

What are the psychological effects of social, technological, economic, and political change? What is the nature and consequence of value conflicts engendered by new societal institutions? What is the nature and consequence of intergroup conflicts in newly emerging nations, and how do they affect the relationship between sub-units (such as tribes) and the national system? How do leadership patterns evolve in developing societies, and how are new elites recruited and new roles defined? What form does political socialization take and what are the consequences of different socialization patterns? What are the conditions for increasing the level of participation among members of the society? What are the reactions to international contact, assistance, and exchange in developing societies, and what conditions are conducive to effective international cooperation? More specifically, what types of economic and educational assistance are most effective in building the capacities of the local population and in encouraging the development of patterns of participation?

I have raised these questions in very general terms, without distinguishing between different types of developing countries and without suggesting the specific variables that might enter into our answers to the various questions raised. But the list suffices to make the point that relevant contributions can come from many kinds of social-psychological research. The type of research I am speaking of here is basic research, although there are, of course, valuable and legitimate contributions that can come from applied research as well. It is basic in the sense that it is concerned with long-range issues rather than specific programs, and that it is designed to answer general questions rather than questions posed by specific operating agencies relevant to their particular missions. At the same time, I do not pretend that I am speaking of research that is neutral and independent of value preferences. The research is based on the assumption that social change is desirable. It is designed to contribute to the understanding of ways to facilitate constructive change in the direction of meeting human needs and of expanding the participation of people all over the world in the political, economic, and social processes of their respective societies, and of ways to minimize the coercive, destructive, and psychologically disabling consequences of rapid social change.

My central thesis is that our discipline ought to invest a major effort in research along these lines. In the preceding chapter, I spoke of this type of research as a contribution to radical thinking about societal processes. It is radical because it seeks to identify the causes of existing social arrangements and policies, to specify the conditions that would make alternative arrangements and policies possible, and to ask what these arrangements and policies, both existing and alternative, mean to concrete human beings. In short, it goes to the roots—and recognizes that "the root is man."

My reasons for urging that we invest a major effort in research on social change are partly scientific. The investigation of these problems offers very special opportunities for theoretically significant research about social behavior, to which I shall return below. Aside from these scientific reasons, however, I also urge this line of research as a contribution to work on vital social issues.

For social scientists in developing countries these issues are obviously at the heart of the problems faced by their societies. They are equally vital, however, for social scientists in the more fully industrialized nations. I have already mentioned the continuity between the problems of social change in developing and industrialized societies, even though these problems are more pronounced and more dramatic in the less developed parts of the world. Most highly industrialized societies, for example, contain within them pockets of poverty and regions that are economically less developed, ethnic or cultural minorities that are not fully integrated into the opportunity systems and the political life of the country, and internal conflicts that inhibit growth and integration. Moreover, these issues are vital for social scientists in industrialized nations for the simple reason that the problems of social change and development, wherever they may occur, are world problems. We all share in the responsibility and we are all confronted by the necessity to deal with these problems for both moral and prudential reasons. The welfare of all is everyone's concern, and in this increasingly interdependent world the fate of one nation is inextricably linked with the fate of all others.

The struggle for social change in developing countries is part of a worldwide struggle to extend human rights and to improve the conditions of human life. Speaking quite personally, I regard this as a struggle of which I want to be a part and to which I want to contribute in the best way I can—which is, I believe, through my activities as a social psychologist. As a citizen of the United States I feel a particularly strong moral obligation to be concerned with these problems because of the special role of my country in world affairs. I feel that my government has shown, especially in the cases of Vietnam and the Dominican Republic, a lack of sensitivity to and understanding of the struggle for social change in the developing world. It has, therefore, acted in ways that, in my opinion, are likely to impede this struggle and to push it into less constructive directions. Thus, I feel a special sense of responsibility to contribute to the development of broader perspectives for viewing the process of social change—and this is precisely what social science research can accomplish.

For both scientific and social reasons, then, the study of social change is of mutual interest to psychologists in both more and less developed countries. This convergence of interest should provide the necessary motivation for cooperative endeavors in this area. Furthermore, a high degree of cooperation between these two groups is essential if research is to proceed effectively, because of our mutual interdependence. On the one hand, problems that we wish to investigate and the detailed knowledge of the nature of these problems and their social and cultural context reside in the developing countries. On the other hand, the human and material resources for investigating these problems are more fully developed in the industrialized nations, where trained research personnel, accumulated research experience, research facilities, and research funds are far more readily available.

There is thus clearly both a basis for international cooperation in research on social change and a strong necessity for organizing such cooperative efforts. In urging, then, that we place psychological research on social change high on our professional agenda, I would urge as a corollary that this research be built, as indeed it must be built, on international cooperation.

As we begin to think about mounting such an effort, there are some basic scientific and ethical questions that we must consider. What are the implications of this kind of effort for the development of psychology—particularly social psychology—as a discipline, and what special problems of scientific objectivity does it raise? What are the ethical implications of research on social change in developing countries and what barriers do these create to cooperation among psychologists from the less and more developed countries? The rest of this chapter will be devoted to a discussion of these scientific and ethical issues and of their further implications for the way in which cooperation in research on social change must be organized.

SCIENTIFIC IMPLICATIONS

Development of the discipline. Is there a danger that attention to the study of social change might distract psychologists from their primary task and might impede the advancement of psychology as a science? It is my contention that the study of social

change is by no means incompatible with the development of our
discipline. As a matter of fact, I would guess that just the opposite
holds true for the growth of psychology within developing countries themselves. Research that is relevant to pressing social problems is most likely to gain support within these societies, given
their limited resources. Moreover, problems of social change can
probably provide the most exciting opportunities for significant
research in this setting and capture the imagination of the most
promising students. Thus, this kind of emphasis is most likely
to contribute to the growth of psychology in developing countries
—by promoting acceptance for it, by demonstrating its relevance,
and by stimulating significant psychological research. With time
it would then become possible for psychological research on a
variety of other problems to gain increasing support.

Two important qualifications are in order here. The favorable development that I am predicting would be far less likely to
materialize if we make exaggerated claims about the immediate
and direct relevance of psychological research to problems of social change. These claims cannot be sustained and would only
discredit us. A large part of the value of psychological research in
this area rests on its cumulative effect and on its contribution,
along with other sources of knowledge, to basic thinking about
the processes of social change. By the same token, psychology as
a discipline would be far less likely to advance if its potential contributions to problems of social change became narrowly defined,
in terms of answering specific operational questions of various
agencies involved in one or another aspect of social change. I do
not question the value and importance of such applied research,
but this is not at the heart of the effort I am advocating. If psychological research on social change is to gain support within
developing countries and at the same time contribute to the development of the discipline, we will have to stress that basic
research, even though it may not answer certain immediate operational questions, may be more fruitful in the final analysis than
applied research that narrowly focuses on problems of the moment. Such research may build the framework for fundamental
answers to long-range problems, and may be highly relevant to
problems that are likely to arise in the future but have not yet
been recognized by policy-makers. In short, we will have to demon-

state what I believe to be true: that theoretical research, and the development of the discipline in which it is embedded, can have important practical implications, although these may not always be readily apparent, particularly if one takes a short-range view.

Going beyond the question of the advancement of psychology in developing countries, what is the probable impact of concerted efforts in the study of social change on the further advancement of psychological, and particularly social-psychological, theory and research in general? It should be evident from my emphasis on theoretical problems that what I am proposing is not a distraction of the social psychologist from his role in basic research, but one way of carrying out this role. Not only is a concern with facilitation of social change and with the social problems surrounding it compatible with basic research, but indeed there are some interesting and significant theoretical problems for which such a starting point may actually represent the most productive way of carrying out basic research (see Tajfel, 1966). Research that addresses itself to such broad questions as, for example, "How can economic development be facilitated in highly traditional, agricultural societies?" or "How can the psychological and social dislocations resulting from rapid social change be minimized and counteracted?" can certainly be a source of important theoretical advances that would not derive from studies formulated in more neutral terms and carried out in more antiseptic settings.

From a methodological point of view, there is a special type of opportunity that research in developing countries can offer to the theoretically oriented social psychologist. This opportunity is linked to the very occurrence of major and rapid changes within these societies. It becomes possible to observe social change and related phenomena in extreme form and in the process of emergence. Because of the discontinuity and the rapidity with which these changes occur, it is sometimes possible to approximate a before-and-after design—that is, to obtain measurements before the introduction of some major innovation and after it has taken its course. The effects of certain variables whose history is known almost in its entirety can thus be observed in detail and in relative isolation from contaminating factors. Even if it is difficult to pin down specific causal connections, it is possible to observe the development of certain new values, beliefs, or social institutions.

For example, my own research on national role conceptions and nationalist ideology can benefit greatly from observations carried out in new nations where the sense of national identity is often just in the process of emergence.

Another special type of opportunity that research in developing countries can offer to the theoretically oriented social psychologist is that it can extend the range of cultures in which theoretical propositions can be put to the test. For example, it ought to be possible to test hypotheses about the determinants of different reactions to social change—of different processes of acceptance and diffusion of change, or of differences in capacity to adjust to rapid societal transformations—by comparing societies that vary along certain relevant cultural dimensions. Cross-cultural comparisons enable us to check the generality of propositions that have been tested in a single culture and to develop theoretical models that can encompass contradictory findings in different cultural contexts (see Tajfel, 1966). Developing countries offer unique opportunities for comparative research, not only because they provide cultural contexts different from those in which social-psychological research has generally been carried out, but also because they often contain a wide diversity of cultures within relatively small geographical units. In sub-Saharan Africa, for example, societies differing greatly with respect to some aspects of culture are, at the same time, characterized by many uniformities, both in culture and in conditions of life. It thus becomes possible to conduct natural experiments, to observe the effects of certain cultural differences on the process of social change and reactions to it with some degree of quasi-experimental control.

Cross-cultural comparisons of this sort are significant, of course, not only for the study of social change, but also for the study of many other social and psychological processes. A useful dividend of participation in research on social change in developing countries may be that it gives the researcher access to comparative data on a wide variety of other phenomena not directly related to social change as such. In some cases, these data may be obtained as part of the research design in a study of social change, but also analyzed for different purposes. For example, in studying the sources of differing reactions to social change, one might examine different patterns of child-rearing, which in turn would provide a pool of data applicable to various other problems as well. In other cases, it may be possible to add to the design of a study on social change some procedures relevant to a different problem. For example, at the end of an interview, respondents may be asked to give a few more minutes to a perceptual experiment. In yet other cases, an investigator's colleagues in the host country may be more willing to help him carry out a completely unrelated study because he has been collaborating with them on research on social change which is of mutual interest. These are some possible indirect benefits that this kind of research may yield, above and beyond its inherent theoretical significance.

Scientific objectivity. In describing the type of research I have in mind, I indicated not only that it was basic research, but also that it was rooted in certain value commitments. Implicit in the research questions raised at the beginning of this chapter is the assumption that "constructive social change"—an admittedly vague phrase whose meaning, I hope, is clear from what has come earlier—is desirable. The existence of such a value preference brings up another scientific issue: Is it possible, under these conditions, to maintain the scientific objectivity of one's research?

That value preferences affect the scientific process and are likely to introduce some distortions into it goes without saying. This is true of every line of research, certainly within social psychology, and even more certainly in an area marked by social significance. However, if we are going to do research on social change and other social problems, then we will have to live with this ambiguity and thoroughly re-examine our assumptions about scientific objectivity. The alternative would be to restrict ourselves arbitrarily to the study of phenomena less likely to engage basic values—to the extent that such phenomena exist at all in human psychology.

Some social scientists might argue, perhaps, that one can enhance the scientific objectivity of research on social change if one deliberately excludes value considerations from the formulation of the research problem. According to this view, the researcher merely sets up the conditions for observing the relevant phenomena, and, by the use of objective methods, is able to do so in disinterested fashion. I submit that this view, if indeed anyone takes it, is based on self-delusion. It is impossible to work in the area of social change—or in other areas pregnant with value considerations, such as the area of mental health—as a purely disinterested observer, merely looking at whatever presents itself. Value preferences are inevitably built into the assumptions of the research design, which determine the questions that are to be asked, the events that are to be observed, the variables that are to be assessed, the categories in terms of which the data are to be organized.

I suspect that it is easiest to delude ourselves about the disinterested nature of our research when our assumptions reflect the dominant value preferences within our society. These value assumptions are so thoroughly built into the structure of reality, as we perceive it, that it does not occur to us to question them and to entertain the possibility of alternative assumptions. Thus, we have the anomalous situation that research rooted in the dominant values of the society is less likely to be questioned about its scientific objectivity and yet more likely to suffer from the lack of it.

It is not only impossible to conduct basic research on socially significant problems in a value vacuum, but it is also not necessary to do so. To be maximally objective, research need not be value-free. There is no reason why the choice of problem cannot be based, as it generally is, on certain value preferences, and why the study cannot be designed to answer questions that have definite value implications. Thus, for example, questions about the conditions favorable to the development of mental health in an individual or about the procedures conducive to improvement in mentally ill patients are deeply immersed in value suppositions, yet they can be approached through objective research. In large part, of course, it is a matter of using methods that are objective, in the sense of being explicit, reliable, and replicable. As I have already pointed out, though, this does not prevent the intrusion of value preferences into the assumptions on which the design is built, for the intrusion of values cannot be prevented. The issue is not whether the investigator has value preferences, but how he takes account of them.

There are several essential steps that can help us take account of our values in the interest of maximizing the genuine objectivity of value-laden research:

(1) We must recognize and make explicit the value prefer-

ences underlying our research, in order to protect ourselves from unwittingly letting these slip into our assumptions and in order to allow others to reconstruct the basis of our design and conclusions.

(2) We must distinguish clearly between commitments to certain valued end-states and commitments to certain specific paths for achieving these states, particularly if these paths represent vested interests concerned with maintaining or achieving power within the society. Thus, for example, there is an important difference between research based on the assumption that social change is desirable and research based on the assumption that the program for social change developed by Party X is desirable. Similarly, there is an important difference between research based on the assumption that political stability is desirable and research based on the assumption that a powerful military establishment as the protector of political stability is desirable. I would not argue that research based on commitment to specific paths is illegitimate, but it has a totally different scientific status in that it tends to limit the investigator's ability to question basic value assumptions. It is thus essential to make such commitments explicit. The question of the auspices under which the research is done—to which I shall return later—becomes central here.

(3) We must be prepared to review our value assumptions, to test the limits of these assumptions, and to explore the possibility and reasonableness of alternative assumptions. For example, if we assume that social change is desirable, we must question whether this is necessarily so, whether it is always so, and what further assumptions lie behind this preference.

(4) In this process of questioning our assumptions, we must be particularly alert to the possibility that our preferences are based on certain further assumptions about facts, which may in themselves be questionable or at least unquestioned.

(5) We must constantly re-examine our definition of the desired end-state, whether it be mental health or constructive social change. If we fail to do so, we can easily slide into the assumption that our way of defining the concept is *the* way of defining it—for example, that adjustment or freedom from symptoms *is* mental health—and thus allow our value preferences to slip out of our awareness and into the very definition of the criterion.

The steps I have outlined are a mere hint of the kind of re-examination of the relationship between scientific objectivity and value commitments that I consider necessary. There is no easy solution to the problem of objectivity in research on socially significant problems. Certainly the avoidance of such research is an unsatisfactory answer, nor ought we to pretend that it is possible to conduct such research in disinterested fashion. One of the coming tasks for social psychology is to learn how to work in areas in which important values are engaged, how to combine social commitment with scientific integrity.

⚜ ETHICAL IMPLICATIONS ⚜

So far, much of the research on social change in developing countries has been done by social scientists from industrialized nations, who have come into the country of concern, set up their project, collected their data, and then taken them home for analysis. This has been accomplished with varying degrees and kinds of cooperation on the part of social scientists in the host society. These activities of foreign scholars have often and understandably created suspicion and resentment among local social scientists and other elements in the society. If we are going to continue to do research in developing countries, and particularly if we hope to establish long-term collaborative relationships, we will have to become more sensitive to the concerns of members of the host societies—and above all to those of our colleagues and potential colleagues there.

Dealing with suspicion and resentment of the scholar who is intruding is not merely a public relations problem. There are, of course, many reasons for these reactions, and no doubt some of them can be ascribed to the sensitivities of intellectuals in developing countries. But to the largest extent, I submit, these problems are rooted in the ethical ambiguities inherent in the situation of the North American or European scholar coming into a developing country to carry out his research.

I would like to describe five issues around which resentment and suspicion may focus, point to the ethical concern that each brings into play, and then say something about possible ways of arranging the relationship between the visitor and his hosts that might reduce ethically questionable behavior and the resentments that follow upon it. The five issues are: imposition of foreign values; invasion of privacy; use of research for purposes of intelligence or intervention; exploitation of the host country; and diversion of local research talent.

Imposition of foreign values. The problem of imposing foreign values is endemic to research on change, wherever it is conducted, particularly if the research is linked to an action program designed to induce change, or if it attempts to develop specific recommendations for facilitating change (see Chapter One). Planned change is typically based on certain values of the change agent, which are not fully shared by the target population. The ethical implications of this state of affairs are more or less acute, depending on the nature of the influence process used. In any event, however, such change does involve at least some threat to the existing values of the target population and a certain amount of tampering with these values. Even when the change agent is a member of the same society, the values governing his influence attempt are likely to be somewhat foreign to those of the target population because usually the two represent different social classes. When the change agent is a member of a foreign society, the problem clearly takes on more serious proportions.

The investigator must keep himself constantly aware of the danger of such imposition. He must develop an informed respect for the people who are being investigated or influenced, for their values and their way of life, understood insofar as possible within their own terms. He must repeatedly question his assumptions about the desirability of the changes he is promoting. Perhaps these changes do not justify the extent to which they disrupt existing values. He must review the methods for inducing change that are employed from the point of view of the degree of manipulation and imposition that they represent. When the foreign scholar works closely with local counterparts, which is generally true in those situations in which the research is tied to an action program, then the problem is lessened, since the local colleague will be more sensitive to the general values of the society that are being threatened and to potentially disruptive consequences. Even in this case, however, the foreign investigator cannot escape the responsibility of confronting the problem of imposition of foreign values. Because of the class differences that I have already mentioned, the local scholar may himself not be fully aware and appreciative of the values of the target population. In fact, it is conceivable that an outsider, because of his distance and lack of indoctrination in class-based assumptions, may at times have a sharper appreciation of the special character of the target population than his local colleague. I can well imagine, for example, that a foreign social scientist might learn things about the values of lower-class Negroes in the United States of which most white middle-class North American scholars simply have no conception.

Invasion of privacy. The problem of invasion of privacy, which confronts social research in general, takes on a special character when the investigator is a representative of a more developed society. Members of the host society may resent the implication that their country is being looked upon as a specimen and studied because of the "quaintness" of its primitive culture and the "backwardness" of its social life. It ought to be possible to persuade our colleagues, and through them other members of their society, that we do not regard them with this kind of patronizing superiority if, indeed, we bring to our research a deep respect for the integrity of the culture that we have come to observe. This is the attitude that is second nature to the well-trained cultural anthropologist. Such resentments can also be overcome to the extent to which the research is clearly placed in a comparative context, so that it becomes quite apparent that our interest is not in the oddities of a particular culture but in the way in which different cultures handle problems common to all of them.

It is particularly important to the development of a cooperative relationship that we not only communicate our awareness of the continuity between more and less developed societies with respect to problems of social change, but that we also build opportunities for mutual exposure into our research plans. Thus, if we are interested in studying tribal conflicts in Africa, we should try to provide an opportunity for our African colleagues to study race relations in the United States. Similarly, if we are interested in studying the social consequences of rapid urbanization in Asia, we should try to provide an opportunity for our Asian colleagues to make direct observations in the slum areas of U.S. cities. Such reciprocal arrangements would help to overcome the potential resentment that one-sided exposure might arouse. At the same time, they would provide excellent opportunities for training young investigators and enhance the contributions of colleagues from developing countries to the larger research enterprise.

Use of research for purposes of intelligence or intervention. Suspicion about the use of social research as a cover for espionage or intervention in foreign countries arose dramatically in the now famous case of Project Camelot (see Horowitz, 1965; Silvert, 1965). While there are no indications whatsoever that either espionage or intervention was involved in this case, it helps to bring into focus some of the ethical problems arising out of the political relationship between the foreign scholar's country and the host country.

I do not need to dwell on the obvious point that no social scientist ought to participate, directly or indirectly, in any operation that uses social science research as a front for intelligence work or intervention in another country. If he engages in such activities, he is not working as a social scientist and he certainly must not pretend to be doing so. I would also regard it as clearly inconsistent with scientific ethics for a social scientist to work for an academic or research organization that serves as a cover for intelligence operations, even if he himself does not participate in them, since he is allowing his scientific standing to be used to legitimize these activities.

The problem, however, goes beyond the obvious and ethically straightforward question of whether a piece of social science research is an act of intervention in disguise. Given the nature of the relationship between the United States and Latin America, for example, a perfectly legitimate study, carried out by honest investigators, may in subtle ways reflect an interventionist policy and contribute to it. This may happen, as it seemed to happen in the case of Project Camelot, when a study, though free and independent in its operations, is carried out for a military client and uses military policy objectives as its frame of reference and source of assumptions (Horowitz, 1965).

The important question that the social scientist must ask himself when he enters into a foreign country to do research on politically sensitive matters is whether he is truly an autonomous agent, not only in the sense of being free to choose his own methods, but also in the sense of being free to question certain basic assumptions and to entertain a totally new set of assumptions—in other words, in the sense of being free to function as a scientist. He must ask himself whether the auspices under which he is doing the research are such that he is really bound, even in the absence of an explicit contract to that effect, to take a particular perspective as his point of departure and to continue within its terms. To the extent that he is, he is not really operating as an autonomous investigator and should not present himself as such. As Silvert (1965) points out, "the peculiar attribute and unique scientific virtue of the university-affiliated social scientist is his freedom. Once [it is] abridged, for whatever reason, then the people relying on his objectivity are in serious danger of accepting a misrepresented product. . . ." (p. 224).

The crucial issue, it should be noted, is not the sponsorship of the research or the source of funds, but the nature of the explicit or implicit contract under which the funds are obtained. It is a good general rule, incidentally, to be very clear about both the source of funds and the nature of the contract, in order to allow colleagues in the host society to make their own estimates about the political implications of the research and in order to allay their understandable suspicions. In this connection let me again quote Silvert (1965), in his comment on the aftermath of the Camelot affair:

> . . . The first step toward rebuilding the consciously extended confidence of Latin American scholars and governments is to be willing to reveal the sources of our funds, the premises of our studies, the nature of our data, and the bases of our conclusions. We should also make every effort to go beyond making data and findings available; we must help to make effective the ability of trained Latin Americans to use those materials, for clearly simple revelation is not enough. The skill to understand is also required (p. 228).

Beyond sharing information, the foreign investigator ought to engage in close, frank consultation with colleagues in the host country. This would enable him not only to allay their suspicions and answer their questions, and to learn through them about the suspicions and questions that others have, but also to discover certain implicit assumptions that he might have been making un-wittingly. Even more desirable would be full participation of colleagues in the host country in the formulation, conduct, and analysis of the research, not as consultants or specialists, but as collaborators, sharing in basic decisions. Under these circum-stances, it is less likely that subtle reflections of an interventionist policy would slip into the research design.

Exploitation of the host country. The researcher from an industrialized country often engages in activities that his col-leagues in the host country regard as exploitative and that thus arouse their resentment. The foreign scholar may come into the country, arrange to get help from local social scientists in the col-lection of his data, give them fair compensation for their help, and then go home with his data to analyze them and write them up. He is too busy and task-oriented and thus not sufficiently thoughtful to view these activities as exploitation. The local scholar, however, resents the fact that he is working on problems of others, without advancing his own career and without being left more capable to initiate research on his own. He sees the foreign scholar as "an exporter of data" (Silvert, 1965, p. 227), who takes all that is valuable out of the country to use for his own ends.

Such feelings of exploitation are less likely to develop if research collaborators in the host country are not merely assigned a specific task in the project and trained to perform it. To the extent to which participation in the project contributes to their general training and provides them with broad experience, they will come away from it feeling more capable to initiate their own research on problems of their own choosing. Such an outcome is most likely to occur if colleagues from the developing countries have maximum opportunity to participate in all phases of the re-search, including the definition of the problem and the initial planning.

Aside from the ethical problem and the feeling of resent-ment engendered by the more exploitative relationship, the growth of social psychology as a discipline within the developing countries is at issue here. The growth of the discipline can be advanced only if the capabilities of personnel in developing coun-tries for initiating and carrying out their own research relevant to their own interests are enhanced. Research projects organized by North American and European investigators are particularly likely to contribute to this end if they are carried out within the context of a training program. That is, if investigators from other countries come not merely to carry out a specific project, but to help set up or to contribute to an ongoing training program— along the lines of the program being developed by Syracuse University and Makerere College (Kampala) under the direction of Marshall Segall—they are more likely to make a long-range contribution, while at the same time pursuing their research interests. It is important to stress, in this connection, that an arrangement that is one-sided in the other direction—that is, one whereby the North American or European psychologist comes to a developing country entirely for the purpose of serving that country, without viewing this experience as relevant to his own research interests— is also untenable in the long run. A cooperative relationship in which one side is always the benefactor and the other the beneficiary will not be acceptable for long to either side. The most promising relationship is a reciprocal one, in which participation by colleagues from the developing countries enhances their own capabilities, while at the same time advancing in concrete ways the research goals of the visiting scholar.

Diversion of local research talent. The foreign scholar is usually in a better position to offer financial and other inducements and may thus divert local research talent to work on his problems. Members of the host society may resent the use of their limited human resources for research on the theoretical problems of the outside scholar rather than on the pressing immediate problems faced by the society. To the extent to which this resentment is based on a perceived conflict between theoretical research and research that has social utility, I would argue, as I have already done earlier, that social-psychological research certainly can have and typically does have practical implications, even if they are not immediately apparent. We can respond to the concern about the social relevance of psychological research by integrating our theoretical interests with research that takes the problems of developing societies as its starting point, and by demonstrating convincingly that some theoretical studies that have no obvious immediate utility do have long-range relevance to these problems.

Beyond that, the remedy that I have already mentioned several times is equally applicable here: If colleagues from the host society participate fully in the formulation of the research, then there is a greater likelihood that it will in fact be relevant to the special problems of their societies as they see them.

Conclusion. Most of the ethical problems that arise in the relationship between social scientists from more and less developed societies can be linked to the pseudo-imperialist character that these relationships sometimes take on. While I doubt that most North American social scientists have imperialistic values or character structures, the realities of their own situations and of the situations into which they come tend to cast them into imperialistic roles. Many of us have assumed, implicitly and without questioning, that the other society is simply there for us to research upon it, and that we can take what we wish from it as long as we pay the fair market price. In the process, we have too often displayed a lack of respect for the values of the society, the sensitivities of its members, the dignity of our respondents, and the personal and professional aspirations of our colleagues. Such an attitude simply will not do. The *sine qua non*, it seems to me, for coming to grips with these ethical problems, and by the same token for extending psychological research on social change, is the development of patterns of truly participatory and reciprocal cooperation. We need to experiment more actively with exchanges that involve mutual exposure, with collaborative research projects built on full participation and reciprocal benefit, with international institutes for research and training, with closer integration between research and training efforts, with international boards to review projects that may be politically sensitive. Needless to say, the degree and type of international cooperation will have to differ from project to project, but the participatory and reciprocal relationship must become our norm—the background against which ethical conduct can be defined and mutual trust can develop.

CHAPTER 4

INTRODUCTION

How can social scientists enhance their ability to carry out effective research in foreign areas and increase both its scientific value and its ethical sensitivity? Two fundamental requirements emerge out of the discussion in Chapter Three. First, we must make certain that our research is truly independent and that we are free not only to choose our problems and methods but also to question the basic assumptions underlying the institutions and policies that come under our scrutiny. Secondly, we must internationalize social science and carry out our research within the framework of an international community of scholars. These two conclusions represent the starting point of the present chapter.

Chapters Three and Four differ in their substantive focus: Chapter Three dealt with research on social change, while Chap-

ter Four deals with research on foreign policy. Both, however, are concerned with research in foreign areas, and particularly in developing countries. Moreover, both emphasize the potential contributions of social research to basic thinking about social problems and policy questions. The two chapters are really companion pieces and were written in close proximity to each other—though with different audiences in mind. In Chapter Three I address myself primarily to my colleagues, while Chapter Four is largely directed to government agencies and policy-makers. Chapter Three tries to show that, from an ethical point of view, research in foreign areas must be truly independent and international; Chapter Four calls on government decision-makers to make such independent and international research possible, and points out why it is in the long-range interest of the nation to do so.

Part of the background of both chapters, as I pointed out in introducing Chapter Three, is the debate generated by Project Camelot and its aftermath. I go into this affair more fully in the present chapter, although it is merely a case in point for more general questions about needed directions in foreign policy research.

Another part of the background are the disclosures, around the time these pieces were written, of academic involvements with the Central Intelligence Agency. I touched on this problem only lightly at the time, because I regarded such involvements as so blatantly and self-evidently beyond the pale that I saw no need for elaboration. Now, alas, it has become evident that the problem is far more serious and pervasive than most of us realized. As I write these lines, I am still stunned by the recent disclosures of CIA support of the National Student Association and various other cultural and educational organizations. I am shocked by the discovery of how profoundly the values of an open society have been perverted by our obsession with the Cold War; and I am distressed by the realization that I no longer know who can and who cannot be trusted. In the relationship of American scholars and intellectuals with their counterparts abroad, the whole basis for trust has now been shattered. The American social scientist pursuing research in foreign areas can expect to find many doors closed to him. His colleagues abroad will, for good reason, regard him with deep suspicion and be afraid to become entangled with

him. *Under these circumstances, the central message of this chap-*
ter—the need to establish the independent and international
character of foreign area research—becomes crucial to the very
survival of this line of research. It will be necessary to consider
very seriously some of the proposals at the end of Chapter Four
for conducting research under international auspices and for estab-
lishing international review boards, if we can ever hope to find a
basis for rebuilding a relationship of trust.

Finally, I should mention the war in Vietnam as a third
part of the background that strongly affected me as I was writing
Chapters Three and Four and other pieces in this volume. My
dismay about American policy in Vietnam gives added depth to
my desire to contribute to constructive social change in develop-
ing countries, as I note in Chapter Three; and strengthens my
sense of urgency about the input of new ideas and assumptions
into the foreign policy process, as I note in the chapter that fol-
lows. Some of my concerns about the war in Vietnam will be
expressed more fully in Chapter Eleven.

The present essay is based on an address presented at the
meetings of the Society for Applied Anthropology in Milwaukee,
Wisconsin, on May 6, 1966. It was also published in the International Studies Quarterly, *1968, 12, 16–37.*

The Use of University Resources in Foreign Policy Research

My purpose here is to call on the federal government and
its various agencies—both legislative and executive—to make a

major commitment to a new kind of basic research. What I am advocating is a large-scale investment in behavioral science research, centered in the universities and concerned with foreign policy issues and foreign areas. The research would be marked by two central characteristics: (1) It would be a completely and genuinely independent effort, built on the understanding that any assumptions may be freely entertained, no matter how heretical they might appear, and any ideas may be fully pursued, no matter where they might ultimately lead. (2) It would be defined as a task for the international community of behavioral scientists, so that, to the maximum degree possible, research would be designed, reviewed, carried out, and analyzed by American scholars in collaboration with their colleagues from other parts of the world.

I shall try to show why such an investment in an independent and international research effort is of crucial importance to our society. I will then proceed to point to the almost total absence of government support for such research at the present time, using Project Camelot and its aftermath as points of reference for the distance that we have yet to travel. Finally, I shall spell out some of the implications of this analysis for what I would regard as a desirable pattern of government support for foreign policy research.

⌘ CRITERIA FOR RESEARCH ON FOREIGN POLICY ⌘

Our foreign policy must confront the fundamental truism that we are living in a revolutionary age. Of special relevance to our international relations are the revolution in weapons systems, and what is variously called the revolution of human rights, or the revolution of rising aspirations—in short, the emergence of Africa, Asia, and Latin America (see Chapters Two and Three). These changes have presented and continue to present our policymakers with new problems and new possibilities—with new realities that the policy process must take into account. Patterns of interaction among nations have been changing and new international institutions have been emerging. Power relationships within the international system have been shifting and new centers of power have arisen. The position of the United States within the

international system, in particular, has undergone radical changes
in the postwar period, and we find ourselves in new roles for
which our earlier history has not adequately prepared us.

It is part of the nature of the revolutionary situation in
which we find ourselves that the failure to understand the new
realities and to adopt policies that are consistent with them—
and to adjust these policies as circumstances keep changing—can
have disastrous consequences. It may lead to a nuclear war that
no one desires and from which no one can benefit; it may lead, as
I said in Chapter Two, to a world dangerously divided along racial
lines, in which our nation is the chief protagonist of the rich
and arrogant white world; and it may lead to an erosion of democratic processes within our own society, as secret bureaucracies
take on increasingly important functions. The current impasse in
our Vietnam policy illustrates the danger of a foreign policy that
is out of touch with new realities and that fails to adapt itself to
changing circumstances. We find ourselves committed to a policy
in which means and ends are badly out of balance, and which has
deeply disturbing long-run implications for our relationship to
China and the rest of the Communist world, our relationship to
the developing nations, and the relationship of our administration
to the American public in the formulation and conduct of foreign
policy.[1]

If we are to achieve a proper relationship between means
and ends in our foreign policy, then we must have a constant flow
of new inputs into the policy process. We need new ideas, new
facts, new analyses, new perspectives—and a continuing effort to
re-examine our goals and formulate our policies in the light of
these. Too often, however, our policy-making machinery is not
equipped to generate these new inputs or to utilize new ideas and
data generated elsewhere. There is a strong tendency for our
policy-makers to be caught within a limited factual and analytic
framework, and to select their ends and means in terms of this
framework, and thus to ignore new developments, new realities,
and new possibilities that might be quite apparent if they were
able to view the problem from a different perspective. For example, I would argue that our policy vis-à-vis the developing

---

[1] These issues are discussed more fully in Chapter Eleven.

world is guided almost exclusively by the Cold War framework, which certainly has some validity but is far too limited and hardly applicable to that situation. As a result, our policy tends to be unrealistic, self-defeating, and inconsistent with our traditional national values.

Behavioral science research represents one source of new inputs into the policy process and can be extremely useful in providing different approaches and different ways of looking at problems, which can form a basis for adapting policies to changing circumstances. Behavioral science is certainly not the only source of potentially useful inputs. Historical scholars and area specialists can often provide data and insights that have not entered into the formulation of existing policy and that can contribute significantly to the policy process—as was demonstrated, for example, by a recent statement on American China policy prepared by a group of scholars in the field of Asian affairs, operating entirely outside of the decision-making apparatus.[2] There are, however, certain unique contributions that behavioral science research can make.

Behavioral science not only provides a special set of concepts and methods, capable of yielding relevant data and interpretations, but it also represents a special analytic approach. It regards any particular state of affairs as only one of a range of alternatives and is concerned with the conditions under which different arrangements emerge. Therefore, it is more alert to the possibilities for changing the existing situation by changing the underlying conditions. For example, the behavioral scientist would regard the assumptions underlying our international institutions or our relations with the developing world as only one of a number of possible sets of assumptions, and hence open to change. This kind of analysis can thus contribute to the development of new international institutions, or new patterns of international relations, that are more in keeping with the new realities. Moreover, the conceptual framework that behavioral science can

---

[2] The statement, the names of the 198 Asian scholars who signed it, and large portions of a position paper prepared by Betty Goetz Lall as background to the statement were published in the *New York Times* on Monday, March 21, 1966.

bring to bear on a particular policy issue may provide a new handle for identifying the dimensions of the issue and developing policy alternatives.

If behavioral science research is to fulfill these functions of providing new inputs into the policy process and offering new approaches and perspectives, then it must operate outside of the apparatus charged with policy-making and execution. Research that is tied to foreign policy or military operations is, of necessity, conceived within the framework of existing policy. While it may be legitimate in its own right, it does not fulfill the function of providing new frameworks that would not normally emerge out of the policy-making apparatus itself. Research carried on by policy-making agencies—like all other operations carried on by these agencies—tends to perpetuate the existing framework, rather than discover its limitations. For research that is capable of questioning the assumptions of current policy and of introducing new perspectives, it is necessary to turn to independent outside agencies, and particularly to the universities.

The mere fact that the research is carried out at a university does not, of course, make it truly independent. It goes without saying that, to be independent, the research must be free from external interference—from direct or indirect control, censorship, or pressure by government agencies. But beyond such freedom from interference, the task of the investigator must be so defined and his relationship to the sponsoring agency so structured that he is free to formulate his problem in terms that transcend the existing policy framework. It is often true in a contractual relationship between an operating agency and a university scholar that the agency defines the questions that are to be asked and the assumptions on which these are to be based—in short, that it determines the framework within which the research is to be carried out. In such a relationship, the investigator may be entirely free from external interference, he may be free to determine the methods of investigation, the form of the analysis, the interpretation of the data. He is not free, however, to question basic policy assumptions, to make these assumptions themselves open to debate and investigation. He is not free to bring entirely new ways of thinking to bear on the problem. And, as a consequence, he is not free to come up with conclusions that question existing policies in fundamental ways.

To be maximally useful, the research should not only be independent in all the ways that I have described, but it should also be carried out, as far as possible, within the context of an international community of scholars. Even the independent American scholar tends, to varying degrees, to approach foreign policy issues from one of the perspectives dominant in our society and to be limited by prevailing assumptions. Scholars differing in national background, however, can bring different perspectives to bear on analyses of international relations. We are able to develop new insights into our own foreign policy process when we see it through the eyes of representatives of other nations. Obviously, each scholar, whatever his nationality, is likely to have a somewhat limited perspective, determined by the situation in which his own country finds itself. But, through the confrontation of different perspectives provided by international collaboration, new and more balanced inputs into the policy process may be generated. Conceptualizations of the relationship between the United States and Africa, for example, can clearly be sharpened and enriched by the assumptions with which our African colleagues are likely to approach the problem and the dimensions they are likely to introduce. Similarly, our understanding of the functioning of international organizations is bound to benefit from the exposure to varied orientations of scholars whose respective nations play different roles within the international system.

So far I have argued that research that is truly independent and informed by international perspectives is crucial as a source of the new ideas needed by our government in the conduct of our foreign policy under present world conditions. A second reason why the independent and international character of foreign policy research becomes important applies to those problems that require research in foreign areas, particularly in developing societies. I might add that the kinds of issues that arise here are involved not only in research that is directly related to foreign policy problems, but to any social science research carried out in foreign areas.

American scholars have been descending upon foreign

countries with increasing frequency. In developing countries, in particular, their arrival is often greeted with an understandably high degree of suspicion and resentment on the part of local scholars and other members of the host societies. There has been an increasing, though probably still insufficient, awareness of the reasons for these reactions, of the ethical problems surrounding foreign area research that they bring into focus, and of their implications for the proper relationship between American scholars and their counterparts in other countries (see, for example, Silvert, 1965; Diamond, 1966; and Hance and Curtin, 1966). The increased awareness and discussion of these issues is in part a consequence—and, in my opinion, one of the positive consequences —of the Camelot affair. The basic issues that arise here involve the sensitivity, responsibility, and professional ethics of American social scientists. There is clearly a need for stock-taking by individual scholars and by the profession as a whole. That this is a matter of central concern to me is evident from the preceding chapter, a large portion of which is devoted to the ethical issues that tend to generate resentment and suspicion. For the present purposes, however, I merely want to point to the implications of these problems for the kind of foreign policy, and other social science, research that can be carried out in foreign areas.

The visiting American scholar is readily suspected of neo-colonialism. In part, this suspicion is rooted in the nature of the reality situation. American scholars are representatives of a richer and more powerful society, which is perceived as having an interest in influencing and controlling the affairs of other nations for its own benefit. Moreover, the individual American scholar, in his relation to his local counterparts, often reflects the perceived relationship between the two countries. He comes into the host society with his seemingly unlimited means and exploits it for his own benefit, perhaps at the expense of or at least without commensurate benefit to the local scholar who helps him collect his data.

Suspicions of neo-colonialism are also rooted in the nature of the historical relationship between the host country and the former colonial power (or, in the case of Latin American countries, between the host country and the United States itself). Thus,

Hance and Curtin (1966) point to some of the historical reasons why American scholars in African countries are sometimes seen as threats to the independence of the host society. In the colonial period,

> . . . the School of Oriental and African Studies in London and equivalent schools and institutes of the other colonial powers had teaching and research programs directly tied to the needs of colonial administrations. Privately endowed research by foreigners was rare. With this background it is hardly surprising that most Africans outside of academic circles assume that American research in Africa today is at least semiofficial. Those nations that are strictly nonaligned are all the more likely to fear the flood of American scholars: it appears to be inconsistent with their international posture (p. 26).

Perceived threats to national independence are likely to arise even when the research is in fact privately sponsored and deals with subjects that are politically neutral. Clearly the problem becomes exacerbated when the research is sponsored by an agency of the American government and when it deals with matters that are politically sensitive.

There is no simple formula for handling these problems. However, to the extent to which the research is truly independent and international in character, we have at least a basis for arriving at a solution. A scholar who in fact does not operate, directly or indirectly, as an agent of the American military or foreign policy apparatus, and who is truly free, as an independent scientist, to question basic policy assumptions, should be able to allay the suspicions of his colleagues in other countries, even if the source of his funds happens to be the federal government of the United States. His ability to do so should be further enhanced to the extent that he sets up truly collaborative relationships with these colleagues and asks them to share in the formulation of the research problem and in the execution of the various phases of the research.

In short, then, the independent and international character of research in foreign areas is a central condition for eliciting the trust of local colleagues and other members of the host society.

Without such trust it is doubtful that the research can have much
validity, and that it will be possible, in the long run, to carry it
out at all.

⚛ THE PAUCITY OF INDEPENDENT AND
INTERNATIONAL RESEARCH ⚛

I have tried to show that foreign policy research must be
independent and international in character if it is to serve as a
source of the new ideas that are so desperately needed in the
foreign policy process and if it is to elicit the trust of the populations—and particularly the scholars—in the various foreign countries in which much of this research has to be carried out. Very
little support for research that meets these criteria, however, is
available from federal sources—nor, for that matter, is support
from private sources overly generous. Just how far we are from
meeting the conditions for effective behavioral science research
on foreign policy issues was revealed by Project Camelot and its
consequences.

Project Camelot has been useful in that it has alerted the
social science community to a number of fundamental issues that
we really could not have ignored much longer. I have already
mentioned one set of such issues, with which I only deal in passing here—the ethics of research in foreign areas. Another set of
issues, highlighted by the debate over Camelot, relates to the character of the research on foreign policy and foreign areas that is
being carried out, and the nature of the support available for such
research. Project Camelot exemplified a type of research which,
by its very nature, cannot meet the criteria of true independence
and international conception. These failures are by no means
unique to Cameolt; Camelot has merely helped to dramatize the
great need for a different model of foreign policy research, especially when conducted in foreign areas, and for a different type
of support for such research.

It would be a mistake to think of Project Camelot as a
simple case of university scholars carrying out research for the
Army in support of its counterinsurgency activities. No one with
any intimate knowledge of the Project has ever suggested that it
was a cover for intelligence work or intervention. Nor did Project

Camelot make any attempts to conceal the sources of its funds, as is true for the far more questionable research activities that some social scientists have apparently carried out under the auspices of the CIA. It so happens that the beginning of the end of Project Camelot did involve a misrepresentation of the Project's sponsorship on the part of a spokesman for it in Chile, but the directors of the Project were always completely open about Army support and even about the nature of the Army's interest in the Project. In fact, they have been criticized for allowing the Army's language of and concern with counterinsurgency to suffuse their own theoretical documents.

The social scientists connected with the Project clearly conceived of it as an opportunity for carrying out basic research. As a matter of fact, it is precisely because support for basic behavioral science research of this scope is so difficult to find that many investigators were attracted by what seemed to them to be a real breakthrough for the field. Moreover, there is no indication that the investigators were deliberately designing the study in such a way as to find specific answers to the question of how to put down rebellion or facilitate the Army's counterinsurgency activities; or that the Army expected them to design the research in this way. This, of course, does not absolve the investigators of responsibility for the fact that the Army was indeed interested in the research because of its implications for anticipating and putting down rebellion. As Charles Tilly (1966) notes in a recent letter to *The American Sociologist,* "The Army—and, behind it, the Department of Defense—supported Camelot in hopes of getting some guides to policy. The organizers of the project knew all this, and to that extent took responsibility for the probable use of any reliable findings. Where the sponsor has a visible interest in the outcome and a significant likelihood of acting on the findings, any one of us takes on a measure of responsibility by accepting his support" (p. 84). Nevertheless, we are not dealing here with a case of operational research conducted for the Army.

The real issue raised by Project Camelot is not that the sponsoring agency was dictating the research. The investigators were free to choose their own theoretical orientations and research methods, and to conduct their research in whatever way they saw fit. The nature of their relationship to the sponsoring agency, however, was such that they were not free to question the basic assumptions of existing policy, and to formulate the research problem in terms of a totally different perspective. The Army did not dictate to the directors of Project Camelot how they should go about their research task, but the nature of the contract, at least implicitly, was such that the research would take the Army's counterinsurgency perspective as its point of departure and would continue within its terms. For example, the assumptions of American military policy—such as the assumption that forces toward social revolution are dangerous and pathological manifestations in developing societies, that maintaining political stability is more important than meeting the needs that may precipitate unrest, that contributing to nation-building in developing countries is part of the mission of the U.S. Army—were accepted without question and built into the design. Thus, the investigators were not able to approach policy issues as truly independent social scientists, for whom any existing set of assumptions represents only one of several possible sets of assumptions and must itself be placed under scrutiny. Their tendency to intermingle counter-insurgency jargon with behavioral science jargon was not just an error in public relations, but a symptom of the degree to which the sponsor's perspective set the tone for the entire research effort.

I. L. Horowitz (1965), in his excellent discussion of these issues, describes the nature of the relationship of the Army to Project Camelot in the following terms:

> . . . The Army, however respectful and protective of free expression, was "hiring help" and not openly and honestly submitting a problem to the higher profes-sional and scientific authority of social science.
>
> The propriety of the Army to define and delimit all questions, which Camelot should have had a right to examine, was never placed in doubt. This is a tragic precedent; it reflects the arrogance of a consumer of in-tellectual merchandise. And this relationship of inequal-ity corrupted the lines of authority, and profoundly limited the autonomy of the social scientists involved. It became clear that the social scientist savant was not so much functioning as an applied social scientist as he was supplying information to a powerful client (p. 47).

What is crucial here is not the sponsorship of the research or the source of funds per se, but the nature of the explicit or implicit contract under which the funds are obtained. To quote Horowitz again:

> . . . The sponsorship of a project, whether by the United States Army or by the Boy Scouts of America, is by itself neither good nor bad. Sponsorship is good or bad only insofar as the intended outcomes can be pre-determined and the parameters of those intended outcomes tailored to the sponsor's expectations. Those social scientists critical of the project never really denied its freedom and independence, but questioned instead the purpose and character of its intended results (p. 47).

To return to my central thesis, it is clear that research organized and conceived along the lines of Project Camelot is not likely to generate the new inputs into the foreign policy process that are so essential. The investigators do not bring truly independent frames of reference to bear on the problem, but operate largely within the frame of reference of their military sponsor. Thus, the research is far more likely to aid in the perpetuation of existing policies than in the development of alternatives. Similarly, the nature of the enterprise precluded the possibility of including local scholars as true collaborators in the research, in the sense of involving them in the formulation of the problem and giving them an opportunity to raise basic questions. Thus, the policy process is also unable to benefit from the potential new inputs that international collaboration in such research might provide by allowing for a confrontation of a variety of national perspectives and for a discovery of unwitting assumptions that American investigators may be bringing to the problem. The fact that the research is not truly independent nor international in character also makes it difficult to elicit the trust of the host society, as the fate of Project Camelot has so dramatically demonstrated.

If Project Camelot has helped to bring to our attention the limitations of so much of our research on foreign policy issues, the response to it has done hardly anything to correct for these limitations. There has been considerable criticism within the government of Camelot-type operations, but by and large it has not been based on the kinds of considerations that I have been raising. Far from expanding the support of research that is truly independent and international in character, the official response to Project Camelot suggests a constriction of such support.

To begin with, the cancellation of Project Camelot itself, despite the Project's shortcomings, constitutes a blow to behavioral science research. The value of behavioral science approaches is a matter of considerable controversy within the foreign policy apparatus, and on the whole, though there are many exceptions, the military agencies have been more favorably inclined toward behavioral science than the civilian agencies—particularly the Department of State. Thus, the cancellation of Project Camelot represents, in a sense, a victory for the opponents of behavioral science. There are indications that it will be even more difficult to obtain support for behavioral science research on foreign policy issues than it has been in the past, and that granting agencies have become even more cautious in their reactions to new proposals. Moreover, we can expect a cutting back of *all* behavioral science research in the foreign policy area, not just research of the Camelot variety. Decisions about the support of research are not likely to be made in terms of the criteria that I would favor—the independent and international character of the proposed research—but in terms of short-run questions of possible embarrassment to members of the foreign policy apparatus. As things stand now, then, the cancellation of Camelot is likely to result in less rather than more of the kind of behavioral science research that our foreign policy process so badly needs.

The major official consequence of the furor over Project Camelot has been the establishment of machinery, within the Department of State, for reviewing research proposals of other government agencies involved in foreign policy operations.[3] There are many reassuring signs that this review process will not take

---

[3] Research supported by the National Institute of Mental Health or by the National Science Foundation is not included under this directive, since these agencies are concerned with basic research rather than mission-related research.

the form of blatant censorship, heedless of the requirements for freedom in scholarly work (see Hughes, 1965; Fendrick, 1966). Nevertheless, the review process is likely to have an inhibiting effect on behavioral science research on foreign policy issues. Projects are evaluated in terms of their potential for touching sensitive areas within foreign governments, and thus creating incidents that might be embarrassing to the United States government. These considerations are certainly not irrelevant, particularly since, as Project Camelot has illustrated, researchers have often been completely oblivious to the sensitivities of the host societies. This is, however, a very narrow and limited criterion to use in the evaluation of foreign policy research. It is likely to lead to a situation in which federally supported research—at least the research supported by the agencies subject to State Department review—will be restricted to innocuous problems that are unlikely to upset foreign governments or American diplomats. Research selected on the basis of such a criterion does not seem conducive to the new ideas that our foreign policy requires.

It is reasonable that research directly related to the operations of an agency involved in an aspect of foreign policy be reviewed by a central board within the Department of State. By this criterion, Project Camelot is probably a proper subject for such review since it was not sufficiently separated from the actual operations of the Army. Not all of the research activities sponsored by agencies in the broad foreign policy field are of this nature, however, nor would such a state of affairs be desirable. For example, it would be useful if such units as the Agency for International Development and the Arms Control and Disarmament Agency were able to sponsor research that is more basic in the sense that it is less tied to the specific missions of these agencies. In this connection, one of the fascinating anomalies is that some of the military agencies, specifically research offices within the Navy and the Air Force, have stood out in their support of truly independent, basic behavioral science research in foreign areas. While it is true that their relative freedom of movement in supporting such research derives from the important role of the military in our society, the fact remains that these agencies have made valuable contributions to the kind of behavioral science research in foreign areas that is needed.

Thus, it is likely that the new review process within the State Department will inhibit nonoperational research that is now sponsored or that might have been sponsored in the future by some of the agencies under its jurisdiction. We see again, then, that the response to the Camelot affair has the effect of restricting existing sources of potential support for independent and international research without opening up new opportunities to take their place.

⋛ A PATTERN OF FEDERAL SUPPORT ⋚

What are some of the implications of this analysis of the situation for the development of a more desirable pattern of federal support of behavioral science research on foreign policy issues? That is, what type of support would make the most effective use of university resources by promoting research that is truly independent and international in conception—the kind of research for which, as we have seen, federal support has been extremely scarce and may be even scarcer in the future?

First, let me consider some of the negative implications, that is, implications for types of research support that should be *avoided*. It is improper and dangerous to use universities as a way of lending legitimacy and an aura of scientific objectivity to research activities that are in fact designed to carry out the policy objectives of a particular operating agency. Blatant examples of this kind of abuse are research projects and research centers that are secretly supported by the CIA. At worst, these might involve operational research designed to promote CIA policies while parading as independent scholarly endeavors. But even at best (where, for example, an investigator carries out presumably legitimate research, say in the area of Russian studies, under the auspices of an agency that fronts for the CIA) it is difficult to imagine that the research is unaffected by the source of support. Of course, since the scholarly community and the public are not apprised of the CIA sponsorship, they cannot take it into account in evaluating the research. Research that is secretly supported by the CIA, however, represents only the most extreme case of a more general problem exemplified by Project Camelot. For Camelot too, despite its commendable openness and concern with basic research, was in essence designed to carry out the policy objectives of its military sponsors.

There is, of course, nothing improper about an operating agency's doing research that is designed to implement its policy objectives, as long as it does so openly and avowedly. But, in general, contracting with universities for such research does not represent a good use of the special resources of the university, which center in its ability to question existing policies in terms of different and genuinely independent frames of reference. The problem becomes more serious when this type of operational research is carried out by a university under the guise of independent scholarly pursuits, or even when the role of the investigator—as independent university scholar or agent of the operating agency—is allowed to remain ambiguous. Under these circumstances, the function of the university is perverted and its credibility is undermined, so that it becomes less and less able to carry out independent research in the future and to serve as a source of new inputs into the policy process.

The basic responsibility for preventing the poor use and the abuse of university resources and for avoiding the involvement of university personnel in improper and ambiguous activities rests with the individual scholar, the university administration, and the professional association. They must establish principles and draw lines; they must question themselves and others and be prepared to feel and express moral indignation. Government agencies, however, must also take responsibility for the kinds of requests they make of university scholars and the kinds of temptations they place before them. They must take into account, in their own planning, that the improper use of university resources is self-defeating in the long run, in that it destroys the independence and credibility of the university scholar, which are the major bases of his potential contribution to the policy process.

Now let me turn to some of the positive implications of the preceding analysis, implications for the type of research support that, in my opinion, the federal government *should* provide. I have argued that we need behavioral science research that is truly independent and international in character. There is very little support for such research at the moment and a major investment in this type of activity will have to be made. Whether we like it or not, a large part of the support for this research will have to come from the federal government, given the size of the investment that is required.

This situation presents a special challenge to Congress and the administration. They must recognize that it is in the long-range interest of the country to promote foreign policy research that is truly independent, research that is free to question in fundamental ways the assumptions on which our foreign policy is based and to entertain radically different sets of assumptions. They must be willing to provide funds for basic research with no strings attached and to allow the investigators to follow their studies wherever they may lead, without any direct or indirect political interference. They must be prepared for the possibility that the findings of such research may fail to support some of the assumptions of existing policy and may, by implication, be highly critical of certain current policy directions.

It would take a real breadth of outlook for a government to support, on a large scale, research that may challenge some of the basic assumptions behind its policies. Yet such research is indispensable if our foreign policy is to adjust to the constantly changing circumstances of the present world. Support of such research would be both an indicator of and a contributor to the health of our society. Moreover, various precedents suggest that the proposed arrangement is feasible, that governments are capable of supporting activities which are potential sources of criticism of their own policies. Thus, Western European universities have been operating under a long-standing tradition of governmental support without governmental interference, and their right to question and criticize official assumptions is securely established. In many countries, the broadcasting system is financed by public funds and yet free of government control. In our own country, federal funds have supported activities of civil rights agencies, poverty agencies, or the Peace Corps, which have often been ahead of official policy. It ought to be possible to establish a tradition of public support for foreign policy research whose freedom to explore and criticize is fully protected.

The best mechanism for providing this support would be through some agency that is clearly outside of the realm of foreign policy operations and is charged, instead, with the funding of basic research. The National Science Foundation or the recently proposed National Foundation for the Social Sciences (U.S. House of Representatives, June 6, 1966; U.S. Senate, October 11, 1966) would meet these criteria. Funds should be made available to such an agency or agencies directly and explicitly for the purpose of behavioral science research on these problems. There has been talk, after Camelot, of developing possible procedures for transferring funds from operating agencies to an agency like NSF, to reduce both the operating agency's control over the research supported by these funds and the suspicion that the research generates. I am not quite clear what these procedures would involve and what implications they carry. I must confess that when such procedures are described in terms like "fumigation" or "purification" of funds, they do not inspire much confidence in me. In any event, such transfers of funds, if they can be justified at all, are no substitute for the direct and explicit provision of funds for truly independent, basic research.

One possible mechanism would be establishment of a special program devoted to basic research on foreign policy issues and in foreign areas within the NSF. The opportunity to establish such a program exists now, in connection with a bill aimed at revising the structure and functions of the NSF that has been recently introduced in the House of Representatives by Congressman Daddario (U.S. House of Representatives, March 16, 1966). The report of the Committee on Science and Astronautics (1966), which served as the basis for the proposed bill, calls for a greater investment in social science research, as well as for "a more active role for NSF in international affairs and in the support of international scientific activities" (Daddario, 1966, p. 45). An NSF program specifically devoted to behavioral science research on foreign policy issues and in foreign areas would seem to be quite consistent with these objectives, and ought to be included as a provision of the new bill.

It is essential, of course, that the terms under which such a program is set up are completely unambiguous about the independence of the research that it supports. It must be totally free from direct or indirect control by the Departments of State or Defense or other operating agencies. In this connection, the statement in the Daddario bill that the Foundation is authorized and directed *"at the request of the Secretary of State or the Secretary of Defense*, to initiate and support specific scientific research activities in connection with matters relating to international cooperation or national security by making contracts or other arrangements (including grants, loans, and other forms of assistance) for the conduct of such scientific research" (U.S. House of Representatives, March 16, 1966, p. 2; italics added) is very disquieting. To be truly independent, a program on foreign policy research must exclude all political considerations in setting priorities, in reviewing proposals, and in making grants, and must base its judgments on the scholarly and scientific merits of the research. To do otherwise would undermine the very purpose to be served by such a program.

A research program of the type envisaged here could also be carried out by the National Foundation for the Social Sciences, if Congress passes the bills before it that call for the establishment of such an agency. There is no reason, of course, why programs of this sort could not be developed both within NSF and within the proposed new agency, perhaps with slightly different emphases. NSF has the advantage of a well-established tradition of support for basic research; the fact that this tradition takes its model from the natural sciences, however, may lead to a tendency within NSF to define as basic research only those investigations that are divorced from policy relevance and hence relatively non-controversial. The proposed new agency, on the other hand, has an advantage in that it could, from the outset, plan its research support in full cognizance of the special nature and requirements of the social and behavioral sciences.

Much depends, of course, on the terms under which the proposed National Foundation for the Social Sciences is established. In this connection, the bill introduced in the Senate by Mr. Harris and twenty other Senators (U.S. Senate, October 11, 1966) seems very promising. In its declaration of purpose, it states

> . . . that it is necessary and appropriate for the Federal Government to support, complement, and assist the accomplishment of social science research which is entirely separate from the operating departments and agencies of the United States Government; [and] . . . to help sustain among social scientists a climate encouraging

freedom of thought, imagination, and inquiry based on the democratic belief that the long-range interests of our Nation will best be served by a free and independent academic community (p. 2).

The House bill (U.S. House of Representatives, June 6, 1966), introduced by Mr. Fascell, parallels the Senate bill in many respects, but also contains some provisions that would seriously undermine the type of program that I am proposing here. It requires the concurrence of the Secretary of State before the Foundation can "support any research or other activity relating to international cooperation, foreign policy, or foreign area research" (p. 19). It also authorizes the Foundation to carry out research that requires a security classification—in contrast to the Senate bill, which explicitly and very wisely prohibits the use of any security classification by the Foundation.

In short, whether the kind of research program that I am proposing here is set up within the framework of the NSF or of a new Social Sciences Foundation, it would not serve its purpose unless its complete independence from the State Department, the Defense Department, and other operating agencies were assured. Furthermore, in line with my stress on the importance of foreign policy and foreign area research with an international base, I would urge that the proposed program be receptive to and in fact encourage applications from international research teams and research centers. It is my conviction that the feasibility and usefulness of foreign policy and foreign area research are greatly enhanced when it is built on international collaboration; and that the full development of this field of research requires that it be rooted in a cross-cutting international community of social scientists. Any moves in this direction should be supported in every way possible. This may very well mean that an American funding agency will have to turn over the control of a research project— from the initial formulation of the problem to the final interpretation of the results—to an international group of scholars. It may even mean that international bodies will have to be drawn into the process of deciding on the allocation of funds and selecting the projects to be supported. There may indeed be barriers to such arrangements, but again they are not without precedent. United States participation in various UN activities certainly involves the relinquishing of control to international bodies; and the recommendations of Senator Fulbright and others for the increasing internationalization of foreign aid are clearly in the same spirit.

This leads me to another recommendation, which is probably more controversial. While I regard it as essential that a major research program in this area be developed in the context of an agency outside the foreign policy apparatus, I would not want to see a reduction in the support for independent, basic research that is now offered by some of the operating agencies. There is the danger, however, as I have already mentioned, that the new review procedures in the Department of State may result in a cutting-back of the basic research commitments of these agencies, or a limitation of the nature of the research supported through the use of narrow and often irrelevant criteria. To counteract these tendencies, I would propose that a different kind of review process be initiated for those projects that are in fact not operational even though they may be sponsored by an arm of an operating agency. The main purpose of the review procedure is, presumably, to avoid situations in which a research project touches on the sensitivities of a foreign society and thus causes embarrassment to U.S. relations with that society. I submit that this purpose can be met more effectively, and with less inhibiting consequences for the research itself, if the review process is carried out by an international board of social scientists, rather than by a board of State Department officials.

My final recommendation is not very specific, but is meant to call attention to a problem that must not be omitted from the present discussion. If the kind of research that I have been proposing is to generate new inputs into the policy process, then we must develop mechanisms not only for supporting such research under the conditions it requires, but also for communicating the findings of this research to the relevant decision-makers. The method of selecting consultants to the policy-making apparatus and the nature of the relationship between the consultant and the agency that employs him often have the effect of reducing the potential usefulness that an outside consultant might have. Instead of bringing new perspectives to bear on problems, consultants tend to approach them from the perspective of the agency, and thus to reinforce rather than question existing policy. If new research is to have an impact on the policy process, those familiar with its findings must be consulted, even if they are likely to raise uncomfortable questions, and they must be encouraged to raise those questions, rather than give the advice that the policy-maker wants to hear.

I have spoken almost entirely about things the government must do and have touched only in passing on the responsibilities of the social scientist himself. Indeed, the social science community bears a great deal of responsibility for the paucity of truly independent research and for the failures dramatized by Project Camelot. If we are met with suspicion abroad and subjected to scrutiny at home, it is in large part because we have failed to ask ourselves, as individuals, and as a profession, some of the crucial questions about the proper relationships of the social scientist to the agencies that sponsor his research, to the foreign societies in which some of this research is carried out, and to his own society in which he has a unique role to perform. There is much new thinking that we must place on our professional agenda. This does not, however, lessen in any way the responsibility of our decision-makers to confront the kind of challenge that we as social scientists can present to them. It is a challenge to take a courageous leap by supporting and exposing themselves to the systematic questioning of their policies. It is the kind of challenge that an open society ought to be capable of accepting, and that our society must accept if it is to adapt to new realities.

PART

*P*art One was primarily concerned with value questions relating to the *products* of social research as they impinge on social life. In the next set of essays I address myself to some of the value questions that arise in the *process* of social research, that is, as the social researcher goes about his scientific and professional business. The distinction between products and process is, of course, somewhat arbitrary since the two are in constant interaction with one another. Thus, in Chapter Two I spoke in part about the way in which the very procedures of social research may contribute to the creation or extension of certain social forces. In Chapters Three and Four I spoke about the critical importance of maintaining the independent and international character of the research process if certain research products are to be attained.

THE SOCIAL SCIENTIST AS EXPERIMENTER AND SOCIAL THINKER

𝄢𝄢𝄢𝄢𝄢𝄢𝄢𝄢𝄢𝄢𝄢𝄢𝄢𝄢𝄢𝄢𝄢𝄢𝄢𝄢𝄢𝄢𝄢𝄢𝄢𝄢𝄢𝄢𝄢𝄢𝄢𝄢

Similarly, in the essays that follow, I shall often be concerned with the relationship between process and products. What unites the essays of Part Two, however, and distinguishes them, at least in emphasis, from those of Part One, is that they take as their starting point the methods and approaches used by the social researcher as he engages in the daily rounds of his scientific enterprise.

The social scientist is confronted with a variety of value issues in the definition of his research task, the setting of his research priorities, and the selection of his research methods. There are, first of all, questions about the very nature of the enterprise in which he is engaged. The goals that he is pursuing in his own research and, more generally, his conception of the purposes of social research and of its place within the larger context of intellectual activity have a considerable bearing on what he regards as important and worthwhile and what methods he deems appropriate.

Secondly, there are questions about the nature of man, which are always suffused with fundamental value preferences. Every social scientist brings to his research certain assumptions about man, about his essential characteristics and the meaning of his existence. These in turn affect the way he defines his subject matter, what he chooses to study, and how he goes about studying it.

Thirdly, there are value questions surrounding the human relationships that are an inevitable part of the scientific and professional activities of the social scientist. In part, these questions concern his relationships to students and colleagues and to the wider intellectual and scientific communities of which he is a part. To this extent, we are dealing with concerns that the social scientist shares with scholars in all other fields of endeavor. There are, however, some unique problems confronting the social scientist, which stem from the fact that human beings happen to be the subject matter of his research. Some profound ethical issues arise in the social researcher's relationship to the individuals, groups, and communities that serve as the sources of his data. An active concern with these issues must always enter into the social researcher's decisions about the problems he will study, the methods he will use, and the way he will handle his data.

The four essays that comprise Part Two address themselves to some of these different value questions which arise as the social researcher goes about his daily work, designing empirical studies and seeking a systematic understanding of social behavior. Despite the diversity of these essays, they all reflect some underlying concerns that recur in different guises—notably a concern with humanizing the orientations and procedures of social research. This concern is central to my interest in the confrontation between the scientific and humanistic study of man (Chapter Five), my conception of the place of experimental work in relation to the essential task of the social scientist (Chapter Six), my delineation of the roles for which we train our graduate students (Chapter Seven), and my attempt to re-examine the use of deception as a significant feature of our experimental methodology (Chapter

Eight). I start with two basic assumptions: that there is an inevitable tension between the scientific study of man and humanistic values; and that despite, if not because of, this tension, the scientific study of man can make unique contributions to which I attach a great deal of value. Thus, we have a dilemma not unlike that involved in the manipulation of human behavior as discussed in Chapter One. The humanization of social research, for me, cannot take the form of abandoning scientific method or of washing out the distinctions between scientific and humanistic approaches to the study of man. Rather, it requires a rethinking of the larger enterprise in which empirical social research is embedded and an active confrontation of the value conflicts it engenders.

CHAPTER 5

⋇⋇⋇⋇⋇⋇⋇⋇⋇⋇⋇⋇⋇⋇⋇⋇⋇⋇⋇⋇⋇⋇⋇

INTRODUCTION

There is a close and continual relationship between social science and social values. On the one hand, social research has a potentially important impact on the values that are held and achieved within the society. It may contribute to forces favorable to some values and unfavorable to others, as I argued in Chapters One and Two; and it may add to our understanding of social values, to our knowledge about the distribution of values over time and space, and to our ability to identify social patterns conducive to the achievement of various values. On the other hand, values have an important impact on social research. As I pointed out in Chapter Three, it is impossible to carry out social research, particularly on socially significant issues, that is unaffected by the values of the investigator and the groups to which he belongs. The choice of problem, the approach to it, and the interpretation of the findings inevitably reflect the value assumptions and preferences that the investigator brings to his research. As a matter of fact, in view of the closeness of interaction between values and social research, I would maintain that we must rethink our whole conception of social research. We will have to abandon the illusory goal of separating values from the research process and move toward a definition of social science as an activity that is necessarily and deliberately embedded in a value-oriented and policy-relevant process.

There is one view of the relationship between values and social science, however, that I regard as highly questionable. This is the view, held explicitly or implicitly by some social scientists of different persuasions, that social science is and ought to be the source of our values. The notion that values can be scientifically derived rests, in my opinion, on self-delusion, for it gives to values an objective status that they do not possess and blinds us to the various subjective forces that govern our conception of the desirable. Moreover, I regard this view as threatening to humanistic values, even though some of the social scientists who espouse it are themselves deeply committed to such values. Values that derive completely from social science must reflect, at least in the long run, the conception of man that underlies the scientific approach—and this conception, I submit, is inherently antithetical to humanistic values.

A central characteristic of the scientific study of man is that the investigator views man and society as objects, which he places at a distance and differentiates sharply from himself so that he can observe them from the outside. Because of the nature of the object of his study, he can achieve this separation and distancing only to a limited degree, and he is well-advised to be mindful of this limitation. Yet, the rules and procedures of the scientific approach are designed to approximate these conditions as much as possible. It is this objectification of man that represents the special strength of empirical social science and its unique contribution to the study of man.

The very same characteristic of social science, however, also represents its clash with humanistic values. The values held by individuals or societies are closely linked to their conception

*of the nature of man—to the model of man to which they sub-
scribe. Humanistic values rest, at least in part, on a conception
of man as a choosing agent and as an end in himself. The working
model of social science, on the other hand, takes man as an object,
buffeted about by external or internal forces beyond his control.
This is, of course, particularly true of those theoretical approaches
that use a mechanistic or a homeostatic model, but it is inherent
in the deterministic approach common to all scientific models of
man. John Seeley, who has written extensively and widely about
these problems, says in this connection: "I do not think science
can live without the principle [of determinism], and I do not
think men can live with it—as applied, at least, to themselves"
(1960b, p. 6). Elsewhere he speaks of "the peculiar problem posed
by adopting for human behavior the terminology of determinism
. . . in reference to beings whose most immediate intuition of
themselves in their most important matters is the overwhelming
intuition of choice" (1960a, p. 84).*

*The danger is, to quote Seeley once more, that as man "be-
comes to himself . . . a scientific object, an object of mere curiosity or curiosity in the service of manipulation, he ceases pari
passu to be a self, ceases to be an object of libidinal investment,
ceases to be his own habitable home, and becomes what he has
made himself, a true object for engineering, the true fruit of science. . . . It is not at all clear . . . that a science of man in the
traditional sense of the word 'science' is possible without self-
destruction—by each of himself, or of most by some" (1960b, p. 4).*

*Despite this danger, I am committed to the scientific study
of man because of its potential contribution to the understanding
of human behavior and the improvement of social life—as long as
we are clear that it is primarily an effective way of knowing about
man rather than a source of values. The conception of man as an
object is indeed a working model required for social research,
and as social scientists we assume that it captures part of the
reality; but this model does not, by any means, fully encompass
the nature of man. Social science, it must be remembered, is one
way of looking at man, one way of studying him—with certain
advantages and disadvantages peculiar to it—but it is certainly
not the only way. Literature, theology and philosophy, mysticism
and poetry, are all concerned with the study of man, and they*

usually approach it with different assumptions about the nature of man, assumptions that are more consistent with humanistic values. I believe, therefore, that in developing a basis for our values we must, at the very least, supplement and balance the scientific model with models derived from these other sources.

Social scientists occasionally confuse their partial working model of man with man "as he really is." Those who take this position argue that man really is a machine or at best an animal, and that anyone who believes otherwise is deluding himself and is being unscientific. In essence, this represents a particular ideological, if not theological, position about the nature of man. Its proponents, however, make the circular assumption that this view of man, because it is more accessible to scientific operations, is rooted in scientific knowledge and is scientifically validated. They even insist that they, unlike the humanists or the humanistically inclined social scientists, are operating in an utterly value-free context. Needless to say, I reject both this view about the nature of man and its pretension to a special scientific status.

At the same time, I have misgivings about efforts to counteract this mechanistic view with the claim that the humanistic view represents the scientifically valid picture of man "as he really is." The humanistic view does suggest many propositions about human behavior that can be put to scientific test. For example, it would lead us to postulate a need for self-actualization from which a variety of testable hypotheses can be derived. To test these hypotheses, one would have to proceed as one does in testing any other hypotheses, that is, one would have to spell out the observable behavior that would be consistent with a particular hypothesis and the conditions under which it ought to be manifested. If the behavior is observed to occur under the specified conditions, it would add strength to the postulated need for self-actualization, and point up some of the limitations of the mechanistic model. The humanistic view can, in this fashion, exert a great deal of influence on the questions we ask and the answers we obtain in the scientific study of man. What cannot be established, however, within the terms of a scientific analysis, is the validity of the basic humanistic conception of man as a choosing agent and as an end in himself. This has to remain a value assumption, rooted in non-scientific sources of knowledge about man.

To blur the distinction between the scientific and the humanistic study of man, by covering them both with the blanket of psychology, does a disservice to both of them. On the one hand, it dilutes and attenuates the unique contributions that come from the application of scientific method to the study of man and society. On the other hand, it acquiesces to a scientific imperialism which fails to acknowledge the unique and special character of other approaches to the study of man, each with its own methods, its own discipline, and its own traditions. I prefer, therefore, to maintain a clear distinction between the scientific and humanistic approaches, while recognizing that each has a legitimate contribution to make to the study of man and seeking opportunities for interaction and confrontation between them.

Chapter Five represents an exercise in this type of interaction. It is both an attempt to gain some insights about social forces from the analysis of a literary work and an assessment of the implications of that work in social-psychological terms. I chose for this purpose Aldous Huxley's last novel, Island *(1962), which is a utopian novel—one that provides very interesting contrasts with the well-known dystopian novel he published thirty years earlier,* Brave New World *(1932). My interest in the writings of Huxley actually goes back to my days as an English major in college, when I did a term paper on "Huxley as a Satirist." Beyond that, however, utopian and dystopian novels provide a rather natural arena for the interaction between literary and social-science approaches.*

This essay was originally prepared as part of the Western Behavioral Sciences Institute's Lucile P. Morrison lecture series on Science and Human Affairs. It was delivered in La Jolla, California, on April 19, 1964. It appeared in Science and Human Affairs, *a volume edited by Richard Farson and published in 1965 by Science and Behavior Books, Inc. (Palo Alto, California). It is reprinted here by permission of the editor and publisher.*

From Dystopia to Utopia:
An Analysis of Huxley's Island

Literature, like social science, is centrally concerned with the study of man and society. These two approaches to social behavior are sometimes seen as conflicting paths to the discovery of truth. Some humanists accuse psychologists and sociologists of distorting the essential truths about man and society by replacing the richness and concreteness of reality with statistics and jargon. Some behavioral scientists, on the other hand, regard literature as irrelevant to the discovery of truth since it is not based on the rigorous application of scientific method. In the next chapter I shall speak of a closely related debate as the "rigor vs. vigor" controversy and explain why I view it as a false issue. Truth is not a single entity and there are various means of discovering its various aspects. Literature and social science represent two different ways of knowing about man and society, differing in their methods and the types of discipline they use, both with respect to the collection of data and their presentation. Their purposes are neither identical nor conflicting but complementary, for each is uniquely designed to produce a different kind of knowledge.

Both literature and social science attempt to abstract and reflect social reality. But the social scientist, in collecting his data, is self-consciously concerned with rules of evidence—with the steps leading from observation to generalization. He tries to keep himself out of the process of discovery as much as possible, or at least to specify precisely how he has personally entered into it. The novelist, on the other hand, is concerned with the maximal use of himself as a sensitive instrument which absorbs data from numerous sources and then reflects their essential meaning. By the same token, the social scientist uses a very different style of presentation from the novelist's. His approach is highly analytical.

He is obligated to lay bare each step in the process of reasoning that leads from the design of his study to the generalization he makes on the basis of it. He must marshal his evidence and draw his inferences from it in such a way that the reader can reconstruct his reasoning process as fully as possible. The novelist, on the other hand, must make his point by transmitting, in all its richness and fullness, a concrete case that brings alive to the reader the generalization he hopes to make. The novelist too is concerned with generalizations, but he would be considered a failure if he had to spell out, for his reader, the inferences to be drawn from his data and the steps he used in arriving at them.

In both collection and presentation of their data, the social scientist and the novelist have recourse to very different kinds of language. The social scientist tries to strip his language, so far as possible, of all surplus meaning. Eliminating surplus meaning is a major part of his effort to pull generalizable truths out of a world of recalcitrant reality. But the novelist tries to use language that is as rich in surplus meanings as possible. The more numerous the levels and nuances of meaning in the phenomena he selects and the way he describes them, the more he enhances our insight into old truths and our discovery of new relationships.

In view of these differences in method and discipline, literature and social science are each equipped to make different kinds of contributions. The social scientist is bound and inhibited by his concern with evidence—and this is as it should be. Sometimes he is unjustly accused of being dry, pedestrian, or costive, when in effect he is only doing his job. I am not saying here that he need not be imaginative or creative. Far from it. But his imaginativeness and creativity are typically of a different nature from those of the novelist. He may be imaginative, for example, in the type of measurement instruments that he develops, or creative in the theoretical structures that he builds. But to the nonspecialist these accomplishments may be unimpressive.

In any event, the rate at which the social scientist moves qua social scientist—he may, of course, also be a dilettante philosopher, social critic, or even novelist—is determined by the availability of evidence. This, in turn, depends on the availability of theories that can direct the search for evidence, and of methods that can help to pin it down. The novelist is *not* inhibited by these considerations—and this, again, is as it should be. This is not to say that social reality is irrelevant for him, but that his task is to reflect it in a way that concretely captures its essence, not to analyze it and to establish the validity of his observations.

I have exaggerated the differences between the two approaches in order to sharpen my point that social science and literature, though both are concerned with the study of man, have essentially different functions and that we should look to them for different kinds of contributions. I do not feel that it threatens my identity or casts doubt on my loyalty to my own team if I argue that there are certain things about social reality that we can learn much more effectively from the novelist than we can from the social scientist. Even for the social scientist it is often extremely useful to turn to the novel for insights into the operation of social forces. In the development of some of my theoretical ideas about processes of social influence, for example, I was greatly stimulated by *1984*, George Orwell's (1949) frightening dystopia.

⋈ UTOPIAN AND DYSTOPIAN NOVELS AS SOCIAL CRITIQUES ⋉

The utopian and dystopian novels are particularly relevant sources of insight into societal phenomena. I see their major value not in what they predict about the future, but in what they tell us about *current* social reality, about the social forces that are now operative and the directions in which society seems to be moving. By describing imaginary future societies, they can get away more completely from the constraints of current reality and can present existing trends in richer, fuller, and more elaborated form. This the social scientist, by the nature of his methods, is unable to do. He may, of course, turn to the novel as his form of expression—as B. F. Skinner has done, for example, in his *Walden Two* (1948)—although typically he lacks the craftsmanship to do this adequately from a literary point of view.

The relevance of dystopias—like *1984* or Huxley's *Brave New World* (1932)—to the understanding of current trends is quite obvious. Typically they represent critiques of the existing social order. They portray dominant social forces and institutional patterns in exaggerated form, by showing the kind of society to

which they may lead if they are followed to their logical conclusion. But utopias, too, are at least in part critiques of the existing social order. Unlike dystopias, they make their points about
current society not by portraying its dominant trends in exaggerated form, but by portraying an imaginary society that sharply
contrasts with the existing one.

At the same time, one can view the utopian novel as a
product of the very social forces it criticizes and seeks to change.
It goes without saying that the proposed changes are in part products of their time, in the sense that they were developed in response to existing social forces. But, more than that, they may
actually be, in themselves, manifestations of the very forces that
they are designed to counteract. There is often much that we can
learn about the nature of a society and its dominant values by
examining the dreams that it has produced.

It is with this purpose in mind that I would like to turn
to Huxley's utopian novel *Island,* published in 1962. This novel
would, in any event, be worthy of our careful attention, given
the author's stature as a literary man and social thinker. But
there is an additional, very special reason why it arouses interest
in any student of modern society. Huxley is probably the only
writer who, in his lifetime, has produced both a dystopian and
a utopian novel. In 1932 he published *Brave New World,* and
thirty years later he published *Island.* What is the difference between these two novels? What has happened in the intervening
thirty years? What accounts for this shift from dystopia to utopia?
Before turning to these questions, let me briefly review some of
the main features of Pala, Huxley's utopian island.

⧼ LIFE ON THE ISLAND OF PALA ⧽

Pala is a South Sea island which has managed to remain
relatively isolated from the outside world, partly because of geographical conditions, and for the past century or so because of
deliberate design. A little more than a century ago modern Pala
had its beginnings. It was started by the then Raja and a Scotch
physician who saved his life by the application of hypnosis. "Dr.
Andrew was a scientifically trained, anti-dogmatic humanist, who
had discovered the value of pure and applied Mahayana. His

friend, the Raja, was a Tantrik Buddhist, who had discovered the value of pure and applied science" (p. 258). The physician became a close friend and adviser to the Raja and together they initiated a whole series of reforms, based on the desire to make the best of both worlds, to fuse the rationality of experimental science from the West with the applied mysticism of Eastern religion. They began by introducing hypnosis to the population as a pain reliever in childbirth and surgery, and continued with the introduction of English as a second language (for scientific, philosophical, and literary pursuits), the development of a program of agricultural experimentation, and the encouragement of birth control. This work was consolidated and carried forward by the Raja's grandson, known as the Old Raja, who also authored Pala's "bible," *Notes on What's What, and on What It Might be Reasonable to Do about What's What.*

Pala, at the time of the reader's introduction to it, is a constitutional monarchy in which the exercise of power is decentralized. We learn little about the political structure, except that it is based on a federation of self-governing units—geographical, professional, and economic. There is no army, no heavy industry. Pala has refused to develop its apparently extensive oil resources for export. There are various kinds of light industry, to meet internal needs for construction and basic consumer goods. Very little is imported, one of the few exceptions being electrical equipment. The equations by which Pala operates are: "Electricity minus heavy industry plus birth control equals democracy and plenty. Electricity plus heavy industry minus birth control equals misery, totalitarianism and war" (p. 167). Birth control has been a key fixture of modern Pala since its inception, when it was decided "that contraceptives should be like education—free, tax-supported and, though not compulsory, as nearly as possible universal" (p. 95).There have been no sharp increases in population.

Pala's economy is largely based on cooperative buying, selling, and financing. People do different kinds of work at different parts of the year—alternating, for example, between work in the fields and the cement factory—even though this may not be the most efficient procedure. Intellectuals also do some manual work each day. The emphasis in scientific work in Pala is almost entirely on biology, which has direct applications to problems of

health, education, and agriculture. Agricultural experimentation
is extensive and has led to improved breeding, crops, and storage
facilities. The people are well fed and all of their needs are adequately met. Their lives are relatively simple, but they are free
and happy. They do not need the kinds of substitutes that are
provided through overconsumption in capitalist societies, because
they are trained to live here and now—to be fully aware and en-
joy their awareness—so that they can derive satisfaction out of
ordinary things and everyday experiences. By the same token,
they do not need the substitutes for living here and now that are
provided by worship of the state in Communist societies.

Religion in Pala is neither encouraged nor discouraged.
There is no established church. The common religion is a form
of Mahayana Buddhism combined with Shivaism which "stresses
immediate experience and deplores belief in unverifiable dogmas"
(p. 170). There is an attempt to teach children that religious symbols are merely symbols, created by man and subject to his own
control. To emphasize this lesson, scarecrows in Pala are made in
the form of puppets representing gods and Buddhas, and children
are periodically assigned to "scarecrow duty," which requires them
to pull the puppets' strings and make them dance and wiggle.
Pala education also encourages a skeptical and analytical attitude
and discourages youngsters from taking words too seriously.

According to Palanese ideologues, this skeptical attitude
represents one form of protection against the abuse of power and
the rise of tyranny. Another form of protection, presumably, is
inherent in the social structure itself: The absence of a military
establishment, the decentralized political system, the cooperative
economy, and the reality emphasis in religion limit the opportunities for concentration of power in the hands of single individuals.
Finally, a major form of protection against the abuse of power
is provided by biological and psychological efforts to prevent and
control the development of an excessive power drive. Palanese
research has isolated two types of individuals, identifiable at an
early age through their physiological and anatomical characteristics, who are predisposed to develop excessive power drives: the
Peter Pans and the Muscle People. The former receive special
treatment which allows them to mature normally; their aberra-
tions are thus nipped in the bud. The Muscle People are trained

to be aware and sensitive, so that they can find alternative satisfactions to the exercise of power. Moreover, their love of power
is canalized and deflected from the domination of people to the
domination of things. This is accomplished, for example, through
felling trees or climbing rocks. Rock-climbing in Pala is a "branch
of applied ethics," a "preventive substitute for bullying" (p. 186).

Peter Pans and Muscle People are also the potential delinquents and criminals in any society. Their early diagnosis,
treatment, and training thus account in large part for the extremely low rate of crime in Pala. Crime that does occur is dealt
with either through the criminal's MAC (Mutual Adoption Club)
or through medical and mycomystical specialists. The MAC and
mycomysticism are important Palanese institutions to which I
shall return shortly. The rate of neurosis in Pala is also extremely
low. In general, the emphasis in Palanese medicine, including
psychiatry, is on prevention. Both prevention and cure of illness
involve an attack on all fronts, physical as well as psychological.
Hypnotic suggestion is used systematically as an aid to treatment,
conducive to building up resistance.

Turning now to family life—most Palanese couples choose
to have small families, perhaps two or three children. In the typical family, two children might be fathered by the husband while
the third would be acquired by DF and AI—Deep Freeze and
Artificial Insemination. Pala has a central bank of superior stocks
to which families sometimes turn in order to avoid perpetuating
some hereditary illness or defect. More generally, however, families turn to the bank to improve the race, or simply for a change—
to bring a new face into the household. But Pala does not only
extend the range available to parents in choosing their children;
it also extends the range available to children in choosing their
parents. I have already mentioned the MAC or Mutual Adoption
Club. Everyone in Pala belongs to an MAC which consists of
anywhere from fifteen to twenty-five couples; each of these couples
can serve as deputy parents to the children of any other couple.
Thus, children are not inextricably bound to one set of parents.
They can migrate to another home if they have had an argument,
or feel unhappy, or just have the need for a change. Typically,
this change will be temporary, although it may be for an extended
period of time. Consistent with this voluntary orientation, there

is no necessary assumption that children will always love their parents. "In our part of the world," explains one Palanese citizen, " 'Mother' is strictly the name of a function. When the function has been duly fulfilled, the title lapses; the ex-child and the woman who used to be called 'Mother' establish a new kind of relationship" (p. 101). Depending on how they feel about each other, they may remain close or drift apart.

Attitudes toward sex are very matter-of-fact in Pala. Children are taught about sex early and systematically. Premarital relations are expected and encouraged. These relationships apparently tend to be monogamous, although occasional deviations are accepted without guilt. I have already mentioned that contraceptives are distributed freely, but they do not represent the most favored form of birth control. Palanese are encouraged to practice *maithuna,* the yoga of love, which is essentially a form of *coitus reservatus.* Youngsters are taught *maithuna* at school, at "about the same time as trigonometry and advanced biology" (p. 89). Not everyone in Pala practices *maithuna,* but a good many people do, and it is clearly considered a superior and more fully satisfying sexual relationship.

The preference for *maithuna* is not simply based on its being an esthetically more pleasing form of birth control. Rather, it is one of a whole series of yogas—though probably the most popular one—that serve to operationalize the basic philosophy of Pala life. This philosophy calls for complete awareness at all times—awareness of the environment, of one's own sensations, of one's own actions, and of those parts of the self that unite it with ultimate reality. Through such awareness, the person is enabled to live here and now, rather than in the past and future. He is able to liberate himself from the prison of his ego—from memories and daydreams, anticipations and silly notions, sentimentality and self-pity. To provide a constant reminder to the Palanese of the need to be aware of what is happening, there are more than a thousand mynah birds, flying all over the island, who have been trained to say over and over the words: "Attention" and "Here and now, boys." One can be fairly assured that there will always be a mynah in the vicinity to keep him from slipping into memory and fantasy.

The ability to be fully aware is taught to the Palanese from early childhood, through various techniques of concentration. Palanese ideology, if I understand it correctly, seems to value these techniques of concentration at three levels. At the simplest level, they serve as means to control undesirable sensations and emotions—in other words, as techniques in applied ethics and applied psychology. One such technique is DC or Destiny Control, also known as SD—Self-Determination. This is a form of self-hypnosis which allows the person to overcome physical pain, as well as sorrow. The Palanese do not expect to eliminate sorrow. As Susila, a recent widow, says: "DC can give you a completely painless childbirth. But a completely painless bereavement—no. And of course that's as it should be" (p. 112). Yet, one must not allow his sorrow to take over and to keep him from attending to the here and now —and this is where DC can make its contribution. Then there is a set of techniques designed to eliminate anxieties and painful memories by putting them into perspective, manipulating them at will and thus gaining control over them. To control their anger and frustration, children are taught to direct the energy that has accumulated into various breathing games or, in more severe cases, to stamp it out in a specially devised dance known as the Rakshasi Hornpipe.

At the next level, techniques of concentration serve as means of enhancing the joy and meaning that one derives from all of one's experiences. By being completely aware of the experience, unencumbered by interfering thoughts and emotions, one is able to appreciate it to the fullest and find fulfillment in it. This is the function of Palanese grace, which is chewed rather than said. They express their appreciation by giving complete attention to the act of chewing the first mouthful. Similarly, this is the function of the yoga of love which, by permitting attention to all of one's sensations, provides more complete satisfaction. And so on for the various other yogas. In the same sense, the Palanese speak of the yoga of work, as well as of the yoga of death. They are trained and helped to be fully aware even of the experience of dying.

The continued practice of these various yogas increasingly enables you to achieve the highest level of return from the techniques of concentration which, in Palanese language, is "to know who in fact you are." Knowing who in fact you are means moving beyond your individuality and attending to "the universal and impersonal life that lives itself through each of us" (p. 280). It means self-trancendence and liberation from bondage to the ego. This process of discovery is aided, not only by the yogas, but most specifically by repeated meditation, which gradually prepares the person for mystical experiences and ecstatic insights. A quick and direct way of achieving mystical experiences that is available in Pala is the taking of *moksha*-medicine, otherwise known as the truth-and-beauty pill. This is a drug derived from toadstools, which Palanese take on occasion, although it is not viewed as a substitute for the more gradual but also more permanent process produced by meditation. *Moksha* is given to the young to allow them to catch a glimpse of the world of liberation. In fact, the first experience with *moksha,* along with mountain-climbing, are the chief components of Palanese initiation rites. Adults take *moksha* as a special treat when they wish to facilitate the occurrence of mystical experiences and heighten their intensity.

In my description of Pala it has been quite apparent how much emphasis is placed on the proper training of children, so that they will acquire the values and skills that are central to life on the island. The process begins very early, in the home. Thus, for example, infants are deliberately conditioned to love and trust animals and persons by placing them into a warm physical contact with the object to be loved and repeating the word "good" while they are being simultaneously fed and caressed. At an early age, biological and psychological tests are used to assess children's temperaments, and their subsequent training is varied accordingly. We have already seen, for example, that specialized training is accorded to those who are diagnosed as Muscle People. Another group that is selected for special treatment are those who are easily hypnotizable; they are taught under deep trance, which enables them to distort time and thus amass information and solve problems much more quickly.

I have also mentioned before that in Pala's schools children are trained to be skeptical and to recognize the limitations of language. They are taught how language affects feelings and thus, in turn, experience; and that there are certain things one cannot speak but only *be.* The training emphasizes analysis and symbol manipulation, on the one hand, and receptivity, on the other. The attempt is made to build bridges from science to ethics and self-knowledge. There is, of course, specific training in the techniques of control and redirection of emotions. There is encouragement of manual work and training in the proper use of the body. There is direct exposure to the facts of sex, childbirth, and death, and children are trained to deal with the emotions that these engender.

This, then, is Pala, the forbidden island on which the novel's dubious hero, Will Farnaby, is more or less deliberately shipwrecked. Farnaby is a cynical, unhappy, self-hating journalist who likes to describe himself as "the man who won't take yes for an answer" (p. 18). As he is nursed back to health on Pala and exposed to its people and institutions, he is gradually, and despite himself, converted to its ways and its philosophy. At the end of the novel we see him in the midst of his first *moksha* experience, catching a glimpse of who in fact he is. But even as he is about to embrace Pala, this experiment of a hundred years is destroyed before his eyes. The new Raja, Murugan, who was educated—or miseducated, in the Pala view—abroad and utterly rejects Palanese values, has just attained majority. He dreams of himself as a great leader who brings progress, purity, consumer goods, fast cars, heavy industry, and armaments to this benighted island. These dreams are encouraged by Col. Dipa, dictator of Rendang, the neighboring island, who is primarily interested in Pala's oil resources and their potential contribution to the expansion of his own power. In our final view of Pala we find Murugan driving through the island at the head of some of Col. Dipa's troops, proclaiming the formation of the United Kingdom of Rendang and Pala and the advent of Progress. And the mynah birds reply: "Attention."

❧ PARALLELS BETWEEN PALA AND BRAVE NEW WORLD ❧

What I found particularly striking in reading *Island* was the way in which it parallels *Brave New World*. Many of the unique features of the Brave New World can also be found, in modified form, on Pala—except of course that they have changed direction. Whereas in *Brave New World* they were presented as

tools for the ultimate enslavement of man, in Pala they have become tools for his liberation. The contrast is not as drastic as it
might seem to be, if we keep in mind that *Brave New World* is
a benevolent dystopia, which bases its control over the population
on the ability to keep them happy—unlike *1984,* in which control is based on the use of terror. Nevertheless, it is striking that
some of the very features of society that were clearly presented
as sources of dehumanization in *Brave New World* are now presented as techniques that can enable men to realize their humanity
to the fullest degree.

Let us look at some of the dramatic parallels between the
two societies, keeping in mind, of course, that they are by no
means identical. In Brave New World, the family has been abolished and "mother" has become a dirty word. In Pala, the family
persists but it has declined in importance through its absorption
in an MAC. "Mother," as we have seen, is strictly a description
of a function. In Brave New World, eugenics has progressed to a
point that babies are produced in bottles and breeding is strictly
controlled. In Pala, breeding is partially controlled through the
selective and voluntary use of AI out of the central bank of superior stocks. In Brave New World, individuals are deliberately
bred for the specific social roles that they are destined to fulfill.
In Pala, they are selected at an early age, on the basis of their
biological and psychological dispositions, and specifically trained
for the social roles for which they are temperamentally suited. In
Brave New World, infants are systematically conditioned to accept
their places in society and to repeat the official slogans. In Pala,
infant conditioning is applied selectively, and children are trained
systematically, from early childhood on, to verbalize and accept
the basic tenets of the Palanese *Weltanschauung.* In Brave New
World, hypnopaedia is used universally. In Pala, it is used for that
portion of the population that is readily hypnotizable, although
hypnotic techniques in general are widely used. In Brave New
World, death conditioning is introduced, beginning at the age of
eighteen months, so that children will learn to take dying as a
matter of course. In Pala, children are familiarized with death and
trained to overcome their anxieties, as the first part of their in-
struction in how to die graciously.

What about some of the values of the two societies? In Brave New World, there is complete sexual freedom, but it is heretical to become personally attached to one's sexual partner and emotionally involved in the relationship. In Pala, too, there is sexual freedom; personal attachment is by no means discouraged, but the most highly preferred mode of sexual encounter is the emotional detachment of *coitus reservatus*. In Brave New World, emotional involvement of any kind is completely taboo. In Pala, it is expected that one will on occasion become emotionally involved, but every effort must be made to control one's emotions. Sorrow is obscene in Brave New World. In Pala, it is considered human, though not entirely mature. Brave New World gives its citizens regular V.P.S.—Violent Passion Surrogate—treatments, which are the complete physiological equivalent of fear and rage. In Pala, they dance the Rakshasi Hornpipe. In Brave New World, reminiscences and memories are subversive. In Pala, they are considered part of the bondage to the ego which must be overcome through constant attention to the here and now. In Brave New World, one resorts to *soma* quite freely to escape from boredom and experience pleasure. In Pala, one takes *moksha*-medicine, albeit only on occasion, to transcend and be liberated from the limitations of the self.

In Brave New World, guilt has been abolished; the confession of sin in the savage reservation, or Mr. Savage's self-punishment, are considered uproariously funny. In Pala, guilt is made light of. The story of Oedipus, for example, has been turned into a quaint puppet show for the amusement of children. In the Palanese version, a boy and girl from Pala talk Jocasta out of suicide and Oedipus out of blinding himself just in the nick of time. They "tell them not to be silly. After all," as ten-year-old Mary Sarojini explains to Will Farnaby, "it was an accident. He didn't know that the old man was his father. And anyhow the old man began it, hit him over the head, and that made Oedipus lose his temper—and nobody had ever taught him to dance the Rakshasi Hornpipe. And when they made him a king, he had to marry the old queen. She was really his mother; but neither of them knew it. And of course all they had to do when they did find out was just to stop being married. That stuff about marrying his

mother being the reason why everybody had to die of a virus—
all that was just nonsense, just made up by a lot of poor stupid
people who didn't know any better" (p. 286).

In citing these parallelisms between the two books, I do
not wish to imply that Huxley describes these various features
in the two societies in similar terms. The specific techniques or
attitudes may be parallel, but they function in very different ways
in Brave New World and in Pala. They play very different roles
in the contexts of the different societies and they seem to have
rather different consequences. There are differences in who controls the techniques or attitudes, how much choice is left to the
individual in adopting them, to what extremes they are carried,
to what extent they serve as means rather than as ends, and what
ultimate purposes they are designed to fulfill. Clearly, they are
dehumanizing forces in Brave New World. As Huxley describes
their operation in Pala, however, they do appear to be liberating
elements that seem to enhance freedom, creativity, compassion,
and self-understanding in some meaningful ways. Nor is there
anything unreasonable in the proposition that the same techniques can be used either for good or for evil.

What is so striking, however, is that the Huxley of *Island*
seems entirely certain that these techniques will indeed be used
for the liberation of man and that they will not be perverted to
the ends of enslavement and dehumanization as they were in
Brave New World. How can the skeptical and cynical Huxley of
1932—who felt that all the developments in natural and social
science, in biology and psychology, would almost inevitably be
used to enslave men—believe in the possibility, if not the probability, of a social system in which these same forces will be used
only to liberate them? Why is he unconcerned, in the context of
Pala, with the danger that these tools might be perverted and
produce another Brave New World?

The only answer that I can find in the book is that, somehow, the addition of Eastern mysticism to Western science enables
one to have all the advantages of modern science without any of
its disadvantages. I do not find this answer entirely satisfying, and
do not feel reassured that Pala could not become Brave New
World, much as this goes counter to the intentions of its designers.

I can only assume that Huxley was able to maintain his conviction in the inviolability of the Pala way of life because he so deeply desired to maintain it.

As one traces Huxley's development, one is confronted first with the bitter and relentless cynicism and skepticism of his early novels. All human interaction seems to be futile; men try desperately to get outside themselves to find meaning in life, but they fail. The early Huxley is satisfied with observing. Gradually, however, he introduces into his novels the lone individual who is able to transcend the social order through absorption of Eastern mysticism. Finally, in *Island*, he portrays a whole society that is able to transcend the social order. Huxley's former self, in the person of Will Farnaby, came to scoff at Pala but remained to admire and to adopt it as his home. The old Huxleyan ambivalence is not entirely gone, for in the final analysis even this island of sanity disappears. It was viable as long as it could isolate itself from the rest of the world, but the rest of the world insisted on embracing it in its own corruption.

Yet, even though Huxley concedes that his answer is not viable, *Island* represents his quest for an answer, for a way out of the futility and hopelessness with which he started. To achieve a better society, Huxley has concluded, man must transcend his human limitations and seek a direct contact with divine reality, which is immanent in nature, and a direct experience of eternity. In doing so, moreover, it is necessary to transcend Western ways by turning to Eastern mysticism. The irony, I feel, is that in his efforts to transcend Western ways, Huxley exemplifies some of the very forces that he is trying to transcend. Not that Huxley can be considered a typical product of his age. But there is a haunting quality of *déjà vu* to his utopia. His specific attempts at overcoming the sense of futility, it seems to me, represent—in a special and modified form, to be sure—some of the efforts at overcoming the sense of futility that are characteristic of Western society in general.

In short, I am arguing that Huxley's utopianism reflects some of the current general trends of the society that he is hoping to change. In this sense, his utopia may actually contribute to the forces that he fears and opposes. If I may be permitted an exaggeration, let me suggest that *Island* could very well have been the blueprint followed—and, of course, perverted—by the creators of the Brave New World.

❧ HUXLEY'S UTOPIA AS AN ECHO OF MODERN SOCIETY ❧

Let me illustrate my point by examining five trends of the modern world that seem to be echoed in the Palanese scheme, trends that carry the seeds of dehumanization: the attempt at total environmental control; the emphasis on psychological manipulation; the search for panaceas; the avoidance of commitment; and the denial of responsibility.

The attempt at total environmental control. One of the most disturbing characteristics of the modern world is that it has led to the development of social systems that attempt to gain total control over the behavior of its members. The most complete expression of this trend is the totalitarian state of the twentieth century. It is made possible, in large part, by the systematic use of the mass media of communication directed to mass societies. Within totalitarian states, we have seen even more extreme experiments in total control, directed to more limited subpopulations. The German concentration camp and the Chinese methods of thought reform or "brainwashing," though differing from each other in procedure and purpose, both represent such experiments. Even in political systems that cannot be characterized as totalitarian, the mass media have the capacity of achieving near-total control over the informational environment and hence the subjective world of masses of people. It is significant that Huxley seems to miss this point in his discussion of brainwashing and mass communication in *Brave New World Revisited* (1958). He speaks of the effects of these processes purely at the psychological level, in terms of their lowering of the individual's resistance. It seems to me, however, that the key element of the brainwashing situation is not that the person's psychological processes become weakened, but that his beliefs, values, and sense of identity are deprived of all social support. He has no access to information that validates his beliefs, to other individuals who share his values, or to social structures that confirm his identity—and under these conditions he cannot maintain them. These conditions, in turn, are made possible by the fact that his guards have complete control over the information to which he is exposed and the social situations in which he participates.

Pala can certainly not be described as a totalitarian society, nor can it be accused of brainwashing its citizens. It is benevolent and humane in every way. It stresses the importance of self-determination and the enhancement of the individual's choice. Yet, the whole Palanese way of life rests on total environmental control, a control that is exercised from infancy on and that is reinforced by every institution of the island and at every stage of the individual's life. This control is symbolized by the ever-present mynah bird, reminding the citizen of the all-important social norms. Thus, even the *natural* environment has been conscripted into the service of total control.

The individual is trained to take the role in society for which he is biologically suited. While this is certainly a benign type of control, in that it allows the person to make fullest use of his particular capacities and helps him avoid unnecessary frustrations, it is control nonetheless. The individual is prepared in specific ways to handle his various experiences. Even self-determination, spontaneity, and liberation are preplanned. Nothing is left to chance.

The individual in Pala certainly has the right to choose, for he lives in a society that respects his individuality. Moreover, he is psychologically capable of choosing, because he has not been paralyzed by fear and forced into a pattern that is foreign to his temperament. Yet the total control over his environment that the society exercises, both while he is being socialized into it and in the course of his later life, gives him very little to choose from. Freedom of choice cannot simply be built into the psychological structure of the individual, but must also be built into the social structure of the society. Freedom of choice consists not only in the behavior of choosing, but also in the availability of choices. Although the individual may be happy in his lot, he does not exercise free choice if the society predetermines what is right for him and trains him to select it.

This is important to me, in large part, because I regard freedom of choice as a fundamental value in its own right (see

Chapter One). To be human means to choose, which means in turn to have the opportunity to make mistakes, to try out roles that are not suitable and learn about one's self in the process, to explore different values, and to experiment with different ways of life. There is another reason, however, why I worry about a society that does not build freedom of choice into its social structure. Such a society, I fear, is limited in its growth, in its ability to evolve better ways of meeting human needs. Though the insights of the founders may be great, the attempt to carry them out through total environmental control hampers the development of new insights and new experiments. But, what is more, a society that relies on total control is unable to deal with the uncontrollable, and thus likely to fail when uncontrollable elements intervene. And that is precisely what happens to Pala.

The emphasis on psychological manipulation. There are strong tendencies in the modern world to manipulate the state of mind of individuals deliberately and systematically so that they will voluntarily adopt the roles or engage in the behaviors desired by the manipulator. The advertiser creates needs in order to sell his products. The propagandist plays on fears and hatreds. Corporations, politicians, parties, and governments try to project a certain kind of image—in other words, to manipulate the perceiver rather than the object perceived. On another level, the society emphasizes adjustment of the individual to the community in which he lives and the organization in which he works, not simply in the sense of living up to social norms, but in the sense of becoming the kind of person that is socially prescribed. Failure to adjust in this sense is seen as a sign of a psychological disability which the person must work to overcome. It is popular, in general, to explain people's difficulties in terms of faulty psychological processes and to suggest that they be dealt with by manipulation of these processes. Newspapers and best-sellers readily tell us how to stop worrying or how to overcome our shyness. There is a tendency in some organizations to use personality tests in order to select personnel not for their ability to do the job but for their potential as good organization men.

I am concerned about these trends, in part, because they represent external manipulation of human behavior, on a large scale and with little concern for the true characteristics of the person being manipulated. The issue here is essentially the limitation of freedom of choice that I have already discussed. There is, however, another issue involved in the emphasis on psychological manipulation: it points to a social order whose proper functioning relies primarily on the use of psychological techniques—on the selection, training, and adjustment of individuals so that they will readily perform their required social roles. This kind of social order, it seems to me, is not maximally conducive to the health of either individuals or social institutions. From the point of view of the individual, it puts the cart before the horse. It implies that the individual serves the institutions, rather than the other way around. When there appears to be a poor fit between individuals and institutions, it means that individuals have to be adjusted rather than institutional arrangements changed. The actions, attitudes, and images of organization members are revised, not the policies and procedures of the organization itself. This very orientation also implies that the institutions are weakened because they are not responsive to criticism and open to improvement. If they are successful in the psychological manipulation of their members, moreover, they have forfeited the members' creativity which could lead to productive change. If, as is more likely, they are not entirely successful in this manipulation, then they may collapse if some members refuse to remain within their assigned roles, since the organizational structure does not provide for such an eventuality.

The emphasis on psychological manipulation is very widespread in Pala. To be sure, such manipulation is used entirely for good ends. But the whole structure of the society rests on *assuring*, through proper psychological manipulation, that correct or desirable behavior will spontaneously occur. This is the function of the different procedures of conditioning and training; of the various techniques for controlling anger and anxiety; of the early identification through physiological and psychological assessment of Peter Pans and Muscle People and their systematic treatment and training, so that they will not express their power drives in crime or the domination of other people. I am intrigued by some of the educational procedures proposed by Huxley and some of the psychological devices for handling one's emotions— for example, the procedures for dealing with fear by putting the feared object in perspective, which are reminiscent of Viktor Frankl's (1963) technique of the "paradoxical intention." They probably do represent a creative fusion of concepts from Buddhist sources and modern psychology. But what I find disturbing is the presumption that all societal problems can be handled through the use of psychological techniques.

I am particularly concerned, in this connection, with the problem of power, which becomes especially acute if we keep in mind the total control of the environment that is exercised in Pala. Given such total control, it is certainly vital to ask who controls the controllers and what mechanisms there are for preventing and dealing with the abuse of power. Huxley seems to rely on the assumption that such abuses will not occur, partly because the social structure does not provide opportunities for the concentration of power, but largely because individuals have been cured of pathological power-drives or trained to sublimate their power drives. There is, therefore, hardly any attention to the necessity of introducing *corrective mechanisms* into the social order—in the form of political institutions and political values—which would be designed to curtail the abuse of power and to deal with it when it occurs. It is assumed in Pala that if everything is properly set up from the beginning and the appropriate psychological techniques are applied, nothing will go wrong. To my mind this underestimates the fallibility of education and other forms of psychological manipulation, as well as the intensity of human passions. The problem of power cannot be resolved once and for all through the creation of a perfect society and the psychological states that it generates in its members. Freedom depends on the existence of institutional mechanisms that can be used to resist encroachments on it, and of political values that support these mechanisms.

The search for panaceas. Modern society seems to generate a strong tendency to seek panaceas that would provide complete and easy answers to all of life's problems. Faddist cults of all sorts prevail in this atmosphere, and true-believer movements tend to spring up. What many of these panaceas have in common is that they offer a simple route to salvation, to self-esteem, to the battle against futility—simple both in the analysis of the problem and in the solution offered. There is no need to think, to exert effort, to suffer; no need to go through the painful process of examining one's self or the arduous task of working out a solution. A formula for salvation is ready at hand, at bargain prices.

Huxley was far too sophisticated to see any of the techniques or beliefs that he proposes in *Island* as panaceas. The Palanese, in fact, are quite clear that they do not want their favored techniques to be turned into panaceas, into ends in themselves. Thus, for example, they stress that the *moksha*-medicine is just a facilitative agent, to be taken only on rare occasions. The various yogas, too, are viewed as means—as operations designed to produce a certain kind of awareness—not as ends in themselves. The same goes for their various social arrangements, such as AI and the MAC, and their various treatment and teaching devices, such as DC and hypnopaedia. These are all to be used selectively, as the need arises, and in situations in which they promise to have some specific utility.

Yet, here they are: the biggest collection of gimmicks that has ever been found on a single island. To be sure, they are part of a total context in Pala and not fads that are superimposed upon it. Still, they are the things the Palanese point to when they try to explain their way of life. Farnaby's introduction to Pala seems to involve an endless succession of such devices; and while none of them is presented as "the" answer, there is the implication that collectively they contain the answer. When Farnaby asks why the women look so radiant, he is told: because they practice *maithuna*. When someone needs to be convinced that there is something to Palanese philosophy, he is encouraged to take *moksha*. And Huxley does not seem to be too actively concerned about the danger that these various techniques will become perverted, that they will be turned from means into ends. He is not afraid, for example, that *moksha* will become a cheap substitute for meditation and that it may, in fact, turn, like *soma*, into a means of enslavement rather than liberation.

It seems to me that Pala does echo the search for panaceas that characterizes modern society, because in the final analysis it conceives of the good life as resting on a series of specific operations, devices, and beliefs that the person gradually masters. To be sure, it is not the single operations, but the total pattern they form that represents the good life. Moreover, it is not the operations themselves but the state of mind that they produce; and this usually requires much effort and long practice. They are not, then, easy panaceas—but yet they are formulas which, if properly applied, can yield the good life directly. My own preference is for a society in which each individual tries to work out the good life for himself. The function of institutional arrangements, of educational devices, of techniques of self-analysis, is to give the individual the opportunity and the capacity to achieve his own fulfillment, not to transpose him directly into a state of fulfillment. In other words, their function is to help him *achieve* the good life by *mobilizing* the self, rather than *reach* the good life by *transcending* the self.

The avoidance of commitment. There is a strong tendency in our society, though by no means a universal one, to "play it cool," to remain uninvolved and uncommitted. It does not pay to believe and feel too strongly, to become overly committed to certain social values and work for them. As a matter of fact, there is something suspect about such commitment: there is obviously something wrong with you if you feel so strongly about things. At the interpersonal level, too, there is a tendency to remain relatively uninvolved, to establish relationships that are superficially pleasant but emotionally bland. Martha Wolfenstein (1951) once made a fascinating analysis of what she called "fun morality"—the elevation of "having fun" to a moral principle in American society so that one feels inadequate if he has not had enough fun. According to her analysis, the diffusion of fun may be a defense against deeper involvement. By attaining satisfaction at low levels of emotional intensity one can protect himself against the higher ones. This modulation of emotional involvement receives some philosophical backing from popular psychoanalysis—and I am speaking here of psychoanalysis as a way of life rather than as a form of treatment—which often substitutes awareness and analysis of one's feelings for action in terms of these feelings. While the abilty to gain distance from one's self and others is essential, to be fully human presupposes some strong commitments to basic values and some deep involvements with other people.

The tendency to avoid strong emotional involvements runs through many areas of Pala life. There are numerous examples, throughout the book, of techniques and attitudes that deliberately favor the maintenance of emotions at a low level of intensity: the sublimation of anger through such devices as the Rakshasi Hornpipe; the control of sorrow through the application of DC; the training for the dignified acceptance of death—one's own and that of loved ones; the MAC, which does away with the child's dependence on his parents and hence loosens his emotional attachment to them; the general disapproval of sentimentality, memories, and dreams that distract your attention from the here and now; the glorification of the detachment of *coitus reservatus*. There is a strong emphasis in Pala on not letting go, on keeping distance from one's emotions, on maintaining control at all times. The existence and meaningfulness of emotions is certainly not denied. As Susila points out, for example: "It wouldn't be right if you could take away all the pain of a bereavement; you'd be less than human" (p. 112). But the goal is to control these emotions and to keep them at a low level of intensity.

There is a certain contradiction, it seems to me, in the emphasis on increased awareness, which runs through Palanese philosophy and is a key element in the various yogas, in meditation, and in the use of *moksha*. For increased awareness means getting outside of one's self, looking at one's self from the vantage point of an external observer. Thus, while it is designed to increase your attention to everything you are doing and sensing, it reduces your personal involvement in your actions and feelings. Similarly, on the interpersonal side, the detachment implied by complete attention to the other seems to stand in the way of the emotional involvement required for a true meeting between two people.

The value of the various methods of detachment described by Huxley should not be minimized. I have already said that I see intriguing possibilities in some of the training devices for controlling emotions. It is quite likely that future research will catch up with some of the methods for relieving pain and anxiety that Huxley envisages. The sections on death are among the most moving in the book. There is a beautiful contrast between Farnaby's recollection of the dehumanizing effect of death as he has known it, both on the person who is dying and on the survivors, and the dignity of death in Pala. There is much that we have to learn about the art of dying, and there is probably much insight to be gained in this regard from the Palanese methods of detachment.

I do, then, see great potential values in these methods. But the issue is whether they are ways of dealing with situations of great stress, ways of handling disabling emotions, forms of treatment—or whether they become a philosophy of life. As a way of life, I do not feel that maintaining ourselves at a low level of involvement and keeping our distance in our relationships to others and to society at large represent an ideal achievement of our human potential. I am especially concerned that emotional detachment may mean an acceptance of evil. In Pala, of course, there is no problem because evil does not exist—which is precisely what worries me. This brings me back to the point I made earlier about institutional mechanisms for dealing with the abuse of power. I worry about a society that is so convinced it has eliminated evil that it sees no need for building resistance to evil into its institutional structure and its value system.

The denial of responsibility. There is an increasing tendency in our society, though again it is by no means universal, for individuals to deny personal responsibility for their actions. This tendency can be related in part to the popularization of psychological and sociological views of man in deterministic terms. If a person can point to his psychological characteristics, or his home environment, or the social conditions under which he lives as sources of his behavior, then he no longer needs to take personal responsibility for them. At a more sophisticated level, this is expressed very nicely by Jeremy Pordage in *After Many a Summer Dies the Swan* (Huxley, 1965), when he says that there is "nothing like self-knowledge. . . . To know why you do a thing that is wrong or stupid is to have an excuse for going on doing it" (p. 149). At a simpler level, this point of view runs through our culture without even the requirement of self-knowledge. Since there *is* an explanation for one's behavior, in terms of forces beyond his control, it is senseless to feel guilty about supposed wrongdoings.

There is another major source of the tendency to deny responsibility in the modern world. The increase in the size and power of the nation-state and the increased complexity of bureaucratic and technological institutions have increased the feeling of helplessness of individuals and the conviction that things are out of their hands. More than that, these same developments have led to the refinement of a political ideology that gives the state the legitimate right to control many areas of the individual's behavior. Following this ideology, the individual does not merely deny personal responsibility for many actions that have been induced by the state, but would consider it morally wrong to abstain because of personal scruples from these actions, given the legitimate authority of the state. Thus the question of guilt does not even arise.

The tendency to deny responsibility is echoed in Pala by the general attitude toward guilt. Guilt seems to be viewed as a form of self-indulgence which, like other lingerings in the past, ought to be abandoned in favor of closer attention to the here and now. Beyond that, however, guilt seems quaint and senseless and a proper subject for puppet shows to entertain the children. The story of "Oedipus in Pala," which I cited earlier, is an excellent illustration of the treatment of guilt. It is ridiculous to feel guilty when you did not know what you were doing or could not help what you were doing and when you have never been taught to control your temper by doing the Rakshasi Hornipe. It would seem that guilt is irrelevant because responsibility is taken out of the individual's hands. Any wrong that he commits is due to biological and psychological dispositions that have not been properly redirected through early training and availability of the necessary social mechanisms. In a society that has total control over the individual's environment there would seem to be no room for personal responsibility and the concomitant capacity for guilt. Such a society worries me.

I am, of course, completely in favor of methods of child-rearing and penology that do not rely on antiquated notions of guilt and sin, rooted in an authoritarian belief system, and that fully take into account psychological and social determinants in the explanation and treatment of delinquent behavior. But, at the same time, I want to work toward a society that fosters the exercise of individual responsibility, which means, in turn, a society in which individuals are capable of experiencing guilt for their own actions and the actions of their group. While we want to contribute to the liberation of the individual from obsession by neurotic guilts, we also want to enhance his sensitivity to the experience, not only of real guilt, but also of existential guilt—the guilt that derives from our inevitable participation in a world that contains injustice, whether or not it is of our own making.

Our capacity to experience guilt, especially of the existential kind, is closely linked to our recognition of the fundamental ambiguity of human existence and our willingness to live within the terms of that ambiguity. Recognition and acceptance of the ambiguity of human existence carry certain implications for our efforts in developing a better society. Some of these implications are the very assumptions on which the preceding discussion has rested: that there are no easy and total answers in the search for the good life; that a good society can never be considered final, incapable of improvement, and that its institutions must therefore be so structured that there are opportunities for choice and change; that the corruption and abuse of power cannot be completely eliminated, and that it is necessary to develop social mechanisms and political values that will help to check them; that there will always be a struggle against evil and for a world that is more free, more sane, and more just, and that there is no substitute for a measure of passion in the conduct of this struggle; and, finally, that we must never cease in our quest for utopia even though we recognize that utopia can never be achieved.

CHAPTER 6

꧁꧂꧁꧂꧁꧂꧁꧂꧁꧂꧁꧂꧁꧂꧁꧂꧁꧂꧁꧂꧁꧂꧁꧂

INTRODUCTION

In the chapter that follows, I continue my examination of value questions inherent in the methods and approaches of the social researcher as he goes about his scientific enterprise. As in Chapter Five, an underlying concern is with possibilities for humanizing the scientific study of man, while recognizing its unique character and contribution. In Chapter Five, this concern was expressed through an exercise in confrontation between the scientific and the humanistic study of man, two approaches that are quite distinct in purpose and style yet equally valid, and whose interaction can greatly enhance the larger enterprise. In Chapter Six, this concern is expressed through an examination of two different approaches within the scientific study of man. One is the more "scientistic" orientation to social research, which emphasizes precision and quantitative analysis; the other is the more "humanistic" orientation, favoring qualitative analysis and clinical intuition. I speak of this distinction as the "rigor vs. vigor" controversy. It parallels in many ways the distinction between "anemic" and "emetic" analyses in social anthropology discussed by Gerald Berreman (1966).

My basic argument is that this distinction is misleading and represents a false dichotomy. Whether one uses quantitative, experimental methods or qualitative, clinical methods depends on the purpose of one's research, the stage of development of the problem under investigation, and various other considerations. Neither approach has a unique claim to being "scientific," and both are necessary to a scientific analysis. "What is called for . . . is a methodology which combines rigor and insight, verification and discovery, accuracy and empathy, replicability and human relevance" (Berreman, 1966, p. 350). Central to this argument is a particular view of the nature of scientific analysis—a view in which "scientific" is not treated as synonymous with "rigorous," in the sense of quantitative and experimental.

In light of this conception of scientific analysis, the present essay proceeds to re-examine the nature of experimental work in social psychology as it relates to the larger task of the social scientist. I see experimental research primarily as a contribution— and a uniquely valuable contribution—to systematic thinking about social behavior, rather than as a way of establishing verified laws of social behavior. There are some interesting points of contact between this conception of social-psychological experiments and the current concern with the "social psychology" of the psychological experiment and its methodological implications. I shall return to this issue, in a rather different context, in Chapter Eight.

The re-examination of experimental work in social psychology that is offered here may also contribute to a discussion, which is just beginning to take shape, of the basic orientation of experimental social psychology. This discussion was opened by two important and stimulating papers in a recent issue of the Journal of Experimental Social Psychology. *One is a courageous analysis by Kenneth Ring (1967) of the current priorities in social-psychological research, in which he deplores the gradual aban-*

donment of Kurt Lewin's vision of a social psychology that combines a concern for scientific understanding with a concern for human welfare, and the ascendence of a "fun-and-games approach" to research in the field. The other paper, by William McGuire (1967), though intended as a "reply" to Ring, is itself a provocative call by one of the major contributors to experimental social psychology for a reorientation of research and training in the field—away from exclusive reliance on manipulational experiments in the laboratory and toward greater use of natural settings and archival data for the testing of our hypotheses. These are encouraging signs of a readiness for fresh thinking about the task of the social psychologist and about the place of experimental work within that context.

This chapter is based on a presentation prepared in 1957, while I was working at the National Institute of Mental Health, as part of a staff panel on problems of interdisciplinary collaboration. It was thoroughly revised and expanded for the present volume. The current version also appeared as an article in the Revista Interamericana de Psicologćia, *1967, 1, 205–222.*

Rigor Versus Vigor:
The Debate on Research Philosophy

Social and behavioral scientists devote a considerable amount of their time and energy to discussions about alternative philosophies of research. Such discussions are especially prominent in interdisciplinary research settings, where they often take the form of debates between the disciplines. For example, during the past fifteen years, research in mental hospitals has drawn on the contributions of anthropologists, psychiatrists, psychologists, and sociologists. Investigators coming out of these different research traditions have tended to formulate the research problems in different ways, to focus on different units of analysis, and to favor different research methods. These differences tend, on occasion, to take on ideological overtones and to degenerate into contests over the relative virtues of the different disciplines and over their relative faithfulness to the precepts of science or to the phenomena under study.

Debates about alternative philosophies of research may also take place *within* a given discipline. Thus, for example, within the field of political science, a debate between "behavioralists" and "traditionalists" has been going on at least since the end of World War II. The behavioralists favor quantitative research and draw their concepts from such fields as psychology and sociology. The traditionalists are more inlined to follow historical, descriptive, and normative approaches to their subject matter. Again the debate has often tended to be ideological, with each side questioning the very legitimacy of the enterprise in which the other side is engaged.

Within the field of social psychology, which is interdisciplinary by its nature—being rooted in psychology and sociology and influenced by other disciplines as well—it is inevitable that differences in research philosophy would arise. These differences are in part related to the disciplinary origins, that is, psychology or sociology, of those who call themselves social psychologists. Many of the differences, however, cut across these disciplinary lines and arise as much within the two subsets of social psychologists as they do between them.

Social psychologists differ in their view of the proper *level of analysis* for social-psychological research. Thus, some investigators, including some who were originally trained in sociology, regard social psychology as essentially an extension of general psychology. They attempt to analyze social behavior in terms of general psychological principles, operating under the special conditions provided by the social situation. Their strategy is to take as their starting point models developed for the analysis of simple situations and to see how far these can be pushed in the analysis of the more complex situations in which social behavior occurs. Other investigators, including many who were originally trained in psychology, assume that social behavior cannot be effectively reduced to the level of individual behavior and that social psychology must, therefore, develop its own level of analysis. Their strategy, accordingly, is to start out with models that represent, as parsimoniously as possible, the complexity of the phenomena that they hope to illuminate.

Social psychologists also differ in the *research methods* that they prefer to use. Roughly speaking, one might distinguish between those whose orientation is primarily quantitative and those whose orientation is more qualitative—or at least clinical and nonstatistical.[1] Within each of these two sets of orientations, one can make further distinctions, which often reflect important differences in research philosophy. Thus, among the "statistically" oriented social psychologists, there are those who rely primarily on the experimental method, involving the active manipulation of variables to be studied and observation of their effects; and those who rely primarily on the use of survey methods to obtain opinion data and behavior reports from selected samples of the population. Similarly, among the more "clinically" oriented social psychologists, one can distinguish between those who prefer to use structured methods to obtain their data on individuals and groups, such as personality tests, structured interviews, and systematic group observation; and those who prefer to use the methods of participant observation and community study in the anthropological tradition.

As in the case of the other differences in research phi-

---

[1] These terms are only approximations. I would include in the second category studies in the factor-analytic tradition that collect large amounts of data on a single individual or a small number of individuals. These studies are certainly quantitative, in the sense that they work with numerical scores and subject these to various kinds of mathematical operations. They are, however, nonstatistical, in the sense that they are not primarily concerned with drawing inferences on the basis of sampling procedures, whether these be random sampling from a surveyed population or random assignment of subjects to experimental and control groups.

losophy that I have touched upon, the differences among social psychologists are sometimes ideologized. Proponents of one orientation may insist that they alone are truly scientific; proponents of another orientation may counter that they alone are truly relevant. Debates about research philosophy are a healthy and necessary part of any field of investigation, but when they take the form of arguments about the *general* virtue of "my" concepts and methods as compared to "your" concepts and methods, without regard to the specific uses to which these are put, then they are bound to be fruitless. More often than not, when we argue about the relative merits of psychologial *vs.* sociological, or quantitative *vs.* qualitative, or experimental *vs.* naturalistic approaches, we are dealing with false issues.

Sometimes the issues are false because they are based on a misconception of what the "opposing" approach or its particular representative stands for. Thus, antagonists in the debate between psychological *vs.* sociological orientations may be operating with stereotyped and anachronistic notions of how the other discipline approaches its problems. I have heard psychological analysis criticized because, supposedly, it seeks to explain group or collective behavior in terms of the idiosyncratic personality characteristics of individuals. I have heard sociological analysis criticized because, supposedly, it is based on armchair speculation or at best on casual observation. Such conceptions may, perhaps, have been accurate at one time, and they may still be good characterizations of how some psychologists or some sociologists go about their respective tasks. But they are highly distorted pictures of the dominant trends in these disciplines, and one can certainly not assume that they are accurate characterizations of the approach of any given psychologist or sociologist. Above all, such stereotypes ignore the fact that within each of the two disciplines, there is wide diversity in the concepts, methods, and levels of analysis used.

Similar misconceptions may be at the root of certain other dubious controversies. For example, some may be critical of a quantitative approach because they see it as a blind and mindless counting of noses. Others may be critical of a qualitative approach because they see it as an undisciplined selection of illustrations that can support any point the investigator wishes to prove. While we have all seen research that conforms to these unhappy stereotypes, they are clearly caricatures and perversions of the skilled and intelligent use of quantitative or qualitative analysis. Whenever debaters operate on the basis of such mutual misconceptions, there is no possibility for a true confrontation and resolution of issues. The antagonists have not even come to the point of discovering whether a real difference exists between them.

Even when two antagonists are genuinely talking to each other and real differences in research approach do exist between them, they may be debating false issues. This happens when the debate contrasts two alternative approaches that are not really alternatives at all. The debate assumes that they are two different ways of doing the same thing, when in fact they turn out to be two different ways of doing two different things. It makes no sense to argue whether one set of concepts or methods is better than another when the two are designed to deal with different kinds of problems. The question must always be: Better for what? Two investigators, both of whom may, for example, be studying social interaction, may be completely justified in working with different variables and units of analysis, if one is primarily concerned with the effects of interaction on individual personality and the other with its effects on the social system. Similarly, the investigator concerned with defining the contours of a phenomenon cannot reasonably be criticized for his failure to use an experimental approach, just as the investigator concerned with establishing functional relationships between variables cannot be criticized for his failure to use a more naturalistic approach. Debates that ignore the purposes that the competing approaches are designed to serve cannot provide much illumination.

The real issue is whether a particular research approach is appropriate to the questions that the investigator is trying to answer. Beyond that, there is the more complicated matter of whether these questions are worth asking at all. This, of course, raises the larger issues of the definition of the social researcher's task and the nature of the enterprise in which he is engaged. These real issues, concerned with the fit between our research approaches and our research problems, and with the nature of our essential task, form the background for much of the debate on research philosophy that is taking place. They tend to be masked, however, and relegated to the periphery, when the discussion focuses on false dichotomies rooted in competing disciplinary loyalties and scientific models.

Many of the dubious issues that I have already mentioned turn on one or another aspect of what might be called the "rigor *vs.* vigor" controversy. In the pages that follow, I shall try to spell out why the controversy on this level is of questionable validity, and how some of the real issues in the evaluation of social research cut across this particular dichotomy. I shall then turn to one special type of research approach, which is generally seen as the model of rigor, namely the experimental method. By examining experimental work in the context of what I regard as the essential task of the social scientist, I hope to demonstrate that, even in this case, the rigor *vs.* vigor formulation provides a misleading picture.

≥ THE RIGOR VS. VIGOR CONTROVERSY ≤

Some years ago, Kenneth Boulding took certain liberties with the lyrics of W. S. Gilbert to draw portraits of the scientist and the humanist. With a few further modifications, Boulding's lyrics can serve to demonstrate some of the differences between the proponents of rigor and the proponents of vigor. With apologies to both Gilbert and Boulding, then, let me present this brief debate between representatives of the two schools of thought:

R. Conceive me if you can
A rigorous young man,
A physical-causative,
Logical-positive,
White-coat-and-rat young man,
Who has decided bent
Towards experiment,
And oh! what a wrath is his
If a hypothesis
Claims it's self-evident.

V. Conceive me if you can
A vigorous young man,
A most analytical,
If not always critical,
Raw-stuff-of-life young man,
Who is persuaded that

Man differs from the rat.
To pierce men's reality
He views their totality
In their native habitat.

R. A serious-aims young man,
A Theory-of-Games young man,
A very stochastical,
Iconoclastical,
Testable-claims young man.

V. A very unique young man,
A reach-for-the-peak young man,
A flagrantly mystical,
Most unstatistical,
Rather oblique young man.

R. A one-way-screen young man,
A keep-it-clean young man,
A fine-observational,
Most operational,
Truth-is-what's-seen young man.

V. A truly all-round young man,
Yet very profound young man,
An I'll-only-do-it-if-
It-is-intuitive,
Truth-at-a bound young man.

R. A look-at-the-fact young man,
A get-out-and-act young man,
A set-up-a-project-
Where-money's-no-object,
Foundational-backed young man.

V. A very arm-chair young man,
A no-questionnaire young man,
A find-it-out-many-ways,
Know-it-all-anyways,
Devil-may-care young man.

R. A facts-by-the-yard young man,
A punchable-card young man,
Statistical-tabular,
Special-vocabular,
Work-very-hard young man.

V. A fitful-gleam young man,
A beautiful-dream young man,

A most metaphorical,
Highly rhetorical,
Letting-off-steam young man.

Needless to say, these portraits are stereotyped caricatures
of the two sides, but they do transmit some of the flavor of the
debate between them. The proponents of rigor stress the importance of obtaining hard facts through the use of exact methods.
They prefer research situations that are maximally structured and,
if at all possible, based on the experimental manipulation of the
independent variables; research instruments that are impersonal
and do not require too much filtering through the mind of the
investigator; and dependent variables that can be stated in terms
of quantitative indices and subjected to statistical analysis. Objectivity, precision, and replicability are, in their view, the central
requirements of a scientific analysis. The proponents of vigor, on
the other hand, stress the importance of research methods that
will capture the real-life flavor of the phenomenon under study,
in all of its fullness and richness. They prefer to make their observations in natural settings, free from the manipulations of the
investigators; to use themselves as active instruments for sorting,
understanding, and integrating what they observe; and to present
their findings in ways that properly reflect the totality of man
and society and the complexity of social behavior. Precision of
methods is, in their view, less crucial than relevance to the questions that social science proposes to answer and truthfulness to
the phenomena of social life.

The different components of the two syndromes I have described do not necessarily always go together, nor do most social
psychologists clearly identify themselves with one or the other of
these syndromes. Yet this division is at least an undertone in
much of the debate and position-taking on questions of research
philosophy and of the most productive direction for the future
development of the field.

The question of whether experimental or naturalistic approaches are ultimately superior is meaningless, because it cannot
possibly be answered in general terms. The choice of appropriate
methods depends, first of all, on the nature of the problem under
investigation, the kinds of questions that the investigator is ask-

ing. A fetishistic insistence on rigorous methods is bound to close off many promising sources of insight and information. Conversely, a squeamish reluctance to pin things down lest the sanctity of the phenomenon be destroyed is likely to keep us from ever attaining reliable knowledge. Depending on our purposes, a sacrifice in either precision or naturalness may be completely justified. For example, if we are interested in identifying the variables that define a particular phenomenon and in tracing its course of development, then we have to observe it in its natural setting. A less rigorous and more impressionistic approach is clearly called for here, since it yields the data we need and cannot obtain in any other way. On the other hand, if we are interested in establishing functional relationships between two sets of variables, then there is no substitute for an experimental approach, even though this forces us to rely on artificial situations of limited generalizability.

The choice between experimental and naturalistic research depends also on the stage of development of our research area and of the specific problem on which we are working. With respect to the research area in general, the "scientific ethos" requires us to use the best methods available for dealing with the questions we have posed. The unavailability of precise methods is certainly no reason for turning away from these questions. We tackle them as best we can, noting the limitations of our methods and gradually working toward their improvement.

With respect to the stage of development of the specific problem, different approaches are called for at different points in time. In the initial stages of work on the problem, when the investigator is interested in gaining an intuitive understanding of the phenomenon and in developing hypotheses, a clinical-impressionistic approach is most appropriate. When he is ready to test these hypotheses in the form of functional relationships, an experimental approach or some approximation thereof is usually called for. In a later stage, when the investigator is interested in testing the generality of his hypotheses in real-life settings, he may again turn to naturalistic observations or to the use of survey methods.

Finally, the choice of experimental or naturalistic approach must also depend on the preferred style of the investigator. Some are more comfortable with one approach and some with

another, for reasons of personality, training, or esthetic preference. When an investigator uses the approach that is most congenial to him, he is likely, other things being equal, of course,
to be more creative and to make a better contribution. Thus, what
is a productive method for one investigator is not necessarily so
for another. Each investigator should feel completely free to select
his own preferred style, without, however, claiming that it is therefore objectively better for all problems. He should keep in mind
the limitations of the particular approach he has selected, apply
it only to those problems to which it is naturally suited, and derive from it only those conclusions that it is capable of producing.
In short, if he writes musical comedy, he should not try to pass it
off as epic drama.

Two aspects of the rigor *vs.* vigor issue deserve special comment. One is the question of quantitative *vs.* qualitative analysis;
the other the question of a holistic *vs.* an elementalistic approach.

Qualitative analysis is sometimes criticized on the grounds
that the investigator has no conception of what he has really found
and is highly susceptible to the fallacy of the positive instance.
Quantitative analysis, on the other hand, may be criticized for the
investigator's tendency to let the true phenomenon pass him by
while he is simple-mindedly and obsessively counting the irrelevant. Thus, critics of a qualitative approach argue that the conclusions derived from it may be interesting, but are probably not
true; while critics of a quantitative approach argue that its conclusions may be true, but are probably not interesting.

The mere posing of the issue in terms of qualitative *vs.*
quantitative is bound to be misleading. In a very basic sense, all
scientific statements are inevitably quantitative, although the
counting and measurement may be only implicit. Even a case
study, for example, makes some implicitly quantitative statements.
When we describe certain patterns of behavior that are characteristic of the person or community studied, then we are essentially saying that this pattern occurs *frequently* and in *many* kinds
of situations. Often, moreover, we select a particular case for investigation because it is deviant or extreme, in other words, because it possesses a particular trait or set of traits to a greater or
lesser extent than other comparable cases.

Similarly, scientific statements generally have a qualitative component, although it too is not always made explicit. Propositions that state the relationship between two quantitative variables apply only if certain background conditions obtain. For example, the nature of the relationship between social pressure and conforming behavior depends on the nature of the situation in which the pressure is exerted, on the cultural context in which the behavior is observed, and on the motivational set that the person brings to the experience. In principle, these background factors can all be stated in quantitative terms, but in practice we rely—and must rely—on qualitative statements of the limiting conditions of our propositions. In empirical work, it is easy to ignore these conditions, because they are built, as constants, into the natural situations we select for study or the experimental situations we create in the laboratory. Nevertheless, these qualitative factors have an important bearing on our findings and, no matter how strong our predilection for quantitative statements, must be taken into account.

Thus, the crucial issue that cuts across the quantitative-qualitative dichotomy is whether, in any given study, the investigator is collecting the data appropriate to his particular purpose, and whether he is drawing conclusions that his particular data entitle him to draw. Those of us who use quantitative methods must always ask ourselves whether what we are counting and measuring is meaningfully related to the phenomena we are interested in, or whether we are just counting and measuring whatever happens to be readily available. The primitive, simple-minded quantifier, who decides what to measure on the basis of the instruments he has at hand, with little regard to the problems he hopes to illuminate, is certainly deserving of criticism. His culpability is compounded if he mistakes his irrelevant or partial index for the real thing. A hypothetical example of such a misuse of the quantitative approach would be an investigator who is interested in the level and determinants of "religiosity" in modern society, who takes church attendance as his sole index of religiosity because it can be assessed easily and reliably, and who then proceeds to draw broad conclusions about religiosity on the basis of these data. Critics of a quantitative approach would undoubtedly point to a study of this kind as a good illustration of the foolishness of trying to investigate religiosity with quantitative methods. What is wrong with this study, however, is not that the investigator used quantitative methods, but that he based his quantitative indices on the wrong data—or at least on an insufficient range of data—and that the data he did collect did not entitle him to draw the conclusions that he proceeded to draw. These errors are not inherent in the use of quantitative analysis as such.

For qualitative research, too, the basic question is whether the investigator has obtained the data appropriate to the conclusions that he wishes to draw. The primary danger here is not that he will focus on irrelevant data that can be easily measured, but that he will focus entirely on positive instances. Qualitative research does not have as many built-in safeguards against the tendency to find what one is looking for. An investigator eager to illustrate a particular phenomenon may find many cases that are consistent with his analysis, while missing many other cases that might be inconsistent with it. But, again, this fallacy is not inherent in the use of qualitative analysis as such. In qualitative as well as in quantitative analysis, the question is: What kinds of data does the investigator use for his analysis, and does he take the nature of these data into account in drawing his conclusions? Specifically, in evaluating qualitative research, we would ask whether the investigator has deliberately looked for nonconfirming cases as much as for confirming ones, whether he has arranged his observations in such a way that contrary findings have an equal opportunity to emerge.

A second aspect of the rigor vs. vigor controversy on which I wish to comment briefly is the apposition between a holistic and an elementalistic approach to human behavior. One component of the "vigor" syndrome, though by no means a universal one, is the insistence on dealing with "the whole man," in contradistinction to segmental, elementalistic approaches which only deal with parts of man and destroy his basic unity. To my mind, this is a false issue, because I do not regard the whole man as the business of social science. He is the proper business of poetry, philosophy, religion, everyday interpersonal relations, and, to a certain extent, psychotherapy. But the task of the social and behavioral sciences is to dissect and analyze the behavior of men and societies, to break it down in terms of theoretical constructs and genotypical formulations, and in this way to increase our systematic understanding of it. It is in the nature of social research to deal with parts of man, artificially separated out from the richness and unity of the total personality. The uniqueness and wholeness of the individual disappears at the hand of the generalizing social scientist, just as the poet's nature disappears at the hand of the natural scientist.

The holistic *vs.* elementalistic dichotomy is sometimes used to distinguish between psychoanalysis and academic psychology. But certainly psychoanalysis does not deal with the whole man. Among the greatest contributions of psychoanalytic theory are the different ways in which it slices man—and, until recently, the theory has not even concerned itself with some of these slices. It is precisely because of the fact that psychoanalysis is a scientific, hence not a holistic, system, that it is not a proper philosophy of life and cannot substitute for an adequate metaphysics and ethics. Man's ultimate meaning, his place in the universe, the nature of good and evil—all of these must be examined outside the scientific realm.

While social science is, by definition, concerned with parts, the picture of man that emerges from its theory and research must be *consistent* with the nature of man and society as they manifest themselves in their phenotypical wholeness. For example, a theory that cannot encompass such human and societal characteristics as self-sacrifice and love, or power and murder, is obviously of limited value. Another and related issue is whether the units of analysis that are used in a given theory and research program are appropriate to the problem with which they are intended to deal. This, it seems to me, is the real issue behind much of the holistic *vs.* elementalistic controversy. For example, I would question the use of a stimulus-response model for social psychology, not because it is too elementalistic, but because its units, which may be quite appropriate for the study of conditioning, are not equally appropriate to the complexities of social interaction. I would favor such concepts as social role and self-presentation, though they too are analytical and segmental, because I regard them as more appropriate to the level of analysis at which the social psychologist operates.

In sum, I have maintained that the rigor *vs.* vigor controversy and its various subcontroversies—such as those involving the relative virtues of quantitative *vs.* qualitative or holistic *vs.* elementalistic approaches—tend to focus on false issues. The real questions, stated in their most general terms, on which the evaluation of a given line of social research hinges, are how *systematic* and how *imaginative* it is. These questions are often masked by the rigor *vs.* vigor debate, because they sound deceptively similar to that dichotomy, while in fact they cut across it.

To be systematic is not the same as to be rigorous, in the sense of using experimental methods and precise, quantitative measures. Systematic work in social science refers to an organized and disciplined way of thinking about social behavior and of moving back and forth between conceptualization and evidence. Systematicness is not linked to a particular set of methods, although it does imply an awareness of the limitations of the methods one is using and of the conclusions that can properly be drawn from them. It is a relevant criterion in the evaluation of any social research, regardless of its form, and within each research tradition there may be wide variations in how adequately this criterion is met. Thus, qualitative, clinical work may be quite systematic, even though it is not rigorous. Conversely, quantitative, experimental work—though highly rigorous—may be quite unsystematic, if it involves the mere accumulation of empirical data without any attempt to relate these to efforts at conceptualizing social behavior.

The criterion of imaginativeness also cuts across the rigor *vs.* vigor dichotomy. The tendency to credit the "looser," clinical approaches with profound insights and to equate the "cold," statistical approaches with arid recapitulations of the obvious is a romantic notion that does not always conform to reality. The use of naturalistic methods, which attempt to capture the richness and the real-life flavor of the phenomenon under investigation, does not guarantee that the research will be imaginative. Conversely, quantitative and experimental work of the most rigorous kind may well be highly imaginative and imbued with a creative spark.

The real issue in the evaluation of social research revolves, in short, around the quality of the thinking and the imagination that it represents. There is no substitute for good thinking and good imagination, no matter what methods we use. And no method automatically insures us of either one of these.

ᕗ EXPERIMENTAL RESEARCH IN SOCIAL PSYCHOLOGY ᕤ

In distinguishing between the different purposes of different types of research, I pointed out that naturalistic research is particularly appropriate for exploring the dimensions of a problem and developing hypotheses, while experimental research is particularly appropriate for testing hypotheses about the functional relationships between different variables. This is, essentially, the usual distinction between research undertaken for purposes of discovery and research undertaken for purposes of verification. The latter clearly calls for a greater degree of rigor—highly structured designs, quantitative methods, and statistical analysis. By and large, I would agree with this formulation, but I would argue that, at least in social psychology, the distinction between discovery and verification is not as sharp as we sometimes maintain. In line with this position, I would like to propose a somewhat different perspective for viewing the functions and contributions of experimental research in this field.

The central features of research design in experimental studies are based on the assumption that we are engaged in efforts to verify general propositions. To this end, we are concerned about random assignment of our subjects to experimental conditions, about providing appropriate controls for our crucial comparisons, and about eliminating alternative hypotheses. In short, we set up our studies in such a way that they will allow us to verify propositions according to the usual standards of experimental method. If experimental research is to maximize its potential contributions—which, as I shall point out shortly, I regard as very considerable—then its practitioners must follow these procedures faithfully. The value of this work rests on our playing the experimental game according to its rules. And, as long as we do, I feel that we are entitled to the privilege of talking the experimental game—of using the language of testing and verification adopted from the natural sciences.

Let us not, however, deceive ourselves about the status of what we have found when we complete an experiment in social psychology. I would maintain that the findings of social-psychological experiments, even if they have been replicated a dozen times, can hardly be thought of as experimentally verified and established laws of nature. I assume that it is reasonable to view experimental findings in the natural sciences, and perhaps even in certain areas within psychology, in these terms. In social psychology, however, the gap between the laboratory and the real world is so great that one is hardly justified in the conclusion that what has been established in the laboratory constitutes a verified fact about nature. This is not because the laboratory situation is unreal, but because it has its own reality. The characteristics of the experimental situation in which we put our hypotheses to the test are related in ways that are largely unknown to the characteristics of the situations to which we hope to generalize our findings. First of all, the laboratory situation as such has unique characteristics of its own, which are only partly understood—although there has recently been a healthy concern with exploring the social psychology of the psychological experiment.[2] In view of the special characteristics of the laboratory situation, it may well be that the whole array of findings based on laboratory studies is applicable only to behavior in the laboratory—and in a subset of other social situations that are similar along certain crucial dimensions. In addition to the unique characteristics of laboratory situations in general, the situation created for any given experiment or series of experiments has special characteristics of its own. As I pointed out earlier, in discussing the role of qualitative factors, in setting up an experiment we devise certain background conditions that remain constant throughout. It may well be that the relationships found hold only in situations that share some of these background conditions. Similarly, in any given experiment we operationalize our independent variable in a particular way and we measure our dependent variable in a particular way. We know that the particular ways in which our variables are operationalized and measured often make a difference in the relationships obtained. It is very difficult, therefore, to have any reasonable assurance that relationships found in the laboratory apply to the wide range of real-life situations, characterized by

[2] See Chapter Eight for some relevant references.

different background conditions and different manifestations of the independent and dependent variables.

In view of the idiosyncratic and unrepresentative nature of experimental situations in social psychology, and in view of our limited knowledge of the dynamics of those situations, we cannot reasonably equate the confirmation of an experimental hypothesis in the laboratory with the verification of a general principle in nature. Our ability to draw such conclusions may be enhanced as we explore a particular relationship in a wide variety of settings, both experimental and natural, and as we learn about the special characteristics of the laboratory situation. At least as of now, however, our field has certainly not achieved this stage in its development.

Does that mean, then, that our experimental work is really *just* a game, that we are merely playing scientist without contributing anything substantial to an understanding of the general principles of social behavior? My answer is an emphatic no. In my view, experimental research can make enormously important contributions to social-psychological knowledge. These contributions, however, take the form of providing *unique inputs into systematic thinking about social-psychological processes,* rather than of establishing laws about social behavior.

I regard systematic thinking about man and society as the central and essential task of the social scientist. I would not insist that it is his only legitimate task. He may also, for example, apply his skills to the solution of certain practical problems. Or he may devote himself to the collection and processing of various kinds of social data, such as demographic or public opinion data, because of their historical interest or policy relevance, rather than because of their theoretical significance. But systematic thinking —continually confronting all manner of evidence and aiming for the development and refinement of general propositions—is the social scientist's task par excellence. It is in this context that I would want to evaluate the contributions of experimental methods, and it is in this context that I see a unique role for the experimental approach. There are at least four ways in which experimental research can feed into the process of thinking about social behavior more effectively than any other type of method:

(1) The requirement to translate our concepts into experimental operations imposes a discipline on our thinking that might otherwise be lacking. As long as we remain at the level of manipulating words, we can gloss over certain conceptual difficulties and avoid the necessity of really resolving certain ambiguities in our thinking. Once we attempt, however, to specify the conditions necessary for testing our propositions, to create laboratory situaations encompassing these conditions, and to manipulate our variables through concrete operations, we begin to discover ambiguities that had remained unnoticed and we are forced to face difficulties that we had been avoiding. The necessity of devising an experiment forces us to commit ourselves—to state clearly what our concepts mean and to pin down precisely what relationships we expect.

(2) Experiments offer us an opportunity to observe causal relationships, which can usually be inferred only indirectly and tenuously from other types of evidence. An experiment cannot, of course—as I have already stressed—indicate the generality of the relationship found. It may, however, provide a very important input into our thinking by showing that the causal relationship between two variables *can* be in the particular direction found, at least under certain circumstances. This kind of information is useful in identifying the dimensions on which our conceptual efforts ought to focus and in suggesting lines of thought that are likely to be more or less productive to pursue.

(3) Experiments provide operating models of the social-psychological systems that we are interested in exploring. They allow us to study certain processes in situations that we have deliberately created and that, therefore, have some advantages over the real-life situations to which we ultimately hope to generalize. The experimental situations are simpler, being stripped—insofar as possible—of extraneous variables and historical complications; they are situations whose histories and dimensions are more fully known to the investigator; and they are, at least to a limited extent, subject to the investigator's control. It is thus possible to observe the operation of the specific variables of interest in a detailed and relatively uncontaminated fashion. It is also possible to extend our range of observations to hypothetical situations that do not exist and have never occurred in real life. Along

with its advantages, the stylized and artificial character of the experimental situation also contains certain disadvantages, notably the difficulty in generalization. When taken in conjunction with observations from real life, however, the observations of a hypothetical model in action provide unique inputs into our thinking about social processes and their potentialities for change.

(4) If theoretical thinking is to remain productive, it cannot feed entirely upon itself, but requires periodic stimulation by new inputs from outside sources. For the social scientist, his empirical observations constitute the major source of such inputs. Every type of observation has something unique to offer as a stimulus to new thinking. One of the unique contributions of experimental observations is that they often derive from novel, atypical situations. Another unique contribution is the possibility of accumulating findings from a series of systematically interrelated experiments, which together point a new direction. It is interesting to note that unanticipated experimental findings, which are not too desirable from the point of view of verifying propositions, are particularly useful inputs into new thinking. Unanticipated findings call the investigator's attention to variables he had not thought of before and suggest interpretations and qualifications he had not considered.

These are some of the special ways, then, in which experimental work feeds into the process of thinking about social behavior and that make the experimental method such an important tool in social research. It is on their embeddedness in this longer conceptual process, rather than on their direct contribution to the body of verified laws about social behavior, that the significance of experimental studies rests. *An experimental finding, at least in our field, cannot very meaningfully stand by itself.* Its contribution to knowledge hinges on the conceptual thinking that has produced it and into which it is subsequently fed back.

There are several implications to the present view that an experimental finding cannot stand by itself. The most obvious implication, with which no theoretically oriented experimenter would disagree, is that findings from any single experiment cannot stand by themselves. Contributions are of necessity cumulative; only as a series of experiments—either by the same investigator, or by different investigators working on related problems

—build upon each other can we begin to formulate meaningful conclusions. There are different points of view about what constitutes a good research program, likely to produce a cumulative effect. Some experimenters prefer to narrow in on their problem, using a variety of experimental situations that focus on related issues, in the hope that the nature of the phenomenon they are exploring will gradually become clarified. Others prefer to use a single experimental situation, systematically varying all the variables that are, for theoretical or empirical reasons, potentially significant, in the hope that they can thus pin down the whole array of factors controlling the phenomenon under investigation. Both types of experimental programs may provide useful inputs into thinking about social behavior, though each has different strengths and weaknesses. Thus, the "narrowing-in" approach provides a better basis for assessing the generality of the phenomenon, while the "varying all the variables" approach is more useful in systematically identifying the dimensions that ought to be considered.

A second implication of the present view, with which some experimental social psychologists may not concur, is that findings from experimental research cannot stand by themselves. Because of the gap between laboratory situations and the range of real-life situations to which we want to be relevant, we cannot base our general propositions on the findings from experimental research alone. Our thinking must be informed by data from a wide variety of sources: population surveys and correlational research, participant observation and community studies, analysis of documents and of individual cases, historical studies and ethnographic reports. This is not to say that every investigator must work in all of these traditions, or even in more than one. There is no reason why a social psychologist who is trained in experimental work, is good at it, and enjoys it, should not devote himself to laboratory studies. He should, however, be aware of the limitations of experimental work and of its place within the larger context of systematic thinking about social behavior. Moreover, if he is well trained, he should at least be able to draw on observations from other sources as he contemplates his experiment, both in the process of defining his problem and developing his hypotheses before he begins his experiment, and in the process of checking the generality of his findings and exploring what they mean in action after the experiment is over.

Finally, the present view implies that empirical facts in our field—especially, but not exclusively, those based on experimental research—cannot stand by themselves. It is not the facts that constitute a contribution, but what is done with them. It may, of course, happen that an experimenter does little or nothing with his findings himself, but they become the raw material for the conceptual work of others. In any event, the ultimate value of experimental findings depends on the quality of the thinking in which they are embedded. It follows that a study that is procedurally clean and well designed, but unrelated to a serious conceptual problem, is less valuable than a messier study that forms part of a systematic process of thinking about social behavior. In other words, even though rigor is one of the unique and central contributions of experimental method, rigor as an end in itself is self-defeating. In the final analysis, no method can substitute for intelligence and imagination.

CHAPTER 7

~~~~~~

INTRODUCTION

Many social scientists are directly involved, and many more are indirectly involved, in the training of graduate students, the future professionals in the field. In this part of our professional activity, value concerns—and particularly the concerns with humanizing the scientific study of man while preserving its unique contributions—arise in a double sense.

They arise, first of all, in what we as teachers communicate to our students in the course of their training. Both in our personal contacts with our students and in the formal procedures (such as curriculum and administrative mechanisms) that we establish, we convey our rank-ordering of professional values, our conception of the essential task of the social scientist, and our definition of the roles for which the students are preparing. Thus, what we hope to communicate to the next generation of social scientists has important implications for the atmosphere and content of graduate education that we ought to promote.

Secondly, value concerns arise in the very process of training itself, which I regard as essentially a socialization process. As socializing agents, teachers are inevitably engaged in a manipulative endeavor, at least insofar as they come into the situation with some definite ideas about the end state they hope to produce and then try to create the conditions conducive to that end state. I take the position that professional socialization is a necessary and legitimate purpose of graduate education, and that we ought to acknowledge this fact—but turn our attention to the kind of socialization experience we provide. We want to create conditions that will enhance the capacity of our students to operate as independent scholars, fully immersed in the traditions of the field but ready to bend these to their own interests and needs, cognizant of a wide range of alternatives and capable of choosing between them. In short, what we want is a process of socialization that fosters rather than inhibits individualization (see Shakow, 1965).

Chapter Seven concerns itself with some of these issues, with special reference to the training of social psychologists. This chapter also appeared in Higher Education in Social Psychology, *a volume edited by Sven Lundstedt and published by the Press of Case Western Reserve University (Cleveland, 1968, pp. 73–104). The section on "Values conveyed in graduate education" is based on an article entitled "Values for graduate edcation in psychology," published in the* American Psychologist, *1966, 21, 954–956. It is reprinted here with the permission of the editor. That article, in turn, was excerpted from a longer speech that I gave at the Department of Social Relations, Harvard University, in 1962, as part of a discussion of educational issues.*

Socialization for Independence: Training Social Psychologists

A common complaint among graduate students—and among some more senior agitators—is that graduate education has a stifling effect on the students. It blocks their creativity, discourages independent thinking, and fosters a bland and drab uniformity. For example, in a special bulletin of the National Committee on Graduate Education in Psychology (Farrell, Markley, and Matulef, 1967) one finds, among others, such criticisms as these: graduate education encourages students to carry out research along orthodox lines, working only on safe problems and using only safe methods; it encourages them to hook into the research projects of faculty members, rather than to develop their own ideas and engage in original research; it fosters an attitude toward the doctoral dissertation as an instrumental task, leading to a union card, rather than as work on a problem that is of real concern to the student and that can serve as the first step in a long-term research involvement; and it suppresses interest in larger social and intellectual issues, in humanistic questions, and in clinical or applied problems.

The critics vary in the shortcomings of graduate education that they emphasize and in the reasons they cite for this sorry state of affairs. Some see it primarily as a problem of excessive pressures in a formal training program, leaving insufficient time for individual research. Others feel that there is entirely too much emphasis on research, resulting in a devaluation of such other activities as clinical work, community action, and teaching. Some of the critics see the problems of graduate education in a broader context, linking them to certain undesirable trends in the field as a whole, which are partly caused by our system of graduate education and which in turn contribute to it. They criticize the tendency toward conformity and faddism in the research topics that people choose to work on and in the approaches they take to them; the orientation toward techniques rather than toward problems; the preference for small problems rather than big issues; the tendency to "grind out" unimaginative studies; and—in the better, more imaginative studies—the emphasis on flamboyance rather than significance. (For the last point, see especially Ring, 1967.)

I share some of these misgivings about the current state of affairs in our field. I am convinced, moreover, that graduate education must bear some of the responsibility for this state of affairs, since it is the major vehicle by which the dominant norms and values are transmitted to the new generation of workers in the field. Insofar as graduate education does promote and reinforce these trends, I agree that we must re-examine what we are doing and reorient our training efforts.

⚲ DOES GRADUATE EDUCATION HAVE A STIFLING EFFECT? ⚲

Before we engage in a process of re-examining and reorienting our graduate training, based on the diagnosis that it has a stifling effect, we must ask ourselves whether this diagnosis is valid. Is it true, in fact, that a stifling atmosphere prevails in most graduate training programs? And, if so, is our pattern of graduate education primarily responsible for this state of affairs or are there, perhaps, other factors that are at least equally important?

In response to the first question, I have no doubt that some programs are strongly marked by a push toward orthodoxy and a narrowness in outlook which militate against creativity; and that all programs are at least partly subject to these tendencies. My own experience with a number of training programs in social psychology, however, does not match the tales of horror that are sometimes cited, and I seriously wonder how widespread such incidents are. It is obviously very difficult to achieve any kind of consensus on such a judgment, since so much depends on the criteria one uses. For example, should one's judgment about the general state of affairs be based equally on all training programs, or on only those that are widely acknowledged as superior programs? Should one's judgment of a given program be based on the actions of a majority of its faculty members, or should the mere presence of a deviant minority, tolerated within the program, alter our judgment? Obviously, there is no ready way of settling the question whether the atmosphere in graduate training is generally stifling, but I would at least want to keep the diagnosis open.

Interestingly, at a recent Conference on Graduate Education in Social Psychology, most student participants—who represented a number of graduate programs—voiced relatively little criticism of such a basic nature. Their criticisms focused largely on such details as the number of required courses and the number and type of examinations—traditional complaints, which are almost *de rigueur* for class-conscious students—and only rarely touched on the fundamental assumptions that underlie graduate training in the field. Perhaps this was a function of the basis on which the student participants in the Conference were selected. They were, after all, the successful students, who may already have been co-opted by the system and may, therefore, reflect its dominant values. On the other hand, the situation would be no less ambiguous if the Conference participants had been selected from the less successful students and they had presented more fundamental criticisms. Their judgment, too, might be suspect, since it might be rooted in the disaffection of those who did not "make it" in the system. Thus, again, it is difficult to know how to interpret either the presence or the absence of fundamental criticism. My experience at the Conference, however, certainly makes me question the accuracy of the diagnosis that a stifling atmosphere prevails—at least in the better-known graduate programs in social psychology. The malaise that many of us feel about where the field is going may be quite justified, but we may be settling too quickly on graduate training as the major source of our problems.

This leads me to my second question, regarding the factors that account for the stifling atmosphere in graduate education, to the extent that it does exist. Although it is difficult to disentangle closely interrelated factors, it is my impression that our pattern of graduate training is not entirely responsible for the tendencies toward orthodoxy, narrowness, and low creativity that we deplore among graduate students and among workers in the field at large. For one thing, these tendencies reflect some of the dominant values in the profession and in the academic world in general. The reward systems that prevail often encourage productivity of research output at the expense of significance, and continuation within well-trodden paths. Graduate students probably sense this early and act accordingly, as soon as they become socialized into the profession. The dominant values are, of course, conveyed to the students as they go through their graduate training, but merely changing our pattern of graduate education would not solve the problem. Educational innovations—such as greater reliance on self-directed work or on group participation—may be very useful, but unless we pay attention to the larger system within which the training program is embedded we cannot expect important changes in the dominant professional values. Educational changes must go hand in hand with changes in the priorities and reward structures within the profession as a whole. Each must be designed to facilitate the other, if we are to counteract mediocrity and conformity.

The tendencies toward orthodoxy and narrowness that we deplore are also due, it must be remembered, to the values and capacities that many students bring to their graduate education. Critics often draw a romanticized picture of the pure and inherently creative graduate student who becomes corrupted by the educational environment in which he finds himself and whose spark is cruelly extinguished. This may, and I am sure often does, happen, but the process is by no means entirely one-sided. First of all, not all graduate students have that much creative potential to begin with and many would, even in the most supportive environment, produce work that is competent but uninspired. Furthermore, graduate students often bring to their training the very values and orientations that critics deplore: an instrumental attitude toward graduate education and a self-conscious concern with manipulating their careers, with doing the proper things that will get them ahead quickly. In advising students, I have found it necessary on a number of occasions to counteract these orientations, to point out that they might be better off, in the long run, if they concentrated on doing good work on problems that held inherent interest for them and allowed their careers to take care of themselves, instead of planning their activities in terms of a deliberate strategy for getting ahead. Such baldly instrumental orientations may be products of anticipatory socialization in the course of undergraduate training, but in large part they probably reflect general values of the culture as applied in this particular situation.

It cannot be denied that at least a certain proportion of students develop such attitudes in the course of their graduate training. Whether or not they work out an over-all strategy of deliberate career manipulation, they may learn, as their training proceeds, that the quickest way to obtain rewards is to do the things that appeal to one or more of their professors. This may lead them to select problems not because they reflect their independent interests or because they impress them as significant, but merely because they fit into the research program of a faculty member. Given such an orientation, students are likely to turn to research that is either methodologically clean and theoretically orthodox, or else methodologically flamboyant and based on a theoretical tour de force, rather than come up with leaps into the unknown. To the extent that the training process encourages such choices, it is certainly having a corrupting influence on the student. But let us not picture the student as the utterly passive victim of his professors' selfishness, narrow-mindedness, and hostility to anything that is new and different. Highly original work, by its very nature, is less likely to gain immediate approval. When we are confronted with a piece of work that is more conventional and fits into a familiar framework, then it is much easier for us to react favorably. If the work is good, then we can appreciate it, because it yields a relatively clear finding or because it is elegant and esthetically pleasing or because it contributes to our own research programs or theoretical models. On the other hand, when we are confronted with something entirely original, we do not know quite what to make of it and we find it difficult to evaluate it in terms of existing frames of reference. We are more likely to respond to the ambiguities and flaws that the work, being in its initial stages, inevitably contains.

Nor would it be desirable and appropriate for professors to react to the work with enthusiasm and praise merely because it is "original," in the sense of never having been done this way before. Certainly, we must avoid any shadow of intolerance toward innovative and original approaches and any tendency, subtle or deliberate, to pressure students into the conventional channels.

Beyond that, we must consistently reward the process of independent thinking and original work. Training would become meaningless, however, if we immediately and universally rewarded the products of such work, regardless of their merit. Original ideas ought to be treated critically and even skeptically. If they are good—and, after all, not all new ideas are good ideas—they will be gradually refined and clarified through this process, and their value will become more apparent to others. A truly creative person must be willing to delay gratification and to absorb the criticism and skepticism of others. He must be prepared to go through a period in which others withhold approval and in which, in fact, he himself experiences agony and doubt about the value of what he is doing. A student who believes that there may be some promise in the new ideas that he is developing must be prepared to explore these ideas and see where they might lead, even if this course entails a certain degree of risk. Indeed, he may have to take risks that have implications for the development of his career, although these risks are much smaller in our field than they are in the fields of creative writing and the arts.

My suggestion that our pattern of graduate education is not solely responsible for the symptoms to which we are reacting is not an excuse for avoiding the thorough re-examination of graduate education that students and others demand, but a call for deepening that examination and going more thoroughly to the root of the problem. I take it as axiomatic that, whenever a group of our graduate students feel called upon to report that we are stifling their creativity, we must take a very serious and careful look at what it is we are doing. At the same time, we must have the courage to raise the possibility that an interaction process may be involved here and to ask our students to look into what they themselves are doing that might contribute to a stifling effect and to examine the values by which they are operating. A joint examination of the values built into our educational programs and the values that the students pursue will help us approach the problem of graduate education in the wider context of the values and reward systems that dominate the field and the academic world in general. Within such an analytic context, we are more likely to develop solutions not merely at the level of changing educational techniques, but also at the level of changing institutional arrangements—not merely at the small-group level, but also at the level of the social system (see D. Katz, 1967).

☙ GRADUATE EDUCATION AS SOCIALIZATION ☙

So far, I have merely raised questions about the prevalence and the sources of the stifling effects that graduate training is said to produce, but I have joined the critics in deploring these effects, wherever and for whatever reason they might occur. I have the impression, however, that some of the critics regard any kind of constraint as stifling and envisage a training program in which a student is merely set free to pursue his spontaneous interests and follow up his creative impulses, in which he is permitted to explore or ignore—as he sees fit—the accumulated body of knowledge and the prevalent concepts and methods of his field, and in which the development of personal standards substitutes for evaluation in terms of external standards. Perhaps I am setting up a straw man, but if such a conception of graduate training does exist I cannot subscribe to it. I feel that there are certain kinds of constraints that we must, of necessity, impose in the course of graduate training, because we are engaged in a process of professional socialization. Moreover, I do not believe that the imposition of certain constraints necessarily blocks creativity and fosters a sheeplike orthodoxy.

One of the primary functions of graduate education is to socialize the student into a professional role. In the course of his training, he turns into a professional in two senses of the term: he becomes a professional in the sense of a non-amateur, a skilled master of his craft; and he becomes a professional in the sense of a person who carries responsibility toward others and toward society at large. Professionalism in the second sense applies most obviously to clinical psychologists, and the question is often raised whether it is appropriate to provide clinical training in the context of a graduate department, rather than in a professional school. This is a legitimate question, but the difference in the professional character of clinical psychology, as compared to other areas of specialization, is largely a matter of degree. Insofar as social psychologists engage in teaching, in consultation, in applied research, or in social engineering, they are acting in professional capacities.

Graduate training, as a form of socialization, must therefore prepare the student to function within certain external restraints, as set by the expectations of society and by those of the profession. The graduate degree, moreover, represents a form of "certification" to society and to the profession that the student has achieved mastery in his field and that he is prepared to take on professional responsibilities. It can be argued that this kind of certification is an inappropriate function for a graduate department to perform, even though there are many historical precedents for vesting the functions of training and certification in the same agency (such as in the traditional relationship between the master and his apprentices or disciples). Whether or not we ought to be involved in what is essentially a form of certification, the fact is that we are; and as long as this is so, we have the responsibility to train students who can meet the requirements of the professional role.

Professional socialization imposes a variety of constraints on the graduate student. He must immerse himself in the history and tradition of his field. He must become conversant in the literature of his discipline, skilled in the use of its techniques, and expert in the manipulation of its concepts. He must acquire competence in operating within a disciplinary framework and sensitivity to standards of workmanship that have gradually evolved. Certainly, the goal of socialization is not to induce blind acceptance of certain ways of thinking and doing research or rigid adherence to a fixed set of concepts and methods. The goal is to enable the student to grow on his own terms, to strike out in new directions, and to approach his discipline selectively as he works out original contributions and draws on other disciplines relevant to his problem. To be enabled to do this, however, there are things he must learn, roots he must acquire, and standards he must develop. He cannot simply be told, as he enters graduate school, to pursue his own interests in total spontaneity and to abandon himself completely to his creative impulses. As he masters a cumulative discipline and learns to use the disciplinary framework as his point of reference, his capability of achieving higher levels of creativity becomes enhanced.

There is no doubt that this is a painful process, as socialization always is. To some degree, at least, the student is molded into a predetermined shape, external demands are imposed upon him, and his spontaneous impulses are inhibited. Inevitably, students will complain—and the better the student, the more likely he is to rebel. It is not enough to respond to these complaints, however, by telling the student that he is just going through an inevitable phase. Since we are involved in a manipulative enterprise, it is particularly incumbent upon us to take all complaints seriously and to re-examine our procedures. It may well be that our training program is unnecessarily restrictive, that it uses methods that are out of keeping with our ultimate goals, and that it contains features we cannot really justify on a rational basis. While we must be responsive, then, to student complaints and welcome them as useful prods, we must also be clear that certain constraints are necessary since we are, indeed, engaged in a deliberate process of professional socialization.

Once we recognize that graduate education is a form of socialization, the crucial question becomes: What kind of socialization experience do we provide for our students? In the terms of my theoretical model for the study of social influence, which is based on a distinction between the processes of compliance, identification, and internalization (Kelman, 1958 and 1961), I would see as our goal the student's internalization of the professional role. It should be noted that I use the term "internalization" not in the sense of passive incorporation of externally induced values and beliefs, but in the sense of an adoption of such induced values and beliefs to the extent that they are congruent with the person's own value system. Internalized behaviors, according to my model, become independent of their original external source and, after appropriate modification, are integrated with the rest of the individual's personal values.

Graduate education, like socialization in other settings, cannot rely entirely on internalization, which often tends to be a more gradual process. In the early stages, in particular, a certain amount of compliance may well be necessary. The student may be required to learn certain skills and information in which he has no particular interest, and to undergo certain experiences that he would rather dispense with. His readiness to comply with these demands is part of his ticket of admission to the training program and a condition for successful completion of the program. He may simply have to accept on faith the assurance that the required courses and experiences will be good for him in the long run. More importantly, graduate education requires identification, which is, in fact, at the core of the socialization experience. Through his relationship with his professors and other representatives of the profession, and—in many crucial ways—through his relationship with fellow students, he learns to take the role of the professional. He not only learns the norms and expectations that define this role, but he also incorporates this role as a basic part of his self-definition. Professors and older students serve as role models and he tends to adopt their language, their attitudes, their values, and their operating procedures. In this process, he takes over the standpoint characteristic of his discipline and learns to see the world within its terms.

Identification with the professional role is a necessary and useful part of graduate training. If the training stops at that point, however, we can consider it a failure. In a paper on psychotherapy (Kelman, 1963), I made the following observations about the place of identification in the therapeutic process:

> Ideally, the adoption of the therapist's standpoint through identification with him represents only a transitional stage in therapy. It is therapeutically very important because the patient must find some new way of looking at things and must have some framework that he can apply to specific situations and in terms of which he can formulate specific new insights. Taking over the therapist's framework represents the only economical solution to this problem during the early stages of therapy. As therapy proceeds, however, and the patient manages to loosen his habitual ways of looking at things and to acquire new insights, he should no longer be dependent on the therapist as an ideological fountainhead. He should be able, at that point, to become more selective with respect to the therapist's standpoint, to accept it not as a total system but as a source of useful hypotheses. He would then modify the therapist's standpoint to suit his own value system; he would accept parts of it and reject others in the light of his own experiences and his attempts to maximize his own values (p. 426).

Though I do not wish to equate students with patients, except in the root meaning of the term "patient" as one who suffers, the conception of identification as an essential but transitional stage is equally applicable to graduate education.

The role for which we hope to prepare our students is that of independent scholar and original thinker, fully immersed in the traditions of his field, but willing and able to move into new and unorthodox directions. Such a scholar is able to confront the concepts, methods, and attitudes characteristic of his discipline with his own value system and intellectual style. In so doing, he is free to accept or reject or modify various aspects of the tradition that he has learned, as they suit his particular interests and needs, and to recombine them in novel ways into a unique product. It is for this kind of role that graduate education must prepare the student. Thus, it requires a form of socialization that is consistent with these ends, a socialization conducive to individualization, or, in other terms, an identification conducive to internalization. The ideal "product" of such a training program is one who, having been fully socialized, is free to integrate his disciplinary orientation with his individual style and his unique intellectual preoccupations, and thus to become an innovator.

I have used the term "product" since this is the common way to refer to one who has completed a graduate training program. It is really a somewhat objectionable term and one that we might do well to replace. It seems to equate graduates with standardized manufactured objects as they come off an assembly line and is, perhaps, symptomatic of the least enlightened approach to graduate training. Yet, at the same time, the term reminds us of a consequence of graduate training that is more prominent the better the program is. A successful program leaves a peculiar mark on its graduates, so that they become, in effect, identifiable products of it, distinguishable from the products of other programs. They should not, of course, be uniform, stereotyped replicas and bearers of a single prescribed ideology. But graduate training is, after all, an important part of their life experience and intellectual development, and should therefore be an integral component of their identity. Regardless of how much they have modified or rejected the basic assumptions of their particular training program, these are issues with which they have had to grapple and to come to terms and which have therefore left an impact on them. Even those who reject the theoretical system in which they were trained may clearly reflect its influence in their style of thinking or even, for that matter, in what they choose to criticize and to differentiate themselves from. In this sense, then, every graduate who has actively related himself to his training experience is and ought to be a recognizable product of his training program. What individualizes him is the unique way in which he combines the influences from this experience with his other concerns and orientations and integrates them in his personal identity.

Given the goal of socialization for independence, the major challenge confronting graduate training programs is "to induce an identification that contains the seeds of its own dissolution" (Kelman, 1963, p. 426). This is most likely to occur if, even during the early stages of graduate training, the emphasis is on encouraging the student to adopt certain intellectual *processes,* rather than a certain set of specific beliefs and formulations. That is, the student's identification with his professional role models should encourage him to adopt a particular way of thinking systematically, of approaching problems, and of setting standards; it should not encourage him to take over a particular ideology and a commitment to a specific methodological or theoretical orientation. In other words, what he should learn through identification is a way of asking questions about man and society, not a predetermined set of answers to these questions. What should ideally remain from this experience is an internalized commitment to those processes that constitute the scientific study of man, based originally on emulation of role models but gradually amplified by each scholar's unique dispositions.

If we are to provide this kind of socialization experience, we must also be sensitive to practices that are incompatible with it and ought to be avoided. I have said earlier that some amount of compliance is necessary in graduate training, in that we require students to take certain courses or undergo certain experiences, even if they have no particular interest in them. We must be especially careful, however, to avoid any arbitrary use of our power to set requirements. We must make certain that we are not retaining requirements that have become anachronistic, or that merely serve as a form of *rite de passage* into the guild.

We must beware of using our power over the student to co-
erce or seduce him into adopting our language and theoretical
framework, working on our problems, and contributing to our
greater glory. Nor are we justified in blocking students from pursuing certain research interests merely because they imperil the
image of the department or the sanctity of the discipline. Perhaps
even more dangerous are the temptations of encouraging or allowing the student to become fixated at the level of identification. In
training students to operate within the conceptual framework of
the discipline, we must in no way encourage them to adopt it as
a rigid party line. We must beware of forcing a particular philosophy of research, theoretical orientation, or methodological approach on our students as *the* correct posture. In our one-to-one
relationships with our students, we must beware of tying them
too closely to us, and recruiting them as disciples who will carry
forward our banners. We should certainly expect to influence our
students, to guide them, to serve as role models for them, and to
work closely with them on common intellectual interests, but we
should encourage them to move beyond identification with us
toward genuine independence.

In sum, I have argued that graduate education does represent a deliberate attempt at professional socialization. In offering
such training, we do more than merely provide an opportunity for
the student to pursue his spontaneous interests. We stand for
something; we try to convey certain values, to prepare the student
for certain social roles, and to build a program that is deliberately
designed to transform the student into a professional. But, a central feature of the role for which we attempt to train our students
is the capacity to engage in independent research and original
thinking. Thus, we need a pattern of socialization that emphasizes
the values of independence and originality and encourages their
exercise. Though relying on compliance and identification, at
least in the early stages of training, we must fashion a socialization experience that is ultimately conducive to internalization.

With these general assumptions in mind, let me now turn
to four issues in graduate education, particularly in the field of
social psychology. Two refer to the end points of our training:
(1) What are the values that we try to convey in the course of
graduate education? and (2) What are the roles for which we train

graduate students? The remaining two issues refer to possible means for achieving these end points: (3) What criteria should we employ in developing a graduate curriculum? and (4) What are appropriate patterns of student participation?

⚛ VALUES CONVEYED IN GRADUATE EDUCATION ⚛

Those of us who are engaged in graduate education in social psychology or related areas typically bring to our professional activities a set of values that are deeply held and of vital importance to us. We do not often verbalize these values, but they are built in as assumptions in everything we do. We try to give expression to them in our teaching, in our research, in our consultation or clinical work, in our personal relationships with students, and in our relationship to society at large. Needless to say, we do not always succeed in living up to these values.

These are the values that we hope to communicate to our students in the course of their graduate training. More often than not, this communication is not explicit; it is based on what we do, rather than what we say. We take it for granted that, by observing us, our students will infer the values we hold, that they will adopt them for themselves, that they will emulate us where we have succeeded and improve on our efforts where we have failed.

The values I have in mind are widely shared among practicing scholars, since they are at the very heart of our common enterprise. Nevertheless, there are—and ought to be—differences in emphasis and tone. At some level, therefore, any statement of values is of necessity a personal statement. With this qualification in mind, let me list seven values that I consider central to the work of a social scientist and that I would like to see conveyed to students in the course of their graduate training. I would, of course, expect each student to adapt these values to his own style and sense of priorities, but hope that he would at least consider them as he defines the personal meaning of his professional role.

The value of intellectual endeavor. The engagement in an intellectual process represents, to my mind, one of the greatest sources of satisfaction and excitment in the life of the scholar. I regard it as a major goal of graduate education to stimulate in the student an active interest in this process: an interest in thinking systematically about some aspect of social behavior, in analyzing its components, finding relationships, achieving integration, and—via these intellectual endeavors—arriving at solutions. Basic to this process are the recognition that insights and creative solutions usually require a systematic and effortful application of one's intellectual skills, a willingness to examine and analyze the many complexly interacting factors that account for social behavior, and an ability to take the open and questioning attitude characteristic of the intellectual.

The value of continuity. It is in the nature of scholarly and scientific work that it is carried out in a tradition, which gives a cumulative effect to the knowledge and understanding that we hope to develop. Each investigator builds on the work of others and relates his work to what has gone before him. In communicating this sense of continuity and interdependency in the scientific enterprise as a central value to our graduate students, it is certainly not our purpose to encourage them merely to imitate the work that has gone before them, or to remain passively within traditional grooves. It is the hope of every scholar that he will add something new to the enterprise in which he is participating (although novelty itself is not of value) and that he will bring the work forward by his own contributions. Sometimes this may require a radical break with a particular tradition, and I would want my students to be prepared to make such a break if they find it necessary. But, even in that case, it is important to know the tradition from which one is differentiating oneself and to relate oneself to it. It is very likely that our own work would not have been possible or would not have been as good if there had not been a great deal of prior work that helped to sharpen the issues and pose the questions. Even the theories that we consider wrong are essential to us in the development of our own positions. In my opinion, a graduate education that is carried out in a historical vacuum, that does not attempt to provide the student with some familiarity of the traditions in his field and invite him to relate his own work to this continuing process, falls short of one of the major criteria of scientific work.

The value of discovery. I use the term "discovery" loosely here to refer to the results of our research endeavors, whatever form these may take. There is a tremendous sense of satisfaction and excitment that comes with the completion of a study, because we feel that we have observed a new phenomenon, or clarified an issue, or gained some insight into a complex process, or discovered a new relationship. The sense of satisfaction may derive from the new understanding that we have achieved, or from the contribution to social welfare that we feel we have made, or from the esthetic enjoyment of an elegant solution. Whatever its source, it is this sense of excitement about the discoveries achieved through our research, through the systematic application of our intelligence to a problem, that I would hope to convey in the course of graduate education.

The value of workmanship. One of the satisfactions that a social scientist, among many others engaged in specialized and creative endeavors, can derive from his activities is the sense of workmanship: the feeling that he knows what he is up to, the ability to define readily the problem with which he is confronted and to choose the appropriate method, the knowledge that he has the necessary skills and expertness to go about the job in a workmanlike way. Graduate training should help to develop this sense of workmanship in the student, both his desire and ability to do a workmanlike job. In short, it should make a professional out of an amateur. Workmanship does not at all mean that the person can do his job easily and automatically, having boiled it down to a simple routine. The job may involve very arduous work, with a great deal of suffering and frustration. What workmanship does mean is the possession of definite standards toward which he is striving and of definite guidelines by which he can evaluate his progress. If work moves in new directions, to which traditional standards appear irrelevant, then it becomes essential that new standards be developed. It is the absence of any standards at all that is the mark of the dilettante.

The value of social usefulness. One of the values that I consider important and hope to convey in graduate training is the concern with the social usefulness of what we are doing. There are, of course, many ways in which a social scientist might consider his work socially useful and I would not want to press for my particular formula. What I would like to do, however, is to

create an atmosphere in graduate training that would lead the
student to pay serious attention to the social contributions that
he could potentially make, contributions to the welfare of individuals and communities or to the solution of pressing social problems. It is essential to keep in mind that the unique contribution
that a social scientist, qua social scientist, can make to human
welfare rests on the systematic analysis of the problem confronting
him—whether it be that of conducting a clinical relationship or
that of resolving a social conflict—and of the variety of factors
that determine its course.

The value of responsibility. Responsibility for the welfare
of our subjects and our clients is, of course, a major value that we
hope to convey in graduate training. Social scientists have many
problems in this area, such as those relating to the use of deception in social-psychological experiments, to which the next chapter
is devoted. There are no easy solutions to these problems, but I
want to make my students aware of their existence and of the importance of active concern about them. At the simplest level, the
issue is one of structuring our relationships so that they will not
have harmful effects on our subjects or clients. Beyond that, however, our students must learn to be constantly aware of the fact
that they are engaged in human relationships with others, and
that assurance of the dignity and enhancement of these others is
part of their professional responsibility.

The value of partnership. The seventh and final value that
I would want to see conveyed in the course of graduate education
is the sense of partnership in an intellectual endeavor and process
of discovery. The opportunity to work jointly with colleagues
whom one respects, to experience the mutual enrichment that
comes from successful collaboration, is, to me at least, one of the
greatest sources of satisfaction in professional life. The ground-
work for such partnership is laid in the student's relationship
with his teachers in the course of his graduate training. I know
that one of the most meaningful experiences in my own graduate
training was my relationship to my major professor, Carl Hovland,
who had the unusual gift of serving as an ideal model while at
the same time encouraging his students to move out in their own
unique directions. I can only hope that I can approximate such
partnerships in my relations with my own students. There is an-

other, broader aspect of partnership that represents an important value and major source of satisfaction, and that is membership in a community of scholars, which not only includes one's immediate colleagues, but extends beyond disciplinary, institutional, and national boundaries.

ROLES TO WHICH GRADUATE EDUCATION IS DIRECTED

I agree with the view that the primary role to which graduate education in social psychology is directed is that of the social-psychological *scientist,* who is prepared to carry out basic research and theoretical analysis with the aim of developing general principles of social behavior. This is, in fact, the role by which our entire training effort is defined and to whose mastery the doctoral degree bears witness. Having said this, however, I must add two important qualifications. First, I do not subscribe to some of the ways in which the role of scientist is conceived, that is, to some of the operational meanings attached to it. Secondly, though I regard it as the defining role, I do not see it as the only role to which our training must be directed.

In the last chapter I described the essential task of the social scientist as systematic thinking about social behavior, fed and tempered by the periodic input of empirical evidence. This is the model I have in mind when I speak of the role of scientist as the primary role to which graduate education ought to be directed. Too often, however, the model of the scientist according to which students are socialized is considerably more narrow and is, in fact, more in keeping with the trappings of science than with its fundamental purposes. I would seriously question several assumptions implicit in such a model:

(1) Scientific social psychology is sometimes equated with the use of a particular set of techniques, such as experimental techniques, or quantitative techniques more generally. Work that uses different methods is classified, by definition, as unscientific. This assumption reverses the usual priorities in scientific work. The starting point for the scientist is a question that he wants to answer, a problem that he wants to solve; he then selects the best methods available for dealing with the problem he has defined,

given the stage of development of the discipline. To equate scientific work with a particular set of methods not only sets artificial limits on the questions that can be asked, but may also encourage arid or trivial undertakings. The use of a particular set of techniques may come to be viewed as not only a necessary but also a sufficient condition for scientific work. That is, science may be confused with methodology, so that a well-controlled experiment or a survey based on a properly drawn sample is automatically defined as an act of science, regardless of its purpose or the problem to which it addresses itself. (See Ring, 1967, and McGuire, 1967, for a discussion of some of these issues as they relate to the role of experimental methods in social psychology.)

(2) Scientific social psychology is sometimes equated with the reduction of social-psychological phenomena to general psychological principles. I do not question the legitimacy of attempts to explain social interaction, for example, in terms of the principles of operant conditioning. I personally feel that such approaches are of limited value and that we have to develop concepts at the level of the phenomena with which we are concerned, but I regard with interest any attempts to see how far one can push basic psychological principles in conceptualizing complex social behavior. What I object to, however, is the notion that *only* by formulating social-psychological phenomena in terms of such simpler concepts can we hope to be scientific. This is similar, of course, to the insistence on physiological or physical reductionism with which general psychology has had to contend. A scientific analysis should be free to develop whatever concepts seem appropriate to the problem under investigation. To insist that explanation must be at the level of individual-psychological processes inhibits the social psychologist's search for the most productive formulation and even makes the posing of certain questions taboo. A parallel and equally inhibiting notion, though it involves the reverse of reductionism, may be observed among some investigators who insist that social-psychological phenomena can only be conceptualized at the sociological level and who therefore reject any formulation that treats participants in social interaction as independent individuals who bring their own motivations and perceptions into the situation.

(3) Scientific social psychology is sometimes equated with

the avoidance of socially significant problems. I have already stressed, in Chapter Three, that scientific research does not necessarily mean value-free research. Many, if not most problems in social psychology cannot possibly be approached in disinterested fashion, nor is it necessary to do so. To be scientific, we ought not to avoid such problems, but to recognize and take account of the value preferences that we bring to their analysis. A scientific social psychology that excludes by definition such central problems as social change or intergroup relations can only be based on a rather naive conception of scientific objectivity.

With this broader conception of scientific social psychology in mind, then, we can define graduate training as socialization for the role of scientist. To say that we are training our students to become scientists means that we are encouraging them to acquire a special set of capabilities, interests, values, and approaches to the study of man and society. It does not mean, however, that the role of scientist is the only social role in which we expect them to function after they complete their training. Social psychologists, like scholars in most other fields, are called upon by society to perform a wide variety of roles, some of which may be closely linked to scientific research, while others may be far removed from it. Demands for the services of social psychologists and other behavioral scientists in a variety of settings, both on a part-time and on a full-time basis, are becoming increasingly urgent. The roles that they are asked to perform involve such varied functions as the following:

(1) Undergraduate teaching, which has, of course, traditionally been a function carried out by scientists. I see no necessary contradiction between the roles of scientific researcher and undergraduate teacher. The active researcher is often the best teacher because he can bring to his students the sense of excitement and immediacy that comes from being involved in producing the new knowledge of the field. On the other hand, active researchers may sometimes be poor teachers because of a lack of skill and interest. Similarly, the man who is not actively involved in research may be an excellent teacher, but this is not necessarily so. The main point is that undergraduate teaching, though typically carried out by graduates of doctoral training programs, represents a different role from that of scientist. Graduate teaching,

of course, can more clearly be seen as an integral part of the scientist role.

(2) Interpretation of social-psychological findings and approaches to the public at large and to special publics, such as members of other professions, of educational institutions, of governmental agencies, of various private organizations, and of international bodies. This function may include not only communication of knowledge, but also advice and assistance in the utilization of that knowledge for social action.

(3) Mediation between the research community and government agencies, foundations, international bodies, and other organizations that have an interest in the utilization of social science knowledge. A social scientist, in the role of mediator, might feed to the research community information about the operating agencies' needs and interests for social science knowledge. At the same time, he might feed to the agencies information about available knowledge, about potential resources in the research community, and about new research that ought to be supported.

(4) Operational research, which may be done by research organizations on a contract basis or by social scientists attached to a public or private agency. This may include action research, or evaluation research, or any other research that is essentially mission-oriented, that is, whose primary purpose is to promote the mission of the sponsoring agency rather than the interests of the researcher. A closely related category is research that consists primarily of the periodic gathering of social data, such as population indices or public opinion polls. The line between operational research and straight data collection, on the one hand, and "basic" research, on the other, cannot always be drawn very sharply. There are many intermediate cases, and certainly many studies carried out for primarily operational purposes yield valuable insights about general principles of social behavior. It is important to keep in mind, however, that operational research, insofar as it addresses itself to problems set by the client, involves a role that is different from that of the scientist.

(5) Social engineering, which may involve some research operations, but in which the social scientist functions primarily in the roles of consultant, clinician, change agent, and community

organizer. Many social psychologists are, for example, actively engaged in sensitivity training and other uses of group methods in a variety of settings. With the increasing emphasis on community mental health and milieu therapy, social-psychological training is becoming an integral part of the preparation for clinical work. There are also demands for people with social-psychological training to work in poverty programs, community relations programs, school systems, and international projects. Social engineering activities may be a source of valuable insights and observations for scientific research, but they do represent a separate function.

(6) Administration, in both educational and research organizations.

(7) Professional exchange, which is becoming a major activity as the volume, the degree of specialization, and the international character of social-psychological research increases. Exchange among colleagues is, of course, an essential element of the scientist role itself. However, with the vast increase in the volume and geographical spread of scientific activities, scientific communication has become a specialized function in its own right. Moreover, every social scientist who wants to be part of a wider community, going beyond the small group of specialists working within the same narrow area, must concern himself with the function of communication between those who, though members of the same or related disciplines, speak different languages, either because they work within very different conceptual frameworks or because they come from very different cultural backgrounds.

Social psychologists ought to be free to respond or not respond to these various demands, as they see fit. We must find ways to protect and support the man who prefers to resist these demands, who can operate effectively only by concentrating on basic scientific research and refusing to be sidetracked from it. At the same time, there is nothing inherently unscientific or disloyal to his calling about a scientist who wishes to respond to social needs and to concern himself with problems of communication, application, and utilization of scientific knowledge. In fact, it is essential that some social scientists address themselves to these concerns, if we want to prevent the work itself from becoming entirely sterile, and if we want to ask society to continue to protect and

support basic research.[1] What *is* crucial is that there be no con-
fusion about the role in which the social scientist is engaged at
any given moment. Thus, when he is extrapolating from scientific
findings, or when he is carrying out mission-oriented research
(see Chapter Four), or when he is engaged in social engineering,
he should not cloak himself with the mantle of science. It can be
assumed, of course, that his scientific training and knowledge
contribute significantly to his functioning in these different situations, but he is not operating in the role of scientist as such.
The principle of multiple roles works both ways. Being a scientist
should not prevent a man from engaging in other functions, but
it also does not permit him to attach the label of science to everything he does.

One might raise the question whether training for some
of the other roles that I have described should not be carried out
under different auspices than the doctoral program. For certain
of these roles such an option would clearly be impossible or undesirable. For example, there are many obvious reasons for having
the functions of administering educational and research enterprises, or mediating between the scientific community and government agencies, carried out by individuals who are fully trained
as scientists and who know the field and can speak for it from the
inside. For others of the roles that I listed, it would certainly be
possible to provide training outside of the context of the doctoral
program. It is possible, for example, to prepare students for undergraduate teaching, operational research, or social engineering
in programs that, compared to the usual doctoral program, give
less emphasis to basic scientific research and more emphasis to
some of the specific skills required in these roles. Even for these
roles, however, there is a great deal of value in retaining close

---

[1] I believe that society should support basic scientific research
as an end in itself, without demanding evidence of its immediate utility. It does have a right to expect, however, some attempt to feed back
the products of scientific research, not necessarily by the individual
scientist who is conducting the research, but by the profession as a
whole. The artist, even when he is absolutely committed to the concept of art for art's sake, also feeds back the products of his work to
society, and at least offers an opportunity to some segments of society
to find something of value and interest in what he creates.

links to the basic scientific discipline. It is highly desirable that at least some of the individuals engaged in these functions be fully trained in basic scientific research and, ideally, move back and forth between the scientist role and these other roles. Such an arrangement encourages constant feedback between scientific developments and the other functions which, though different, are highly dependent on such developments. Thus, it becomes more likely that undergraduate teaching will reflect the best and latest thinking in the field, and that operational research and clinical work will be more self-critical, more innovative, and more sophisticated in their methods.

Another factor to be considered is the nature of the Ph.D. degree. In the United States, at least, the Ph.D. is, in essence, a degree certifying that the student has received advanced training, that he has adequately mastered his field, and that he has achieved a satisfactory level of competence. Even though the doctoral dissertation represents an original and substantial piece of work, it does not attest to the graduate's having made an outstanding contribution to the field or being an unusually creative scientist. It is essentially a witness to professional competence, rather than to scientific creativity. We may deplore this state of affairs, but it is a reality, largely rooted in the general principle of equalitarianism that underlies American education. Thus, even in the best universities, the Ph.D. is sought by and given to individuals who have no particular interest in scientific research or no special talent for it. They are individuals who want to engage in some of the other roles that I have listed and whose often considerable talents lie in those directions, and who work for a Ph.D. because it is a widely recognized symbol of competence and a condition for the achievement of high status in a variety of activities. I do not propose that we change our standards or our goals for graduate training because of this state of affairs; these should remain oriented toward training for the role of scientist. We must, however, accept the fact that not all of the students we train in this tradition will function exclusively or even primarily as scientists. We ought to create an atmosphere that encourages these students to function creatively and effectively in the other roles that are congenial to them, rather than to feel obligated to play scientist, to go through the motions of research, and to clutter up the journals with studies in which neither they nor their colleagues are interested.

The implication of what I have been saying is that we ought to communicate, in the course of graduate education, that a variety of professional roles are legitimate and worthwhile and that those who engage in activities other than basic research and graduate education need not consider themselves failures or traitors to their training. The value of the scientific study of man, of systematic thinking about social behavior, and of research oriented toward the development of general propositions must remain the central core of our training efforts. It must be transmitted through the role models with whom the students associate, through the standards of quality that they acquire, and through the various activities in which they become active participants. These processes are, after all, what the field is all about; they are the processes whereby the discipline can grow and develop and can become more useful and relevant. At the same time, however, it should be made clear that basic scientific research is not necessarily the only way in which training in the field can be utilized. Students should be allowed to learn, therefore, of the availability and validity of other roles, and have some direct exposure to them. Specific and systematic training for these other roles may sometimes be difficult within the context of a graduate program. Training in clinical psychology, for example, has often been a source of difficulty, although in some departments of psychology it has been accomplished very effectively. In any event, wherever possible, there ought to be opportunities within graduate programs for those students who are interested in deepening their experience with other roles to obtain further training in them, through relevant courses, practicum arrangements, and exposure to appropriate role models.

CRITERIA FOR A GRADUATE CURRICULUM

What kind of curriculum would we have to devise to convey to our students the values and prepare them for the roles that I have discussed? How should the curriculum be structured if it is to provide maximum opportunities for students to gain a broad perspective of their discipline, an intimate knowledge of its traditions, concepts, and methods, and an expert grasp of an area of specialization, while developing into independent, creative, and interdisciplinary social scientists? Clearly, there is no single pattern that would meet these requirements, and each institution has to create a program suited to its particular resources and traditions. At the most general level, however, I would describe my ideal curriculum as one that is pluralistic and problem-oriented, and that balances opportunities for specialization with those for integration and opportunities for apprenticeship with those for diversification. Let me comment briefly on each of these four criteria.

Pluralism. The curriculum should ideally reflect the broadest definition of social psychology and should provide a place for the whole range of approaches to problems in the field. This means, first of all, that different theoretical approaches ought to be represented in the curriculum. Social psychology has roots both in psychology and in sociology and these two parent disciplines have historically provided different perspectives on the field, although there is now an increasing convergence between them. In most programs, social psychology is presented entirely within the context of one or the other of these two disciplines. In my ideal curriculum, students would be exposed to both perspectives, as well as to the range of theoretical approaches within each of them. Secondly, the curriculum should provide exposure to the different methodological approaches to social psychology. Too often, the field is almost exclusively identified with a single type of procedure, such as the laboratory experiment or the sample survey. In my ideal curriculum, each student would at least have some experience in each of two broad categories of social-psychological research: systematic research in natural settings, in which design and methods are adjusted to the requirements of the situation into which the investigator enters; and experimental research, in which the investigator manipulates and controls the relevant variables in the laboratory or in a field situation. Finally, the curriculum should provide exposure to the different research traditions with which social psychologists have been identified. This would include various substantive areas, such as attitude research or research on socialization. It would also include the two broad, but by no means mutually exclusive, categories of research oriented toward theory-building and research oriented toward social issues.

I would regard graduate training as particularly successful if it produces social psychologists who are themselves "pluralistic" —whose approach to the field is based on an integration of its psychological and sociological sources, and who are able to move back and forth between the laboratory and the field and between theory-building and research on social issues. I would not expect all students to fit this pluralistic model, however, nor do I see any need for them to do so. They should be free, if they prefer, to work entirely within a Skinnerian framework, or to restrict themselves to survey methodology, or to concentrate on narrow theoretical problems. The idea of a pluralistic curriculum is to provide exposure to the whole range of approaches to the field and to allow the student to choose freely among them. The curriculum should avoid the tendency to identify a single approach to social psychology as the only one that is ideologically correct, and communicate that there are many ways of making significant contributions to the field. Beyond that, the student should be free to choose the approach that he prefers, or to recombine different approaches into a unique package, or to move from one to the other as the occasion demands it.

There are often serious practical limitations to our ability to devise a pluralistic curriculum. Clearly, a small program does not have the resources to offer the entire range of approaches to the field. Some programs try to deal with these limitations by concentrating on a very small number of areas of specialization and developing real strength in those areas. This may often be a reasonable way of maximizing the value of a small program, as long as there is no pretense that its offerings represent the entire field. Under these circumstances, the only way to satisfy the principle of pluralism is to inform the student of the limitations of the program, to acquaint him with the existence of other approaches to the field, to encourage him to broaden his background through work on his own or in other departments or in summer institutes, and to make it easy for him to switch to another program if he finds his present one excessively narrow.

Problem orientation. The curriculum should ideally be organized and areas of specialization be defined in terms of substantive problems rather than in terms of disciplines (that is, psychology *vs.* sociology) or of methods. The basic units into which the field is divided ought to be the domains of social behavior that we wish to explore, the phenomena that we seek to explain, the questions that we hope to answer. The methods and approaches we use ought to be determined by our problem, rather than the other way around. This order of priority should be reflected in the structure of the curriculum.

My assumption is that most social-psychological problems can be investigated most effectively through a combination of methods, by shifting back and forth, for example, from naturalistic observations to controlled experiments (see Chapter Six). This does not mean that any given individual has to avail himself of the entire range of methods. Because of differences in personal style, some investigators are more comfortable and more creative when they use laboratory techniques, others when they engage in interviews, and others still when they derive their data from participant observation. In thinking about his problem, however, each investigator ought to be able to draw on the work of all those who have been concerned with the same general phenomenon, regardless of the particular methods that they have used. Too often, social psychologists define their specialties in methodological terms, so that an experimentalist might automatically dismiss as irrelevant the work of a survey researcher, and vice versa. A curriculum organized in terms of problems can help to counteract such wasteful tendencies.

As far as the disciplinary sources of social psychology are concerned, I see the integration of psychological and sociological approaches as the most promising direction for the future development of the field. This is based on my view that the central and unique concern of social psychology is with those problems that lie at the intersection between psychological and sociological (or individual and institutional) processes (see Kelman, 1965). According to this view, dividing the field in terms of a psychological social psychology and a sociological social psychology misses some of the most important problems to which we ought to address ourselves. The alternative is to organize the field in terms of problem areas that cut across the two parent disciplines and of necessity draw on both of them (as well as on other disciplines, depending on the problem). This was the principle we used, for example, in establishing, in 1966, a new curriculum for the inter-disciplinary Doctoral Program in Social Psychology at the University of Michigan. The three proseminars that constitute the core sequence in social psychology were deliberately defined in terms of three substantive foci, each of which cuts across psychology and sociology and draws on the work of both disciplines—processes of social interaction; socialization and social influence; and organizational and collective behavior.

Balance between specialization and integration. With the expansion of information and the increased volume of work in every area of social research, specialization is inevitably the order of the day. An individual must specialize if he is to gain full mastery over the domain in which his major work lies and if he is to be able to function as an independent scientist, making original contributions. An effective curriculum must, therefore, provide opportunities for specialization, including seminars on specialized topics, research experiences in specialized areas, and preliminary or qualifying examinations defined in terms of special problems. Specialization does not necessarily mean narrowness and parochialism; if combined with problem orientation, it may involve the convergence of a variety of methods and approaches on a specific substantive issue. To counteract any tendency toward excessive narrowness, it is essential to maintain flexibility in the definition of areas of specialization. Thus, it ought to be possible for students to work out various combinations of interests in defining their specialties. In some cases, this may involve a combination of social psychology with inputs from other disciplines, such as political science, anthropology, economics, public health, or law. In any event, insofar as possible each student should be allowed to tailor-make his area of specialization in a way that is most appropriate to the problem with which he is concerned.

While specialization is, thus, both necessary and desirable, it also contains many dangers. If there is too much emphasis on specialization—and, particularly, if areas of specialization are narrowly defined—then the student loses his perspective over the entire field, his sense of continuity between problems, and his ability to see relationships. Under these circumstances, he lacks the secure grounding that would allow him to operate as an independent investigator within his disciplinary framework, and his ability to choose and recombine is restricted. Thus, it is essential that the curriculum balance opportunities for specialization with opportunities for integration, which will give the student an intimate familiarity with his field as a whole and an understanding of the relationships between its various parts.

In my view, it is still possible to treat social psychology as a single, integrated discipline, such that a student can encompass it in its totality and gain a full perspective, though not a specialist's mastery, over its various sub-areas and the relationships between them. The time may come, as it has already come in general psychology, when it will no longer be possible to think of social psychology as a single discipline and when we will have to accept a division into relatively separate subdisciplines. I feel very strongly, however, that we have not yet reached that stage and that it is possible to provide integration and to build bridges between the different approaches represented in the field. In fact, I feel that we are still at the stage of *creating* an integrated discipline, pulling various disparate strands together into a common framework. This is especially true, as I have already noted, for the needed integration between psychological and sociological approaches to social-psychological problems.

In short, it is my view that there is a core of social psychology, which can be defined (though there will, of course, be differences in its definition) and which is sufficiently encompassable so that it can be transmitted in the course of graduate training. This can be accomplished, for example, through a series of basic courses and through a general examination defined in terms of a reading list in the history and theory of social psychology. The definition of the core will differ depending on whether training in social psychology is provided as an integral part of psychology, or as an integral part of sociology, or as part of an effort to integrate psychological and sociological approaches to the field. In the latter conception, which I regard as most promising for the future development of the discipline, the core is distinctively social-psychological and organized in terms of problem areas (as illustrated, for example, by the core sequence of three proseminars mentioned above). It is essential to this conception of an integrated discipline that, as part of his basic background, each student obtain a good grounding in both parent disciplines. It cannot be expected, however, that such an integrated interdisciplinary curriculum would also produce well-rounded general psychologists and general sociologists. It would have to sacrifice some of the thoroughness of training in the core of the parent disciplines in return for training broadly based social psychologists, who have good backgrounds in both psychology and sociology but who define their core as specifically social-psychological.

Balance between apprenticeship and diversification. Apprenticeship is clearly one of the most valuable experiences in graduate training and provides a type of learning that cannot possibly occur in formal courses. It gives the student an opportunity for active participation in the work of the field and for exposure to the subtle details of research that cannot be communicated in books or courses on research methods. It allows him to observe a role model and to collaborate with him in the various phases of a project. It is certainly the most important vehicle for training in an area of specialization and for fostering the transition between novice and craftsman.

It must be remembered, however, that there are also certain dangers inherent in the apprenticeship arrangement. It may tie the student too closely to his professor and it may commit him too completely to a specialized area of research. If this happens, the apprenticeship, instead of being a primary means toward the development of independence and originality, becomes, in fact, a constrictive influence. To counteract such possibilities, it is necessary for the curriculum to balance opportunities for apprenticeship with opportunities for diversification. While encouraged to involve himself deeply in a specific research enterprise and to work closely with the professor who runs it, the student should also be allowed to familiarize himself with the range of activities in the field, to keep his options open, and to develop unique combinations of various methodological and conceptual approaches. No single apprenticeship, in short, should represent the total experience—the only meaningful enterprise—of graduate training; nor should it exclusively set the pattern of the student's own research.

Much depends, of course, on the particular pattern of relationships to his apprentices that any given professor encourages.

Beyond that, however, opportunities for diversification must be built into the curriculum. In part, this is accomplished by exposing students, through courses and other experiences, to a wide range of activities, which would help them place their apprenticeship experience in perspective and provide them a better basis for choice. In addition, it might be a good idea to arrange, as a matter of course, more than a single apprenticeship experience for each student, or, at the very least, to establish a norm that would make it easy for students to shift apprenticeships if they so desire.

⚛ PATTERNS OF STUDENT PARTICIPATION ⚛

Active participation of students in the enterprise is, in my view, a central principle of graduate training. It is necessary, however, to distinguish between different functions, for each of which a different pattern of participation is appropriate. I would like to describe briefly the types of student participation that impress me as appropriate, respectively, for the intellectual functions, the certificatory functions, and the administrative functions of a graduate training program.

Intellectual functions. In seminars, research projects, and other intellectual activities of the training program, the active participation of students in a spirit of colleagueship and their direct involvement in all phases of planning and execution ought to be maximized. The pattern of participation, however, is clearly different from that appropriate to a decision-making context. It must be based on the recognition that the relationship between the teacher and the graduate student is that of a master craftsman and his apprentice. That does not imply, by any means, that teacher always knows best or even most. We all know that our students are often smarter than we are, more up-to-date on new techniques, and more knowledgeable about the latest developments. At the very least, our students represent an additional source of ideas, insights, and experiences, and they can and do make stimulating and important contributions to the intellectual enterprise. My personal experience certainly matches that of Rabbi Judah Ha-Nasi who said: "Much have I learned from my masters, more from my colleagues than from my masters, but most of all from

my students" (Babylonian Talmud, Order Nezikin, Tractate Mak-
koth, p. 10a). Yet, the teacher is older, more experienced, more
seasoned, and more thoroughly integrated in the profession. He
can thus serve as a model, to be emulated in a selective fashion.
He can communicate a certain amount of wisdom and know-how
that he has acquired over the years. Needless to say, there will
always be marked differences in the nature of the teacher-student
relationship, depending on the individuals involved. One cannot
possibly legislate a particular pattern of participation in a teaching or research relationship. One can, however, establish and
communicate the norm that these are collaborative relationships,
which are based on the principle of reciprocal benefit and in
which the active participation of the student, as someone who has
a unique contribution to make, is encouraged.

Certificatory functions. The certification of students and
the evaluation of their performance is clearly the task of the
teacher rather than of the student. The teacher has a responsibility toward others, within the profession and within society
at large, to testify to the student's competence and to indicate
whether he has met certain professional standards and how well
he has done so. There are some who argue that the function of
evaluation ought to be turned over to students themselves, since
they are in the best position to know how well they have achieved
what they set out to achieve. With such an arrangement, I feel,
we would be both imposing an unfair burden on the students and
evading our responsibility to society. I agree that self-evaluation
is important, but it is a different function from that of certifying
to the student's competence in relation to certain external standards. As long as we offer a degree, and as long as this degree is
intended to communicate something to the public about a person's
achievements, we must take responsibility for student evaluation.

It follows that the final responsibility for setting the standards against which the performance of students is evaluated must
also rest with the faculty. It is the faculty which must ultimately
decide on the nature of the tests to be passed and of the requirements to be met. While it is important, as I shall point out shortly,
to seek the advice of students in these matters, such questions as
whether or not there should be a statistics requirement and what
level of proficiency it should call for cannot properly be settled

by a student vote. Decisions about curriculum—for example, about the courses and other experiences to be required—represent a borderline case. To the extent that courses constitute a way of achieving proficiency in a certain area, and that proficiency is measured by examinations, it is completely appropriate for students to participate fully in the setting of course requirements. The faculty's unique responsibility for certifying the student's proficiency is met, in those cases, by the examination and does not extend to the question of how this proficiency is achieved. Certification, however, is not only based on the student's having achieved certain measurable levels of proficiency, but also on his having partaken of certain educational experiences. Thus, curricular requirements are often designed not to prepare the student for qualifying examinations, but to provide him with qualifying experiences. The ultimate responsibility for setting such requirements rests, again, with the faculty.

To say that the ultimate responsibility for evaluating students, for setting standards, and for deciding on requirements rests with the faculty does not mean that students should play no part in these processes. As a matter of fact, I believe very strongly that students should participate in these functions in two important ways:

(1) They should participate as *consultants*. Students can make important contributions to discussions of curriculum, standards, and testing procedures, by supplying relevant information that is available only to them and by providing a different perspective on these questions. To be sure, students have a vested interest in these matters, but faculty members too have a vested interest and can benefit greatly from the challenges presented by students. If students question an existing requirement, for example, and our only defense is that it has always existed, then it is obviously time to take another look. Certainly we should never allow ourselves to fall back on the argument that we know best. Students are in a particularly good positon to tell us, on the basis of their own experiences, what are effective and ineffective ways of preparing for a given examination or acquiring a given skill. They can tell us about experiences they need, in preparation for their own career goals, that are not available in the curriculum at all or that can only be acquired at great sacrifice. They can alert

us to new developments—to which they are often better attuned than those of us rooted in older traditions—that should be reflected in the curriculum offerings. They can tell us, from their perspective, what can realistically be expected from students in the course of a four-year training program. In short, they have so much to offer in the way of new information and challenging perspectives, that their advice must be actively sought and seriously considered in the planning and evaluation of curriculum and in the setting of standards and requirements.

(2) They should participate as *interested parties*. Since the faculty holds the power of evaluation and certification, and since it is in a positon of both setting and implementing the criteria on which these are based, it must keep itself open to the criticisms and complaints of those who are, in a real sense, at their mercy. Students must have an opportunity to express their grievances about the severity of the criteria by which they are being evaluated or the fairness with which these criteria are applied. They should have ways of letting us know if they feel that we are being unreasonable, that we are asking them to do things they cannot possibly do, that we are setting up contradictory demands so that meeting one makes it that much harder to meet the other. Mechanisms that would allow students to participate in the setting of requirements and the process of evaluation by feeding back their reactions and grievances must be readily available.

Administrative functions. Yet another pattern of student participation would seem appropriate when it comes to the general administration of the training program and the government of the community shared by faculty, students, and staff. Many of the decisions in this area have a direct effect on the lives of students and do not involve the issues of professional expertise or student certification. In the making of such decisions, it seems to me, students ought to be full participants. This would include what are probably the key decisions to be made in this context, namely those relating to the allocation of resources and the setting of conditions for their use. Many questions immediately arise as to just how far the participation of students should extend and how much power should be given to them. For example, should they participate in the decisions about hiring and promotion of faculty and staffing of courses? Should they have a voice equal to that of the faculty in decisions about the use of space and facilities? I worry about these questions as much as anyone else, since, at least in comparison with students and members of the nonprofessional staff, I am part of the privileged class and obviously have a great deal to lose.

Many arguments—or rationalizations—in favor of limiting student power suggest themselves. Thus, one can question the appropriateness of giving students control over the careers of people whose task it is to certify and evaluate them. With regard to the use of resources, there is the familiar argument that students have less stake in the community, since they are only temporary residents. (It seems a similar argument was used in years gone by to justify restriction of the vote to property owners.) There are also many reasons for arguing that we, the members of the privileged class, have nothing to fear from graduate student power. For example, students may well be cautious about reducing the privileges of the faculty, even if they had the power to do so, since any precedent they set may come to haunt them when they themselves enter the privileged class. It must be remembered, after all, that their anticipated period of membership in that class is considerably longer than their student years, so that they might hesitate to seek short-term advantage at the expense of their long-term interest.

The pattern of student participation in decision-making that is finally evolved will have important implications, not only for the socialization of graduate students, but also for the future shape of academic life. There are many difficult questions to be resolved. It is time that we give them our serious consideration.

CHAPTER 8

༄ཀ༈ཀ༈ཀ༈ཀ༈ཀ༈ཀ༈ཀ༈ཀ༈ཀ༈ཀ༈ཀ༈ཀ༈ཀ

INTRODUCTION

The social scientist faces a unique set of value questions in his scientific work by virtue of the fact that human beings—or, more precisely, human minds—form the subject matter of his research. He must concern himself with the ethical implications of his treatment of his human subjects and of the relationships that he establishes with them. Chapter Eight addresses itself to this problem, focusing specifically on the widespread use of deception in social-psychological experiments. My concern, as in the preceding chapters, is with finding ways of humanizing the procedures of social research while safeguarding its unique contributions.

In the two years or so since this essay was originally written, the whole question of the use of human beings as subjects in scientific investigations has become a public issue. It has been discussed, not only in professional journals (see, for example, the American Psychologist *of November 1965, May 1966, and May 1967), but also in general magazines (see, for example, Lear, 1966a and 1966b; Goodman, 1967). It has been the subject of congressional hearings (see, for example, Testimony before House Special Subcommittee on Invasion of Privacy, 1966) and of a special panel appointed by the Executive Office of the President (see Office of Science and Technology, 1967). It has been debated extensively at conferences (see, for example, Sykes, 1966), at professional meetings, and in universities and research institutes.*

The most dramatic cases have come from the use of human subjects in medical research. One cause célèbre involved a well-known cancer researcher and his associates, who injected live cancer cells in aged patients after obtaining a perfunctory consent from them (Lear, 1966a). It was evident that these patients did not and could not know what they were consenting to. What was particularly revealing in the investigation of this case was that this kind of procedure had become standard practice among the workers in this field. In this particular case, there was no charge that patients had been harmed by the injections; the issue was the use of patients for the purpose of experiments that had nothing to do with their own treatment, without obtaining their informed consent. Other cases of medical research have been cited which resulted in serious damage or even death for subjects who did not consent to participate in the experiment or did not even know that they were doing so (see Beecher, 1966).

In behavioral research, the possibility of harm to the subject, particularly in the form of psychological damage, may also arise, though this problem arises less frequently and is not as severe and dramatic as it is in medical research. The crucial ethical problem that arises in behavioral research is that of the invasion of the subject's privacy, that is, "the right of the individual to decide for himself how much he will share with others his thoughts, his feelings, and the facts of his personal life" (Office of Science and Technology, 1967, p. 2). By invading a person's privacy we are, of course, harming him in a certain sense and, on occasion, exposing him to the possibility of future harm; but the key issue is that we are depriving him of the personal dignity and freedom of self-determination to which he is entitled. The prob-

lem of invasion of privacy goes far beyond the procedures of be-havioral research. Public discussion has centered most heavily on the use of personality tests in screening employees for government or industry and, even further from the context of research, on the threats to privacy presented by the widespread use of wire-tapping and electronic eavesdropping. In social research, protec-tion of the subject's privacy depends directly on the manner in which his consent is secured and the confidentiality of his data is respected, since the essence of the right to privacy is that the individual himself controls what information about himself he is to disclose, to whom, at what time, and for what purposes. To the extent to which the subject is coerced into participation, or deceived about the purposes of the research, or observed without his knowledge, the principle of consent and thus his right to pri-vacy are violated. (For an excellent discussion of these issues see Ruebhausen and Brim, 1965; also see Lovell, 1967, for a discussion of related issues in the use of personality tests for personnel selec-tion and placement.)

In response to public discussion of these issues, the U.S. Public Health Service has developed a new set of regulations, re-quiring a special review of all research proposals submitted to that agency for financial support in which human subjects are used (Surgeon General's directives on human experimentation, 1967; see also Stewart, 1966). This review, which is carried out within the applicant's institution, is designed to assure that the welfare of the subject is adequately safeguarded and that appro-priate steps are taken to obtain his informed consent. The concern is not only with risks of potential harm to the subject, but also with the issues of voluntary participation, confidentiality, and protection of the subject from misuse of the findings. Researchers are understandably disturbed by these new regulations, since they introduce certain extraneous considerations into the research proc-ess and impose a degree of external control on the conduct of re-search. This control, it is feared, may be exercised by people who are not familiar with the particular area of research involved and who do not know and do not care about the conditions necessary for carrying out effective research in that area. Moreover, regula-tions of this sort may open the door to pressures from various sources, public and legislative, who do not value social and psy-

chological research, who have little conception of what it takes to conduct such research, and whose reactions to research procedures are often uninformed and hysterical.

I share many of the fears and concerns about these new regulations, but I also feel that it is not enough to deplore them and oppose them while ignoring the issues with which they are designed to deal. In a very real sense, we have brought this situation upon ourselves, by our failure to give attention within the profession to the problems of informed consent, invasion of privacy, and the human treatment of our research subjects. We have tended to act as if there were no other values to consider but those of carrying out good research (and sometimes not even that, but merely the values of carrying out publishable research). The rights and welfare of our subjects were often forgotten and treated in cavalier fashion. We have been able to manage this for a long time because we tend to choose as our subjects those elements of our society that cannot effectively talk back: the children and the aged, the mentally ill and the poor, the prisoners and the soldiers, the sophomores and the alcoholics. I do not feel that social and psychological research has caused much damage to individuals, but I feel that we have been remiss in our failure to concern ourselves with the possibilities of such damage and, moreover, with the kinds of broader social values that our treatment of human subjects is fostering.

Because of this absence of internal, that is, intraprofessional, controls, it is not surprising that external controls are being introduced. We should, of course, do everything possible to prevent these external controls from interfering with the researcher's freedom to inquire. "The investigator pursuing knowledge, whether his subject is man or some other aspect of the natural world, must not feel constrained to limit his study to those things which have current social approval" (Office of Science and Technology, 1967, p. 9). At the same time, however, we should regard the new regulations as a special opportunity—as an opportunity for the profession to engage in the extensive and probing examination of these issues that we have so far neglected. I hope that one of the consequences of this process will be to keep governmental regulations from becoming more restrictive than they now are. In fact, since these regulations are still evolving, it is my hope that we can help them evolve in constructive directions. I would like to see us move away from a model in which the ethical behavior of researchers is policed by external agencies, and move toward a model in which researchers themselves give active consideration to the ethical implications of their research procedures and regularly consult on these matters with their peers, including colleagues from other fields, who do not have a vested interest in existing procedures and are able to bring new perspectives to the problem. There are good bases for the belief that this second kind of model can work. The methodological choices of investigators do not have to be policed and subjected to external controls, because the requirements of good methodology are built into the value systems of social scientists as part of their professional training and are constantly reinforced throughout their professional careers. Similarly, there would be no need to police and impose external controls on the ethical choices of investigtors, if the issues involved were seen as an integral part of the researcher's concern in designing and carrying out his studies, if they were given an important place in professional training, and if they were the subject of wide and continuing discussion within the profession.

Fortunately, such discussion has already been initiated. Recent papers have concerned themselves with ethical problems that arise in participant observation studies (Erikson, 1967; Howard, 1965), in community self-surveys (Wolf, 1964), in research with children (Smith, 1967), and in psychopharmacological research (M. M. Katz, 1967). This chapter attempts to contribute to this intraprofessional discussion by focusing on ethical, and closely related methodological, problems that arise in a line of research in which I have been personally involved: social-psychological experiments. Specifically, I am concerned with the use of deception in such experiments, which raises obvious questions about informed consent and invasion of privacy.

There are some interesting parallels between the issues that I am discussing in this chapter and those that I raised in Chapter Three concerning research in developing countries. In both instances, the ethical problems involved are of long standing and have been undermining the relationship between researchers and people with whom they deal in the course of their research, but they were so much built into the procedures of research in the area that they have not been discussed within the profession. In both instances, it was public and governmental reactions to cases that obtained publicity that brought the issue to the fore. In both instances, external controls by government agencies were applied in response to the problem, which immediately triggered strong defensive reactions within the profession, but which also opened the way, for the first time, to a thorough discussion of the underlying issues. In both instances, the ethical problems turned out to be organically related to specific methodological problems and to the broader question of the future of this type of research, that is, of maintaining the conditions (such as cooperation from subjects and from colleagues in foreign societies) necessary for carrying out the research. And, finally, in both instances, I feel, the search for a solution calls for the development of more participatory and more reciprocal patterns of research.

The problem of deception, like many other problems that I have discussed earlier, does not lend itself to an easy and total solution. It reflects, once again, the underlying tension between the scientific study of man and humanistic values. For those of us who see the scientific study of man as an important and socially useful enterprise, deception poses a conflict of values which must be resolved differently in each specific case. Our efforts to deal with this problem, however, can be greatly aided by a more detailed understanding of the effects of experimental procedures that use deception and by an exploration of alternative research procedures. It is very encouraging, therefore, that methodological research on deception and related problems has recently begun to emerge (see, in particular, Brock and Becker, 1966; Fillenbaum, 1966; M. S. Greenberg, 1967; Ring, Wallston, and Corey, 1967; Stricker, Messick, and Jackson, 1967; Walster, Berscheid, Abrahams, and Aronson, 1967; Willis and Willis, in press). These and future studies will help to extend and enrich the debate of the issues raised in this chapter.

This essay was originally prepared for a symposium on "Ethical and methodological problems in social-psychological experiments," held at the meetings of the American Psychological Association in Chicago, September 3, 1965. It was published in the Psychological Bulletin, *1967, 67, 1–11, and is reprinted here with the permission of the editor.*

The Human Use of Human Subjects

In 1954, in the pages of the *American Psychologist*, Edgar Vinacke raised a series of questions about experiments, particularly in the area of small groups, in which "the psychologist conceals the true purpose and conditions of the experiment, or positively misinforms the subjects, or exposes them to painful, embarrassing, or worse, experiences, without the subjects' knowledge of what is going on" (p. 155). He summed up his concerns by asking "What . . . is the proper balance between the interests of science and the thoughtful treatment of the persons who, innocently, supply the data?" (p. 155). Little effort has been made in the intervening years to seek answers to the questions he raised. During these same years, however, the problem of deception in social-psychological experiments has taken on increasingly serious proportions.[1]

The problem is actually broader, extending beyond the walls of the laboratory. It arises, for example, in various field studies in which investigators enroll as members of a group that has special interest for them, so that they can observe its operations from the inside. The pervasiveness of the problem becomes even more apparent when we consider that deception is built into most of our measurement devices, since it is important to keep the respondent unaware of the personality or attitude dimension we wish to explore. For present purposes, however, I shall dwell primarily on the problem of deception in the context of the social-psychological experiment.

---

[1] In focusing on deception in *social*-psychological experiments, I do not wish to give the impression that there is no serious problem elsewhere. Deception is widely used in most studies involving human subjects and gives rise to issues similar to those discussed in this chapter. Some examples of the use of deception in other areas of psychological experimentation will be presented later in this chapter.

The use of deception has become more and more extensive and it is now a commonplace and almost standard feature of so-cial-psychological experiments. Deception has been turned into a game, often played with great skill and virtuosity. A considerable amount of the creativity and ingenuity of social psychologists is invested in the development of increasingly elaborate deception situations. Within a single experiment, deception may be built upon deception in a delicately complex structure. The literature now contains a fair number of studies in which second- or even third-order deception was employed.

One well-known experiment (Festinger and Carlsmith, 1959), for example, involved a whole progression of deceptions. After the subjects had gone through an experimental task, the investigator made it clear, through word and gesture, that the experiment was over and that he would now "like to explain what this has been all about so you'll have some idea of why you were doing this" (p. 205). This explanation was false, however, and was designed to serve as a basis for the true experimental manipu-lation. The manipulation itself involved asking subjects to serve as the experimenter's accomplices. The task of the "accomplice" was to tell the next "subject" that the experiment in which he had just participated (which was in fact a rather boring experience) had been interesting and enjoyable. He was also asked to be on call for unspecified future occasions on which his services as ac-complice might be needed because "the regular fellow couldn't make it, and we had a subject scheduled" (p. 205). These newly recruited "accomplices," of course, were the true subjects, while the "subjects" were the experimenter's true accomplices. For their presumed services as "accomplices," the true subjects were paid in advance, half of them receiving $1, and half $20. When they completed their service, however, the investigators added injury to insult by asking them to return their hard-earned cash. Thus, in this one study, in addition to receiving the usual misinforma-tion about the purpose of the experiment, the subject was given feedback that was really an experimental manipulation, was asked to be an accomplice who was really a subject, and was given a $20 bill that was really a will-o'-the-wisp.

It is easy to "view with alarm," but it is much more diffi-cult to formulate an unambiguous position on this problem. As a working experimental social psychologist, I cannot conceive the issue in absolutist terms. I am too well aware of the fact that there are good reasons for using deception in many of our experiments. There are many significant problems that probably cannot be investigated without the use of deception, at least not at the present level of development of our experimental methodology. Thus, we are always confronted with a conflict of values. If we regard the acquisition of scientific knowledge about human behavior as a positive value, and if an experiment using deception constitutes a significant contribution to such knowledge which could not very well be achieved by other means, then we cannot unequivocally rule out the experiment. The question for us is not simply whether it does or does not use deception, but whether the amount and type of deception are justified by the significance of the study and the unavailability of alternative, that is, deception-free, procedures.

I have expressed special concern about second-order deceptions, for example, the procedure of letting a person believe that he is acting as experimenter or as the experimenter's accomplice when he is in fact serving as the subject. Such a procedure undermines the relationship between experimenter and subject even further than simple misinformation about the purposes of the experiment, since deception does not merely take place within the experiment but encompasses the whole definition of the relationship between the parties involved. Deception that takes place while the person is within the role of subject for which he has contracted can, to some degree, be isolated, but deception about the very nature of the contract itself is more likely to suffuse the experimenter-subject relationship as a whole and to remove the possibility of mutual trust. I would be inclined to take a more absolutist stand with regard to such second-order deceptions—but even here the issue turns out to be more complicated. I am stopped short when I think, for example, of the ingenious studies on experimenter bias by Rosenthal and his associates (for example, Rosenthal and Fode, 1963; Rosenthal, Persinger, Vikan-Kline, and Fode, 1963; Rosenthal, Persinger, Vikan-Kline, and Mulry, 1963). These experiments employed second-order deception in that subjects were led to believe that they were the experimenters. Since these were experiments about experiments, however, it is very hard to conceive of any alternative procedures the investigators might have used. There is no question in my mind that these are significant studies; they provide fundamental inputs to present efforts at re-examining the social psychology of the experiment. These studies, then, help to underline even further the point that we are confronted with a conflict of values that cannot be resolved by fiat.

I hope it is clear from these remarks that my purpose in focusing on this problem is not to single out specific studies performed by some of my colleagues and to point a finger at them. Indeed, the finger points at me as well. I too have used deception, and have known the joys of applying my skills and ingenuity to the creation of elaborate experimental situations that the subjects would not be able to decode. I am now making active attempts to find alternatives to deception, but still I have not forsworn the use of deception under any and all circumstances. The questions I am raising, then, are addressed to myself as well as to my colleagues. They are questions with which all of us who are committed to social psychology must come to grips, lest we leave their resolution to others who have no understanding of what we are trying to accomplish.

What concerns me most is not so much that deception is used, but precisely that it is used without question. It has now become standard operating procedure in the social psychologist's laboratory. I sometimes feel that we are training a generation of students who do not know that there is any other way of doing experiments in our field, who feel that deception is as much *de rigueur* as significance at the .05 level. Too often deception is used not as a last resort, but as a matter of course. Our attitude seems to be that if you can deceive, why tell the truth? It is this unquestioning acceptance, this routinization of deception, that really concerns me.

I would like to turn now to a review of the bases for my concern with the problem of deception, and then suggest some possible approaches to dealing with it.

IMPLICATIONS OF THE USE OF DECEPTION

My concern about the use of deception is based on three considerations: the ethical implications of such procedures, their

methodological implications, and their implications for the future
of social psychology.

Ethical implications. Ethical problems of a rather obvious
nature arise in those experiments in which deception has potentially harmful consequences for the subject. Take, for example,
the brilliant experiment by Mulder and Stemerding (1963) on the
effects of threat on attraction to the group and need for strong
leadership. In this study, one of the very rare examples of an experiment conducted in a natural setting, independent food merchants in a number of Dutch towns were brought together for
group meetings, in the course of which they were informed that
a large organization was planning to open up a series of supermarkets in the Netherlands. In the high-threat condition, subjects
were told that there was a strong probability that their town would
be selected as a site for such markets and that the advent of these
markets would cause a considerable drop in their business. On
the advice of the executives of the shopkeepers' organizations, who
had helped to arrange the group meetings, the investigators did
not reveal the experimental manipulations to their subjects. I
have been worried about these Dutch merchants ever since I heard
about this study for the first time. Did some of them go out of
business in anticipation of the heavy competition? Do some of
them have an anxiety reaction every time they see a bulldozer?
Chances are that they soon forgot about this threat (unless, of
course, supermarkets actually did move into town) and that it
became just one of the many little moments of anxiety that must
occur in every shopkeeper's life. Do we have a right, however, to
add to life's little anxieties and to risk the possibility of more extensive anxiety purely for the purposes of our experiments, particularly since deception deprives the subject of the opportunity
to choose whether or not he wishes to expose himself to the risks
that might be entailed?

The studies by Bramel (1962, 1963) and Bergin (1962)
provide examples of another type of potentially harmful effect
arising from the use of deception. In the Bramel studies, male
undergraduates were led to believe that they were homosexually
aroused by photographs of men. In the Bergin study, subjects of
both sexes were given discrepant information about their level of
masculinity or femininity; in one experimental condition, this

information was presumably based on an elaborate series of psychological tests in which the subjects had participated. In all of these studies, the deception was explained to the subject at the end of the experiment. One wonders, however, whether such explanation removes the possibility of harmful effects. For many persons in this age group, sexual identity is still a live and sensitive issue, and the self-doubts generated by the laboratory experience may take on a life of their own and linger on for some time.

Yet another illustration of potentially harmful effects of deception can be found in Milgram's studies of obedience (1963, 1965). In these experiments, the subject was led to believe that he was participating in a learning study and was instructed to administer increasingly severe shocks to another person, who after a while began to protest vehemently. In fact, of course, the "victim" was an accomplice of the experimenter and did not receive any shocks. Depending on the conditions, sizable proportions of the subjects obeyed the experimenter's instructions and continued to shock the other person up to the maximum level, which they believed to be extremely painful. Both obedient and defiant subjects exhibited a great deal of stress in this situation. The complexities of the issues surrounding the use of deception become quite apparent when one reads the exchange between Baumrind (1964) and Milgram (1964) about the ethical implications of the obedience research.[2] There is clearly room for disagreement among honorable people about the evaluation of this research from an ethical point of view. Yet there is good reason to believe that at least some of the obedient subjects came away from this experience with a lower self-esteem, having to live with the realization that they were willing to yield to destructive authority to

---

[2] The complexity of the problem is underscored in a recent paper by Crawford (1966), in which he argues that the *nature* of the contribution to knowledge made by Milgram's research provides an ethical justification for the procedures he uses. In this connection, Crawford cites my own statement that, to counteract manipulative tendencies, we must study processes of resistance to control and conditions for the enhancement of freedom of choice (see Chapter One). He points out that Milgram's studies, by clarifying the nature of destructive obedience and showing its relationship to various other factors, contribute directly to this goal.

the point of inflicting extreme pain on a fellow human being. The fact that this may have provided, in Milgram's words, "an opportunity to learn something of importance about themselves, and more generally, about the conditions of human action" (1964, p. 850) is beside the point. If this were a lesson from life, it would indeed constitute an instructive confrontation and provide a valuable insight. But do we, for the purpose of experimentation, have the right to provide such potentially disturbing insights to subjects who do not know that this is what they are coming for? A similar question can be raised about the Asch experiments on group pressure (1965), although the stressfulness of the situation and the implications for the person's self-concept were less intense in that context.

Though we are here specifically considering social-psychological experiments, the problem of deception and its possibly harmful effects arises in other areas of psychological experimentation as well. Dramatic illustrations are provided by two studies in which subjects were exposed, for experimental purposes, to extremely stressful conditions. In an experiment designed to study the establishment of a conditioned response in a situation that is traumatic but not painful, Campbell, Sanderson, and Laverty (1964) induced, through the use of a drug, a temporary interruption of respiration in their subjects. "This has no permanently harmful physical consequences but is nonetheless a severe stress which is not in itself painful . . ." (p. 628). The subjects' reports confirmed that this was a "horrific" experience for them. "All the subjects in the standard series said that they thought they were dying" (p. 631). Of course, the subjects—"male alcoholic patients who volunteered for the experiment when they were told that it was connected with a possible therapy for alcoholism" (p. 629)— were not warned in advance about the effect of the drug, since this information would have reduced the traumatic impact of the experience.[3] In a series of studies on the effects of psychological

---

[3] The authors report, however, that some of their other subjects were physicians familiar with the drug; "they did not suppose they were dying but, even though they knew in a general way what to expect, they too said that the experience was extremely harrowing" (p. 632). Thus, conceivably, the purposes of the experiment might have been achieved even if the subjects had been told to expect the temporary interruption of breathing.

stress, Berkun *et al.* (1962) devised a number of ingenious experimental situations designed to convince the subject that his life was actually in danger. In one situation, the subjects, a group of Army recruits, were actually "passengers aboard an apparently stricken plane which was being forced to 'ditch' or crash-land" (p. 4). In another experiment, an isolated subject in a desolate area learned that a sudden emergency had arisen (accidental nuclear radiation in the area, or a sudden forest fire, or misdirected artillery shells —depending on the experimental condition) and that he could be rescued only if he reported his position over his radio transmitter "which has quite suddenly failed" (p. 7). In yet another situation, the subject was led to believe that he was responsible for an explosion that seriously injured another soldier. As the authors point out, reactions in these situations are more likely to approximate reactions to combat experiences or to naturally occurring disasters than are reactions to various "laboratory" stresses, but is the experimenter justified in exposing his subjects to such extreme threats?

So far I have been speaking of experiments in which deception has potentially harmful consequences. I am equally concerned, however, about the less obvious cases, in which there is little danger of harmful effects, at least in the conventional sense of the term. Serious ethical issues are raised by deception per se and the kind of use of human beings that it implies. In our other interhuman relationships, most of us would never think of doing the kinds of things that we do to our subjects: of exposing others to lies and tricks, of deliberately misleading them about the purposes of the interaction or withholding pertinent information, of making promises or giving assurances that we intend to disregard. We would view such behavior as a violation of the respect to which all fellow humans are entitled and of the whole basis of our relationship with them. Yet we seem to forget that the experimenter-subject relationship, whatever else it is, is a *real* interhuman relationship, in which we have responsibility toward the subject as another human being whose dignity we must preserve. The discontinuity between the experimenter's behavior in everyday life and his behavior in the laboratory is so marked that one wonders why there has been so little concern with this problem, and what mechanisms have allowed us to ignore it to such an extent. I am reminded, in this connection, of the intriguing phe-

nomenon of the "holiness of sin," which characterizes certain
messianic movements as well as other movements of the true-
believer variety. Behavior that would normally be unacceptable
actually takes on an aura of virtue in such movements through a
redefinition of the situation in which the behavior takes place
and thus of the context for evaluating it. A similar mechanism
seems to be involved in our attitude toward the psychological experiment. We tend to regard it as a situation that is not quite
real, that can be isolated from the rest of life like a play performed
on stage, and to which, therefore, the usual criteria for ethical
interpersonal conduct become irrelevant. Behavior is judged entirely in the context of the experiment's scientific contribution
and, in this context, deception, normally unacceptable, can indeed be seen as a positive good.

The broader ethical problem brought into view by the very
use of deception becomes even more important when we see it in
the light of present historical forces. As I stressed in Chapter One,
we are living in an age of mass societies, in which the transformation of man into an object to be manipulated at will occurs on a
mass scale, in a systematic way, and under the aegis of specialized
institutions deliberately assigned to this task. In institutionalizing
the use of deception in psychological experiments we are, then,
contributing to a historical trend that threatens values most of
us cherish.

I find myself particularly disturbed by our contribution to
historical trends when I contemplate the massive and blatant use
of deception as an integral part of national policy in the United
States today. I refer, first of all, to what is politely called the credibility gap, the cynical manipulation of truth by the national Administration as a standard and accepted part of its conduct of
domestic and foreign policy. Even more germane to the present
discussion, however, is the recent disclosure of secret CIA support
of various private organizations, and particularly of the National
Student Association, over a period of years, during which the
world public, the American public, and the vast majority of members were led to believe that these were independent agencies.
The message is all around us that systematic deception is the way
to conduct our affairs; that it is utterly acceptable as long as you
manage to get away with it; and that it is wisest never to trust

anyone. As educators and as scientists engaged in the study of man, we ought to be in the vanguard of those who try to counteract this message. Instead, by the procedures we use, we help to reinforce the message, to feed the cynicism and mistrust of our youth and to communicate to them that deception permeates even those of our institutions whose very purpose is dedication to truth.

Methodological implications. A second source of my concern about the use of deception is my increasing doubt about its adequacy as a methodology for social psychology.

A basic assumption in the use of deception is that a subject's awareness of the conditions we are trying to create and of the phenomena we wish to study would so affect his behavior that we could not draw valid conclusions from it. For example, if we are interested in studying the effects of failure on conformity, we must create a situation in which the subjects actually feel that they have failed, and in which they can be kept unaware of our interest in observing conformity. In short, it is important to keep our subjects naive about the purposes of the experiment so that they can respond to the experimental inductions spontaneously.

How long, however, will it be possible for us to find naive subjects? Among college students, it is already very difficult. They may not know the exact purpose of the particular experiment in which they are participating, but at least they know, typically, that it is not what the experimenter says it is. Orne (1962) points out that the use of deception "on the part of psychologists is so widely known in the college population that even if a psychologist is honest with the subject, more often than not he will be distrusted. As one subject pithily put it, 'Psychologists always lie!' " And, Orne adds, "This bit of paranoia has some support in reality" (pp. 778–779). There are, of course, other sources of human subjects that have not been tapped, and we could turn to them in our quest for naïveté. But even there it is only a matter of time. As word about psychological experiments gets around in whatever network we happen to be using, sophistication is bound to increase. I wonder, therefore, whether there is any future in the use of deception.

If the subject in a deception experiment knows what the experimenter is trying to conceal from him and what he is really after in the study, the value of the deception is obviously nullified. Generally, however, even the relatively sophisticated subject does not know the exact purpose of the experiment; he only has suspicions, which may approximate the true purpose of the experiment to a greater or lesser degree. Whether or not he knows the true purpose of the experiment, he is likely to make an effort to figure out its purpose, since he does not believe what the experimenter tells him, and therefore he is likely to operate in the situation in terms of his own hypothesis of what is involved. This may, in line with Orne's (1962) analysis, lead him to do what he thinks the experimenter wants him to do. Conversely, if he resents the experimenter's attempt to deceive him, he may try to throw a monkey wrench into the works; I would not be surprised if this kind of Schweikian game among subjects became a fairly well established part of the culture of sophisticated campuses. Whichever course the subject uses, however, he is operating in terms of his own conception of the nature of the situation rather than in terms of the conception that the experimenter is trying to induce. In short, the experimenter can no longer assume that the conditions that he is trying to create are the ones that actually define the situation for the subject. Thus, the use of deception, while it is designed to give the experimenter control over the subject's perceptions and motivations, may actually produce an unspecifiable mixture of intended and unintended stimuli that make it difficult to know just what the subject is responding to.

The tendency for subjects to react to unintended cues, to features of the situation that are not part of the experimenter's design, is by no means restricted to experiments that involve deception. This problem has concerned students of the interview situation for some time, and more recently it has been analyzed in detail in the writings and research of Riecken, Rosenthal, Orne, and Mills. Subjects enter the experiment with their own aims, including attainment of certain rewards, divination of the experimenter's true purposes, and favorable self-presentation (Riecken, 1962). They are therefore responsive to demand characteristics of the situation (Orne, 1962), to unintended communications of the experimenter's expectations (Rosenthal, 1963), and to the role of the experimenter within the social system that experimenter and subject jointly constitute (Mills, 1962). In any experiment, then, the subject goes beyond the description of the situation and the experimental manipulation introduced by the investigator, makes his own interpretation of the situation, and acts accordingly.

For several reasons, however, the use of deception especially encourages the subject to dismiss the stated purposes of the experiment and to search for alternative interpretations of his own. First, the continued use of deception establishes the reputation of psychologists as people who cannot be believed. The desire "to penetrate the experimenter's inscrutability and discover the rationale of the experiment" (Riecken, 1962, p. 34) becomes especially strong. Generally, these efforts are motivated by the subject's desire to meet the expectations of the experimenter and of the situation. They may also be motivated, however, as I have already mentioned, by a desire to outwit the experimenter and to beat him at his own game, in a spirit of genuine hostility or playful one-upmanship. Second, a situation involving the use of deception is inevitably highly ambiguous, since a great deal of information relevant to understanding the structure of the situation must be withheld from the subject. Thus, the subject is especially motivated to try to figure things out and is likely to develop idiosyncratic interpretations. Third, the use of deception, by its very nature, causes the experimenter to transmit contradictory messages to the subject. In his verbal instructions and explanations he says one thing about the purposes of the experiment; but in the experimental situation that he has created, in the manipulations that he has introduced, and probably in covert cues that he emits, he says another thing. This again makes it imperative for the subject to seek his own interpretation of the situation.

I would argue, then, that deception increases the subject's tendency to operate in terms of his private definition of the situation, differing, in random or systematic fashion, from the definition that the experimenter is trying to impose; moreover, deception makes it more difficult to evaluate or minimize the effects of this tendency. Whether or not I am right in this judgment, it can, at the very least, be said that the use of deception does not resolve or reduce the unintended effects of the experiment as a social situation in which the subject pursues his private aims. Since the assumptions that the subject is naive and that he sees the situation as the experimenter wishes him to see it are unwarranted, the use of deception no longer has any special obvious advantages over other experimental approaches. I am not suggesting that there may not be occasions when deception may still be the most effective procedure to use from a methodological point of view. But since it raises at least as many methodological problems as any other type of procedure does, we have every reason to explore alternative approaches and to extend our methodological inquiries to the question of the effects of using deception.

Implications for the future of social psychology. My third concern about the use of deception is based on its long-run implications for our discipline and combines both the ethical and methodological considerations I have already raised. There is something disturbing about the idea of relying on massive deception as the basis for developing a field of inquiry. Can one really build a discipline on a foundation of such research?

From a long-range point of view, there is obviously something self-defeating about the use of deception. As we continue to carry out research of this kind, our potential subjects become more and more sophisticated, and we become less and less able to meet the conditions that our experimental procedures require. Moreover, as we continue to carry out research of this kind, our potential subjects become increasingly distrustful of us, and our future relations with them are likely to be undermined. Thus, we are confronted with the anomalous circumstance that the more research we do, the more difficult and questionable it becomes.

The use of deception also involves a contradiction between our experimental procedures and our long-range aims as scientists and teachers. To be able to carry out our experiments, we are concerned with maintaining the naïveté of the population from which we hope to draw our subjects. We are all familiar with the experimenter's anxious concern that the introductory course might cover the autokinetic phenomenon, need achievement, or the Asch situation before he has had a chance to complete his experimental runs. This perfectly understandable desire to keep our procedures secret goes counter to the traditional desire of the scientist and teacher to inform and enlighten the public. To be sure, experimenters are interested only in temporary secrecy, but it is not inconceivable that at some time in the future they might be using certain procedures regularly with large segments of the population and thus prefer to keep the public permanently naive. It is perhaps not too fanciful to imagine, in the long run, the possible emergence of a special class in possession of secret knowledge, a possibility that is clearly antagonistic to the principle of open communication to which we, as scientists and intellectuals, are so fervently committed.

DEALING WITH THE PROBLEM OF DECEPTION

If my concerns about the use of deception are justified, what are some of the ways in which we, as experimental social psychologists, can deal with them? I would like to suggest three types of steps that we can take: increase our active awareness of the problem, explore ways of counteracting and minimizing the negative effects of deception, and give careful attention to the development of new experimental techniques that dispense with the use of deception.

Active awareness of the problem. I have already stressed that I would not propose the complete elimination of deception under all circumstances, in view of the genuine conflict of values with which the experimenter is confronted. What is crucial, however, is that we always ask ourselves whether deception, in the given case, is necessary and justified. How we answer the question is less important than the fact that we ask it. What we must beware of is the tendency to dismiss the question as irrelevant and to accept deception as a matter of course. Active awareness of the problem is thus in itself part of the solution, for it makes the use of deception a matter for discussion, deliberation, investigation, and choice. Active awareness means that, in any given case, we will try to balance the value of an experiment that uses deception against its questionable or potentially harmful effects. If we engage in this process honestly, we are likely to find that there are many occasions when we or our students can forgo the use of deception, either because deception is not necessary (that is, alternative procedures equally good or better are available), or because the importance of the study does not warrant the use of an ethically questionable procedure, or because the type of deception involved is too extreme (in terms of the possibility of harmful effects or of seriously undermining the experimenter-subject relationship).

Counteracting and minimizing the negative effects of deception. If we do use deception, it is essential that we find ways of counteracting and minimizing its negative effects. Sensitizing the apprentice researcher to this necessity is at least as fundamental as any other part of research training.

In those experiments in which deception carries the potential of harmful effects, in the more usual sense of the term, there is an obvious requirement to build protections into every phase of the process. Subjects must be selected in a way that will exclude individuals who are especially vulnerable; potentially harmful manipulations, such as the induction of stress, must be kept at a moderate level of intensity; the experimenter must be sensitive to danger signals in the reactions of his subjects and be prepared to deal with crises when they arise; and, at the conclusion of the session, the experimenter must take time not only to reassure the subject, but also to help him work through his feelings about the experience to whatever degree may be required. In general, the principle that a subject ought not to leave the laboratory with greater anxiety or lower self-esteem than he came with is a good one to follow. I would go beyond it to argue that the subject should in some positive way be enriched by the experience, that is, he should come away from it with the feeling that he has learned something, understood something, or grown in some way. This, of course, adds special importance to the kind of feedback that is given to the subject at the end of the experimental session.

The postexperimental feedback is, of course, the primary way of counteracting negative effects in those experiments in which the issue is deception as such, rather than possible threats to the subject's well-being. If we do deceive the subject, then it is our obligation to give him a full and detailed explanation of what we have done and of our reasons for using this type of procedure. I do not want to be absolutist about this, but I would suggest this as a good rule of thumb to follow: Think very carefully before undertaking an experiment whose purposes you feel unable to reveal to the subjects even after they have completed the experimental session. It is, of course, not enough to give the subject a perfunctory feedback, just to do one's duty. Postexperimental explanations should be worked out with as much detail as other aspects of the procedure and, in general, some thought ought to be given to ways of making them meaningful and instructive for the subject and helpful for rebuilding his relationship with the experimenter. I feel very strongly that, to accomplish these purposes, we must keep the feedback itself inviolate and under no circumstance give the subject false feedback or pretend to be giving him feedback while we are in fact introducing another experimental manipulation. If we hope to maintain any kind of trust in our relationship with potential subjects, there must be no ambiguity that the statement "The experiment is over and I shall explain to you what it was all about" means precisely that and nothing else. If subjects have reason to suspect even that statement, then we have lost the whole basis for a decent human relationship with our subjects and all hope for future cooperation from them.

Development of new experimental techniques. My third suggestion is that we invest some of the creativity and ingenuity now devoted to the construction of elaborate deceptions in the search for alternative experimental techniques that do not rely on the use of deception. The kind of techniques I have in mind would be based on the principle of eliciting the subject's positive motivations to contribute to the experimental enterprise. They would draw on the subject's active participation and involvement in the proceedings and encourage him to cooperate in making the experiment a success, not by giving the experimenter the results he thinks the experimenter wants, but by conscientiously taking the roles and carrying out the tasks that the experimenter assigns to him. In short, the kind of techniques I have in mind would be designed to involve the subject as an active participant in a joint effort with the experimenter.

Perhaps the most promising source of alternative experimental approaches are procedures using some sort of role-playing. I have been impressed, for example, with the role-playing I have observed in the context of the Inter-Nation Simulation, a laboratory procedure developed by Guetzkow and his associates (1963) which involves a simulated world in which the subjects take the roles of decision-makers of various nations. This situation seems to create a high level of emotional involvement and to elicit motivations that have a real-life quality. Moreover, within this situation, which is highly complex and generally permits only gross experimental manipulations, it is possible to test specific theoretical hypotheses by using data based on repeated measurements as interaction between the simulated nations develops. Thus, a study carried out at the Western Behavioral Sciences Institute provided, as an extra bonus, some interesting opportunities for testing hypotheses derived from balance theory, by the use of mutual ratings made by decision-makers of Nations A, B, and C, before and after A shifted from an alliance with B to an alliance with C.

A completely different type of role-playing was used effectively by Rosenberg and Abelson (1960) in their studies of cognitive dilemmas. In my own research program, we have been exploring different kinds of role-playing procedures with varying degrees of success. In one study, the major manipulation consisted in informing subjects that the experiment to which they had just committed themselves would require them, depending on the condition, either to receive shocks from a fellow subject or to administer shocks to a fellow subject. We used a regular deception procedure, but with a difference: We told the subjects before the session started that what was to follow was make-believe, but that we wanted them to react as if they really found themselves in this situation. I might mention that some subjects, not surprisingly, did not accept as true the information that this was all make-believe and wanted to know when they should show up for the shock experiment to which they had committed themselves. I have some question about the effectiveness of this particular procedure. It did not do enough to create a high level of involvement, and it turned out to be very complex since it asked subjects to role-play subjects, not people. In this sense, it might have given us the worst of both worlds, but I still think it worth some further exploration.

In another experiment, we were interested in creating *de novo* differently structured attitudes about an organization by feeding different kinds of information to two groups of subjects. These groups were then asked to take specific actions in support of the organization, and we measured attitude changes resulting from these actions. In the first part of the experiment, the subjects were clearly informed that the organization and the information we were feeding to them were fictitious, and that we were simply trying to simulate the conditions under which attitudes about new organizations are typically formed. In the second part of the experiment, the subjects were told that we were interested in studying the effects of action in support of an organization on attitudes toward it, and they were asked, in groups of five, to role-play a strategy meeting of leaders of the fictitious organization. The results of this study are very encouraging. While there is obviously a great deal that we need to know about the meaning of this situation to the subjects, they did react differentially to the experimental manipulations and these reactions followed an orderly pattern, despite the fact that they knew it was all make-believe.

There are other types of procedures, in addition to role-playing, that are worth exploring. For example, one might design field experiments in which, with the full cooperation of the subjects, specific experimental variations are introduced. The advantages of dealing with motivations at a real-life level of intensity might well outweigh the disadvantages of subjects knowing the general purpose of the experiment. At the other extreme of ambitiousness, one might explore the effects of modifying standard experimental procedures slightly by informing the subject at the beginning of the experiment that he will not be receiving full information about what is going on, but asking him to suspend judgment until the experiment is over.

Whatever alternative approach we try, there is no doubt that it will have its own problems and complexities. Procedures effective for some purposes may be quite ineffective for others, and it may well turn out that for certain kinds of problems there is no adequate substitute for the use of deception. But there are alternative procedures that, for many purposes, may be as effective or even more effective than procedures built on deception. These approaches often involve a radically different set of assumptions about the role of the subject in the experiment: They require us to use the subject's motivation to cooperate rather than to bypass it; they may even call for increasing the sophistication of potential subjects, rather than maintaining their naïveté. My only plea is that we devote some of our energies to active exploration of these alternative approaches.

PART **III**

The essays in Part Two attempted, in different ways, to bring humanistic values to bear on the professional activities of the social scientist. Part Three is concerned, in a sense, with the reverse of this relationship—with attempts to bring the social scientist's professional knowledge and orientation to bear on humanistically motivated social action.

There are various ways in which a social scientist may relate himself to social action. At one end of the continuum, he may participate in action programs simply as a citizen, concerned with advancing his own value positions, without any direct involvement of his professional role. At the other end of the continuum, he may be concerned with social action in his capacity as a social researcher, although this relationship itself may represent

THE SOCIAL SCIENTIST AS PARTICIPANT IN SOCIAL ACTION

ᚴᚴᚴᚴᚴᚴᚴᚴᚴᚴᚴᚴᚴᚴᚴᚴᚴᚴᚴᚴᚴᚴᚴᚴᚴᚴᚴᚴᚴᚴᚴᚴ

different degrees of distance from the groups engaged in the action. For example, he may be carrying out research in the particular policy area that the action group is trying to influence, be it race relations or foreign affairs; or he may be studying the characteristics of social movements as a participant observer; or he may actually be involved in a piece of action research.

The three essays that follow exemplify a relationship of the social scientist to social action that falls somewhere between an involvement in the role of citizen and one in the role of scientist. It can best be described as an involvement in the role of "observing participant," to contrast it with the more purely professional role of participant observer. The purpose of the participation is clearly to act on a public issue and to promote a preferred

227

policy, not to carry out social research. The social scientist brings to this action concern, however, the special skills, information, and perspective that are part of his professional background and preoccupation.

There are various forms that this type of participation in social action can take. Let me distinguish three, each of which makes use of some of the conceptual skills and accumulated knowledge that social researchers are able to offer.

(1) Social scientists can speak to the *techniques* of social action. They can help to predict the probable outcomes of different programs and to evaluate their relative effectiveness in achieving the desired goals. They can attempt to define the characteristics of the action approach that—given a particular set of circumstances—is most likely to meet with success.

(2) Social scientists can speak to the *context* of social action. They can analyze the societal conditions conducive to different types of social action and thus contribute to an understanding of the possibilities and limitations of a movement or program. Daniel Katz, for example, recently (1967) presented such an analysis, comparing the civil rights movement and the anti-Vietnam war movement in the United States.

(3) Social scientists can speak to the *substance* of social action. They can provide inputs in the form of data, theories, and insights to the analysis of the substantive problem with which the action program is concerned and to the development of proposals for alternative policies. This was a major function of the teach-ins that were originally organized in opposition to the war in Vietnam.

Each of the essays in Part Three touches on each of these three types of contributions. In terms of primary focus, however, Chapter Nine addresses itself to the techniques of social action, Chapter Ten to its context, and Chapter Eleven to its substance. Moreover, each chapter is concerned with a different issue area: Chapter Nine with racial conflict, Chapter Ten with civil liberties, and Chapter Eleven with foreign affairs.

CHAPTER 9

꧁꧂꧁꧂꧁꧂꧁꧂꧁꧂꧁꧂꧁꧂꧁꧂꧁꧂꧁꧂꧁꧂

INTRODUCTION

My interest in the application of nonviolent action techniques to the problems of racial conflict in the United States
began more than two decades ago. My first experience in a CORE-
sponsored direct action campaign was in the summer of 1947, at
Palisades Park in New Jersey, when CORE conducted a tough but
finally successful campaign to integrate the Park's swimming pool.
My initiation, incidentally, was complete and helped to bind me
to the movement in that I was arrested, along with a number of
other participants. In 1951 I moved to Baltimore and had my first
experience in an officially segregated community. I joined with
other Baltimoreans to establish a CORE chapter which, by the
time I left in 1954, had succeeded in desegregating lunch counters
in all of Baltimore's variety stores and drug stores. I continued to

be active in CORE, serving as a National Field Representative between 1954 and 1960.

I believe in nonviolent action, of course, because it is consistent with my basic values about human relationships and social change. At the same time, I am convinced that nonviolent action represents a potentially effective way of producing social change, based on principles that are social-psychologically sound. As a social psychologist, I know very well that one cannot make blanket statements about the effectiveness of this or any other form of action. All one can say is that nonviolent action, if it meets a specified set of conditions and is carried out under a specified set of circumstances, is likely to produce a specified set of effects. This is, essentially, the kind of argument I try to present in Chapter Nine, even though it takes the form of advocacy rather than of a neutral listing of propositions. The propositions can be readily inferred from my description of the characteristics of nonviolent action that account for its effectiveness, of the nature of the changes that such action is likely to produce, and of the reasons why I regard it as uniquely relevant to our current racial crisis.

I developed my ideas about the social-psychological bases of nonviolent action in the course of several talks that I gave at various times. One was an address presented in March 1960 at a mass meeting of Boston EPIC (Emergency Public Integration Committee), which had been set up to support the lunch-counter sit-in movement in the South. Another was a joint presentation with Gordon W. Allport before the Social Relations Society at Harvard University, also in March 1960. A third was a paper read on September 7, 1964, at the meetings of the American Psychological Association in Los Angeles, as part of a symposium on "Pacifism, martyrdom, appeasement: On influencing an 'intractable' adversary by nonviolent means." In preparing the present chapter, however, I was able to draw on these earlier papers only insofar as they dealt with general principles of nonviolent action. My attempt to apply these principles to the problems of race relations had to take account of the tremendous changes in the situation of 1968 as compared to that of 1960 or 1964. The final version of the essay was written shortly after the assassination of Martin Luther King, Jr., and tries to grapple with the implica-

tions of this cataclysmic event for the continued relevance of nonviolence.

I experienced a great deal of difficulty in writing this essay, not because of its content, but because of its political meaning in the context of current pronouncements about violence and "law and order." I was concerned about the possibility that it might be interpreted as another admonition to Negroes that they must refrain from the use of violence. As I point out in the essay, I regard such admonitions, coming from white men, as highly questionable from a moral point of view. Moreover, anyone who is concerned with the prevalence of violence in our society should direct his admonitions to the real perpetrators and sources of this violence in white America, not to its major victims in the Negro community. In speaking about nonviolence to the Negro community, nothing could be further from my purpose than a wish to moralize. My purpose, rather, is to point to what I believe to be an effective instrument of social change in Negro Americans' current struggle for justice.

The Relevance of Nonviolent Action

The early 1960s were a period of excitement and exhilaration in the history of social protest in the United States. The country was emerging from the long winter of the Joseph McCarthy years. A new generation of young people, who had not learned the habit of caution, rediscovered the meaning of personal commitment and social action. The civil rights movement captured the imagination of Negro and white students who, in turn, gave courage to their elders and brought them back into the struggle.

Perhaps the most exciting feature of the civil rights movement during these years was the pattern of social action that it pursued. Though activist and militant, it was firmly committed to nonviolence; though dedicated to creating a new pride and a new image for Negro Americans, it was built on collaboration between the races. Organized nonviolent and interracial struggle against segregation and discrimination was not, of course, invented in 1960. It goes back to the formation of the Congress of Racial Equality in Chicago in 1942. By 1960, CORE chapters had almost two decades of experience in breaking down segregation through the use of the techniques of nonviolent direct action, with many local successes to their credit, mostly in Northern and border states. Nonviolent action became a major force in the South in 1956 with the Montgomery bus boycott, under the leadership of Martin Luther King, Jr., and the formation of the Southern Christian Leadership Conference. It was in the early 1960s, however, that nonviolent civil rights action began to take on the character of a national mass movement, mobilizing support throughout the country and exerting major influence on official policy.

⊱ PRINCIPLES OF NONVIOLENT ACTION ⊰

What is nonviolent action? One thing that surely ought to be clear is that nonviolence does not refer to the mere absence of violence—though it seems that both militants, who castigate nonviolence as a counterrevolutionary strategy, and establishmentarians, who embrace it as part of the process of orderly change, are not always aware of that fact. Nonviolence is not to be equated with passive yielding to superior force or with working only through established channels. It is a positive, active, and in fact militant strategy, designed to produce thoroughgoing changes in social patterns.

Though it respects the adversary as a human being and attempts to mobilize his conscience, nonviolent action is not just a moral appeal and a petition to the other than he do the right thing. It is very definitely and deliberately an exercise of power. Barbara Deming (1968) puts it very well:

> To resort to power one need not be violent, and to speak to conscience one need not be meek. The most effective action *both* resorts to power *and* engages conscience. Nonviolent action does not have to beg others to "be nice." It can in effect force them to consult their consciences—or to pretend to have them. . . . One brings what economic weight one has to bear, what political, social, psychological, what physical weight. There is a good deal more involved here than a moral appeal. It should be acknowledged both by those who argue against nonviolence and those who argue for it that we, too, rely upon force (p. 14).

Indeed, a nonviolent confrontation presents real threats to the adversary. By dramatically exposing his unjust practices, by refusing continued cooperation with them, and by replacing them with new patterns, it may threaten him with embarrassment and adverse publicity, with reduction in his economic or political power, and with disruption of the orderly processes he cherishes. It does not, however, threaten to destroy him, and thus leaves open the way for reappraisal, for negotiation, and for rebuilding.

Nonviolent campaigns are most readily identified by the use of techniques of direct action. Various other techniques, however, have always been important parts of the repertoire of nonviolent action, even though they may not be unique to that strategy. Thus, nonviolent action programs overlap with and utilize protest demonstrations, educational campaigns, legislative lobbying, judicial suits, community organization, and negotiations with employers or unions. Typically, they rely on a combination of methods, which vary in dominance, depending on the nature of the problem under attack, the stage in which the campaign finds itself, and the opportunities for action that are available. What defines nonviolent action is not the specific array of techniques that have evolved, but the effort to utilize and develop appropriate techniques that are consistent with a set of basic action principles.

If we view nonviolence as a pragmatic strategy for intergroup conflict, rooted in a Gandhian philosophy of action (see Janis and Katz, 1959), we can describe these principles as follows:

(1) Nonviolent strategy is built on an active effort to empathize with one's opponent and to understand the perspectives, goals, fears, expectations, and preconceptions that he brings to the situation. To understand the adversary's point of view does not mean to accept it or to compromise with injustice. Rather, it avoids the type of escalation of conflict that is caused by misperception, and permits actions that are informed by the facts, that are not unnecessarily threatening, and that are conducive to a resolution of conflict in which both sides benefit.

(2) Nonviolent strategy includes continuing efforts to maintain and broaden channels of communication, to step up the level and depth of communication, and to discuss and negotiate all disagreements directly. Even when the conflict has reached a stage of sharp confrontation, there is a readiness to enter into negotiation and to explore mutual interests and possibilities for cooperation.

(3) Nonviolent strategy calls for the deliberate initiation of steps that help to decrease tension, hostility, and reliance on violent means. Janis and Katz stress, in this connection, the importance of "adopting a consistent attitude of *trust* toward the rival group and taking overt actions which demonstrate that one is, in fact, willing to act upon this attitude" (p. 86). By exhibiting trust toward the adversary, by refusing to treat him as an enemy, and by dealing with him in a straightforward and above-board manner, one can often induce a reciprocal response on his part.

(4) Nonviolent strategy is committed to eschewing violence in response to hostile moves initiated by the opponent. This commitment is clearly formulated and publicly pronounced. It means refraining from acts of physical or verbal violence against members of the other group and from acts that have the effect of humiliating them, even in the face of clear provocation. It does not, however, mean a passive yielding to coercion on their part. Typically, the strategy involves disciplined nonviolent resistance, marked by a readiness to make personal sacrifices in defense of one's cause.

(5) When it becomes necessary to initiate conflict moves and to engage the opponent in a direct confrontation, nonviolent

strategy continues to rely on nonviolent techniques. These techniques are aimed not at defeating the adversary, but at trying to "convert" him, while working for the achievement of concrete, positive objectives.

(6) Wherever possible, nonviolent action confronts a specific practice or law or institutional pattern that is unjust, and consists in a direct or symbolic enactment of an alternative pattern that corresponds to the desired state of affairs. This effort to give concrete expression to the desired state of affairs—to bring into reality, even if only in symbolic and rudimentary fashion, a pattern consistent with social justice—represents the most characteristic and most dramatic feature of the "classical" nonviolent action campaign. Thus, participants in lunch-counter sit-ins or in Freedom Rides refused to accept the established pattern of segregation and—by sitting where they were not supposed to sit—acted out the new pattern with which they hoped to replace it.[1]

A fundamental feature of these six principles is that they combine firmness and militancy with a conciliatory and open attitude. Participants in nonviolent action try to capitalize on the opponent's strengths rather than his weaknesses, to mobilize his sense of justice and self-interest in support of change rather than resistance to it, to win him over rather than to win over him. At the same time, they are utterly clear about their goals, they are

---

[1] Such direct action techniques, however, are usually preceded and always accompanied by a variety of other activities. For example, in Baltimore CORE's campaign against segregated lunch counters in the early 1950s, we went through a series of other steps—including tests to determine existing practices, leaflet distribution, efforts to mobilize the support of various community agencies, and repeated discussions and negotiations with store managers—before mounting a sit-in campaign. Even after sit-ins began, we continued to utilize various other techniques, such as attempts to initiate negotiations between store management and some established community agencies, and attempts to put pressure on the national headquarters of a local store by picketing branches in other cities and by raising the issue at stockholders' meetings. The existence of a direct action campaign, of course, served as an important lever for the other approaches, but it was the convergence of different approaches that finally produced the desired change.

firm in their commitment to a new social pattern, they insist on
the opponent's responsibility to accept and promote change, and
they leave no doubt that they themselves are prepared to follow
through even at great personal cost. They express their militancy
not by the suffering that they are prepared to inflict on the opponent, but by the suffering to which they are willing to subject
themselves in order to achieve justice. In short, theirs is a militancy that is not confounded with violence and hatred. Their
strategy for social change relies on power directed to two tactical
purposes: (1) to confront the adversary with the fact that he can
no longer rely on their willing cooperation with existing practices
and that, at least in symbolic and rudimentary fashion, a new state
of affairs has been instituted; and (2) to force the adversary to take
active steps in reciprocating the respect, trust, openness, and objectivity that they have shown toward him.

These principles have been applied most readily and effectively in the area of public accommodations, the context in which
nonviolent action was originally tailored to the struggle for racial
equality in the United States. In campaigns designed to integrate
public facilities it is relatively easy to define the specific practice
that needs to be changed, to identify a specific adversary, and to
find a dramatic and yet self-evident way of symbolically enacting
the alternative desired pattern. Other areas, such as discrimination
in employment or segregated housing, are not as ideally suited for
a classical nonviolent action campaign. In particular, it is difficult
to find a focus for direct action and confrontation that has a clear
and intrinsic relevance to the old pattern under attack and to the
new pattern designed to replace it. An open housing march, for
example, is a mechanism of nonviolent confrontation that is only
indirectly linked to the housing pattern itself; by marching
through a hostile neighborhood the participants are symbolically
insisting on their right to be there. If they actually erected houses
on vacant lots, or moved into abandoned buildings, the link between action and issue would be as obvious as it was in the case
of sit-ins and Freedom Rides. Opportunities for such actions, however, are not readily available.

The challenge to those of us who believe in the efficacy of
nonviolent strategy is to develop creative new techniques, em-
bodying the principles of nonviolent action, that are suited to the

central problems and the new realities of today—that address themselves to the issues of poverty, of economic and political participation, of the improvement of ghetto life, of the upgrading of educational facilities. Efforts in that direction are under way. The Poor People's Campaign, planned by Martin Luther King before his assassination and now led by Ralph Abernathy, is the major example of such efforts. Proponents of nonviolent action (for example, Swann, 1968) have also suggested "constructive programs"—that is, ways of instituting new states of affairs—that can accompany the Washington campaign. Various self-reliance projects, such as cooperative businesses and services, and community organization efforts in the black ghettoes, though not conceived as components of a nonviolent action campaign, are in fact governed by or at least compatible with the principles of nonviolent action. The question is, Are such efforts relevant to the current situation? Is there still a place for creative innovation in nonviolent action or is nonviolence dead?

THE RELEVANCE OF NONVIOLENCE TODAY

By now almost everyone who is willing and able to listen realizes that, despite the dedication and sacrifices of the civil rights movement, justice and equality for Negro Americans are nowhere in sight. This does not mean that the civil rights movement has failed. Rather, it means that the task is far more difficult and the changes required are far more fundamental than most of us realized. The exclusion of Negroes from American society is so systematic and racism is so thoroughly built into public attitudes and institutional arrangements that a meaningful solution requires a restructuring of the system.

This newly recognized wisdom and the new rhetoric that accompanies it, however, often blind us to the tremendous changes, both in law and social pattern, that have in fact taken place during the past ten years. In his last book, Martin Luther King (1967) summed up the important contributions that nonviolent action had made to these changes in the following words:

> It is not overlooking the limitations of nonviolence and the distance we have yet to go to point out the remarkable record of achievements that have already

come through nonviolent action. The 1960 sit-ins de-
segregated lunch counters in more than 150 cities within
a year. The 1961 Freedom Rides put an end to segregation in interstate travel. The 1956 bus boycott in Montgomery, Alabama, ended segregation on the buses not
only of that city but in practically every city of the
South. The 1963 Birmingham movement and the cli-
mactic March on Washington won passage of the most
powerful civil rights law in a century. The 1965 Selma
movement brought enactment of the Voting Rights
Law . . . (p. 58).

The civil rights movement not only has a series of concrete
accomplishments to its credit, but it also revolutionized social
action in this country by militantly working toward social changes
without resort to violence and hatred. King and other Negro
Americans have thus taken the lead in reshaping and revitalizing
the whole of American society. White America could hardly expect nonviolence in return for the systematic violence to which
Negroes had been subjected over the centuries; it surely could not
expect the leadership of Negroes in giving new vitality to a society
that had excluded them from its benefits. This was indeed an
unanticipated blessing, perhaps grounded in part in the very suffering to which the Negro community has been subjected and
which prepared it for this unique role in experimenting with
radically new and more human forms of social action.

It is not surprising, at least in retrospect, that, as the
struggle progresses, its emphasis has moved away from the principles of nonviolence and interracial collaboration as the central
pillars of the movement. This development can be traced to the
dynamics of the struggle itself, as well as to the new realities that
it has created or revealed. Despite many successes, and in large
part because of the hopes that these very successes engendered (see
Pettigrew, 1967, pp. 295–297), there came a growing realization
of the painful and costly process by which every small change had
to be hammered out, of the dependence of the Negro community
on white support and good will, of the profound hatred and violence that the movement elicited among some elements of the
white community, of the limits beyond which even the "white
liberal" was unprepared to go, of the divergencies in interest—
and yet communalities in fate—between the Negro middle and

lower class and between the Negro populations in the rural South and the urban North, of the irrelevance of civil rights advances to the Negro ghetto dwellers in Watts and in the large cities throughout the country, and of the desperation and isolation of the vast Negro underclass. These conditions ushered in a nationalistic phase of the struggle, in which black unity, black pride, black self-determination, and black leadership have become the central instruments. This nationalistic phase was perhaps inevitable, but its advent was hastened and intensified by the impact of the Vietnam war on our domestic programs.

The current phase is marked by the emergence of a new group of militants, committed to a transformation of the movement and bidding for its leadership by an appeal to nationalist sentiments. As is so often true in nationalist movements, some of these appeals take on an aggressively ethnocentric character. They express contempt and hatred for the white man and are often phrased in the idiom of violence and surrounded with the mystique of guerrilla warfare. The strength and influence of militants of this school are easily exaggerated, in part because they are so vocal and colorful. They represent only one branch of the nationalist revival in the Negro community, and their interpretation of Black Power is certainly not typical of all those who use the term. Charles Hamilton (1968) and Nathan Wright (1967), for example, have something quite different in mind when they speak of Black Power. Yet the militant separatists have shifted the center of gravity in the movement and have laid down a powerful challenge to the doctrine of nonviolence. They have contributed to a widespread feeling, particularly in the younger generation, that nonviolent action is irrelevant to the current realities, a relic of the past that only "Uncle Toms," "counterrevolutionaries," and "white liberals" would think of unearthing.[2]

The assassination of Martin Luther King, the most eloquent spokesman for nonviolence and the most beautiful human

---

[2] Barbara Deming (1968) quotes a man who said to her: "You can't turn the clock back now to nonviolence!" She comments, wistfully: "Turn the clock back? The clock has been turned to violence all down through history. Resort to violence hardly marks a move forward. It is nonviolence which is in the process of invention, if only people would not stop short in that experiment" (p. 12).

being in American public life, has added a new poignancy to
questions about the relevance of the philosophy for which he
lived and died. Again and again we are told that this act of total
violence demonstrates the futility of nonviolence and marks the
end of the nonviolent phase of the struggle. This is a natural reaction to the anger, to the bitter hurt, to the sense of meaning-
lessness and despair evoked by the assassination. But once we turn
from grief to analysis, can this reaction really be maintained?

Certainly the assassination of Martin Luther King does
not provide proof of the ineffectiveness of nonviolence as a strategy, any more than did the assassination of Mohandas Gandhi
twenty years ago. It is true that a nonviolent strategy is designed
to call forth reciprocal behavior in the adversary, and that proponents of nonviolent action expect the number of casualties to
be far lower than those suffered in a violent confrontation. Nonviolence, however, as Gandhi knew, and as King knew and repeatedly said, offers no guarantee against injury and violent death.
Nonviolent action is a form of struggle, often carried out in areas
in which tensions are high and emotions deep. Proponents of such
action are cognizant of the fact that it may activate efforts of
ruthless suppression and bring into the open blind hatreds and
fears. It is quite possible, therefore, that the level of violence on
the part of the adversary may at first increase after a nonviolent
action campaign has been initiated, although certainly not to the
same extent that it increases after rioting or other forms of violent
action.

Although violent responses by the adversary are by no
means necessary to the success of a nonviolent action campaign,
they may in fact further it. They may mobilize widespread support for the campaign among those who were previously neutral
or inactive, as they did in Birmingham and Selma. They may also
bring about a gradual change in the adversary himself, as he finds
that his own violence continues to be met with nonviolence and
with increasing disapproval on the part of bystanders. But whether
or not it furthers the campaign, a violent response is an eventuality for which nonviolent actionists must be and have been prepared.

To cite the assassination as evidence for the failure of nonviolence reveals a lack of understanding of what nonviolence

means and what Martin Luther King stood for. It is similar to the lack of understanding betrayed by a number of publicists, who, in discussing King's assassination, referred to the "irony" that this nonviolent man met with such a violent death. Nonviolence for King meant active participation in controversy and struggle; he was not dedicated to keeping things calm, smooth, and orderly, but to a militant pursuit of change. As activists, practitioners of nonviolence like Martin Luther King are unique in that they refuse to inflict violence on others but are prepared for the possibility that they may bring it upon themselves. Thus, there was neither irony, nor proof of the inefficacy of nonviolence, in the fact that King met with violent death; it was consistent with his profound commitment and indicative of his extraordinary courage.

Granting, however, that the assassination did not prove the failure of nonviolence, did it not at least demonstrate that the conditions for nonviolent action do not exist today? The assassination, it can be argued, brought out dramatically the profound violence of white America and its determination to crush every effort of the Negro population to achieve a measure of justice. An atmosphere in which the internationally acknowledged spokesman for nonviolence, the man who more than any other refused to abandon faith in America, becomes a prime target for assassination may not be suited to the practice of nonviolence. In this view, then, the assassination as such does not constitute a reason or justification for abandoning nonviolence, but it serves as a symbolic reminder that such a strategy is irrelevant.

I find this a compelling position because I too reacted to the assassination of Martin Luther King with a sense of despair at the relentless violence of American society, both in its internal and external affairs. Yet, on closer reflection, I cannot accept as valid the conclusion that nonviolence is irrelevant to the present situation of our society. In fact, I shall try to show why militant nonviolent action is specifically relevant to our present dilemma, given the changes that need to be achieved and the available means that are capable of achieving them. I am convinced that nonviolent means are far more likely to be effective in producing real changes than the violence now being elevated into a positive value in the romantic mystique and the revolutionary rhetoric of some black militants and their white supporters and provokers. What is wrong with the cult of violence is not that it is too radical, but that it is not radical enough. It relies on the slogans, the methods, and the ways of thinking that have characterized all of the old nationalisms, and, in advocating violence, it is—to use King's words (1967)—"imitating the worst, the most brutal and the most uncivilized values of American life" (p. 64). The advocacy of violence may be radical in the sense of using an aggressive style and calling for "extreme" actions. The advocacy of nonviolence, however, is truly radical in its insistence on an analysis that goes to the roots, on a redefinition of ends and means, and on a search for innovative approaches.

Black militants are, understandably, suspicious and resentful of calls for nonviolence that come from—or are seen as coming from—representatives of the establishment. It is indeed hypocritical to demand of Negroes, in a moralizing tone of voice, that they renounce violence when the rest of the society is so saturated with it, particularly at a time when the very men who make these demands are responsible for the brutal and systematic uses of violence in Vietnam. Clearly, these demands derive from a vested interest in maintaining the status quo, which the black militant certainly does not share. It is from the same perspective that some political figures have declared in recent months that "no one has a right to riot." They reveal their complete lack of comprehension of the meaning of the riots by appealing to the legitimacy of the system, when the essential message of the riots is precisely that the system—being unjust—is illegitimate.

My own questioning of the mystique and rhetoric of violence derives, of course, from a very different perspective, formed by a concern with fundamental social change. Nevertheless, as a white man, I hesitate to urge Negroes to commit themselves to nonviolence because of its moral superiority, or even because of its pragmatic advantages. I feel that only Negroes can decide whether they prefer the risks of armed self-defense to the risks of going unarmed, whether they prefer erring in the direction of undue trust of the white society to erring in the direction of undue suspicion, or even whether they prefer expressing their anger to being effective. White men, no matter how deeply involved they may be in the struggles of the Negro community, are not exposed to the same provocations, nor subject to the same consequences, and they have a freedom to withdraw from the struggle that is not available to their Negro comrades. They must be wary, therefore, of any attempt to impose their own moral or strategic preferences on Negroes, for whom these questions represent basic existential choices.[3] But, just as it would be presumptuous for white men to pass moral judgment on the actions of black nationalists, so would it be patronizing to withhold criticism of the premises on which these actions are based, if that criticism derives from an honest and thoughtful analysis of the issues and options.

My analysis has convinced me that violence is self-defeating in Negro Americans' struggle to achieve justice and that nonviolence is ultimately more conducive to genuine change. This analysis is based on the following considerations: (1) The current phase of the struggle calls for tactics of confrontation directed to a realignment of power relationships within the society; (2) Such confrontations, however, can create meaningful and lasting changes only if they induce white Americans to re-examine their attitudes and to open up the system to full Negro participation; (3) We face, therefore, a real dilemma in that confrontations and demands for changes in power relationships—particularly if they use the postures and rhetoric of violence—tend to alienate white Americans from the Negro population and its cause and to strengthen the barriers to Negro participation through repression and separation; and (4) Nonviolent action offers the most promising resolution to this dilemma, and is thus singularly relevant to the current situation, because it provides confrontations without unduly alienating the white population and challenges to existing power relationships without unduly threatening the integrity of the system.

---

[3] By the same token, white "revolutionaries" ought to think twice before urging the Negro to adopt a strategy of violence and to form the vanguard of their revolution. In their often self-righteous conviction that they are the only true spokesmen for the oppressed, they may fail to notice that they are imposing their *own* revolution on the Negro rather than supporting *his* struggle.

❧ REALIGNMENT OF POWER AND TACTICS OF CONFRONTATION ❧

There can be no effective resolution of our current domestic crisis until the white community becomes aware of the steps that must be taken to restructure our social system. If our society is to be both stable and democratic, the power relationships of different groups within it will have to be drastically altered. The fact of the matter is that Negroes and other groups permanently locked into poverty have been denied access to all of the normal channels for attaining and exercising power. Excluded from participation in the political and economic life of the society, they have no way of applying effective pressures to meet their needs and interests. Their concerns can be ignored with impunity. Moreover, social patterns and the educational system perpetuate their exclusion from the system and make their powerlessness permanent. They are thus deprived of institutionalized means for changing their situation, either in the short run or in the long run.

Meaningful social change can come about only as the rightful power of the Negro community grows along with steady improvement in its conditions of life. That is, the needed massive programs for expanding economic opportunities, for assuring basic income, and for creating decent housing, educational facilities, health care, transportation, and recreation must all be of such a nature as to increase the power of Negro citizens. They must be able to maintain and renew these programs through their own actions, both locally and nationally, and be freed from total dependence on white generosity and white supervision. The "white power structure," therefore, must be prepared to give up many of the powers that it now holds to the Negro community. The exercise of these powers is illegitimate as long as it is held by men who do not represent Negroes and do not have their interests at heart, but who are mainly concerned with maintaining the smoothness and orderliness of the society so that they can benefit from their own advantageous position and proceed with their own business without undue disruption. In short, power in the Negro community must be transferred from those who use it primarily to maintain law and order to those who wish to use it primarily to attain justice.

It is important to understand, in this connection, that "law and order" has a very different meaning for the black ghetto than it does for the larger society. Law and order are indeed essential to the health of the society, but their appeal is relevant only to those who are integrated into the system and who recognize its legitimate authority. Being committed to the system, because it represents them and meets their needs and interests, they are concerned with maintaining orderly processes so that the society can continue to function effectively.

What is law and order to those who are integrated into the system, however, is basically coercion and tyranny to those who are excluded from it. They have no investment in maintaining the orderly processes of a system that does not represent them, that does not meet their needs and interests, that does not even offer them protection. To those who share power, the demand to maintain law and order is morally compelling and, at least in the long run, it is in their self-interest to meet this demand. For those who have no power, however, the demand to maintain law and order is coercive and is seen as an effort to keep them in line so that those who wield the power can go about their business and maintain their illegitimate authority.

The police in the black ghetto represent the most visible symbols and agents of this illegitimate authority. They are perceived, and usually with justification, as being in the ghetto not to serve its inhabitants, but to control them—not to protect the interests of the community, but to protect the interests of the white establishment. Thus, they are no different from a colonial police force, assigned to maintain "law and order" for the benefit of an outside power. Ghetto life is filled with experiences of injustice, violence, and repression carried out by the police. Under these circumstances, it is cynical or naive to ask ghetto dwellers to respect law and order as the obligation of citizens.

Law and order will become a meaningful concept once Negroes achieve their rightful share of power in the society and are able to exercise control over the agencies that function in their communities, including the police force. Thus, a top priority is to work for a thorough redistribution of power within our society. Whites, who currently hold exclusive control over most bases of power, can contribute to this process by removing all barriers to the full participation of Negroes in the country's economic and political life and in its educational and social institutions. They must, in fact, make positive efforts to assure greater participation by Negroes if the effects of a long history of systematic exclusion are to be overcome. Furthermore, whites must turn over the power that they now hold in the Negro community and in poverty programs to those who can represent the interests of the relevant constituencies more legitimately.

There has been little awareness in the white community of the nature and extent of the changes in power relationships required if our racial problems are to be solved. With the advances in civil rights that began with the Supreme Court ruling on school segregation in 1954, white America, particularly its liberal and official sectors, settled down comfortably into the illusion that the solution was around the corner. Over the years they saw more and stronger laws being enacted, visible signs of segregation increasingly being removed, opportunities for Negroes opening up, and Negroes and whites working cooperatively in the civil rights movement. While it was clear that a great deal of further work and continuing pressure on recalcitrant elements (particularly in the South) would be required, the back of the problem had, in their view, been broken, and all that was needed was continued effort in the same direction.

For many middle-class Negroes, the civil rights movement did, indeed, provide meaningful changes. Their opportunities did increase and more doors were opened to them. At times, for men with special qualifications, black skin color even became an advantage, as government, industry, and the universities began to search for Negro talent. These developments, however, left the lower-class Negro in a situation that was in many ways worse than it had been before. The changes that had been instituted by the civil rights movement did not seem to touch on his problems in any meaningful way. They brought about no improvement in his educational facilities, his employability, his housing, his transportation, his daily life. Many lower-class Negroes found themselves, in fact, in an increasingly unfavorable position, as the need for unskilled labor declined.

The rhetoric of civil rights had raised their hopes and also their conviction that they were entitled to a better deal. Moreover, they saw that the middle-class segment of the Negro population was making progress and their sense of relative deprivation, therefore, became more and more pronounced. But, above all, it became increasingly clear to them that nothing was going to change. The white man, despite his liberal policies and pronouncements, simply did not understand the problems of the black ghetto and what needed to be done to improve the conditions of its inhabitants. Thus, the lower-class Negro felt more isolated than ever. He saw himself as the forgotten man, who was bypassed by the changes that had been set into motion.

This sense of isolation and abandonment was made even more intense by the fact that advances in civil rights had deepened the gulf between lower-class and middle-class Negroes. Middle-class Negroes, it seemed, were getting what they wanted out of the civil rights movement, since they were able to exploit the opportunities that were being opened up. They, therefore, lost interest—or seemed to lose interest—in the problems of the lower-class Negro and the more thorough restructuring of the system that these required. As discrimination based on race as such declined in importance and only the disadvantages caused by race (which middle-class Negroes had somehow managed to overcome) remained, the two classes no longer shared a common fate as clearly as they had before. Thus, lower-class Negroes felt abandoned not only by white society and its officialdom, but also by the Negro middle class. This feeling was less prevalent in the South, where the Negro community is more cohesive and cuts across class lines, where the church is still a more effective social force and kinship structure is more intact, where most of the Negro middle class is economically dependent upon the Negro community itself, and where skin color as such remained more clearly a source of common fate for all Negroes that it did in the North. In the Northern ghettoes, however, the lack of community and the social distance of the Negro middle class made the sense of abandonment more oppressive.

This sense of abandonment—the feeling that your problems have not been understood or even been noticed, the realization that changes that you had a right to expect are passing you by—provides the mood that favors resort to confrontation tactics. The riots can be seen, in part, as a spontaneous attempt by ghetto dwellers to force themselves on the attention of white America and the black establishment, to communicate that they are hurting badly, that they regard the situation as serious, and that they will no longer put up with it. Thus, Dynes and Quarantelli (1968) suggest that "the looting that has occurred in recent racial outbreaks is a bid for the redistribution of property. It is a message that certain deprived sectors of the population want what they consider their fair share—and that they will resort to violence to get it" (p. 14). Similarly, the burning of houses in their own oppressive neighborhoods may well be the ghetto dwellers' way of communicating that they feel permanently locked into intolerable living conditions and that they must somehow find a way out. These confrontations, then, are desperate ways of saying, "You are not hearing us," by people who have become convinced that there is no other way of getting their message across.

This reaction in the ghettoes has, in turn, activated many elements of the Negro middle class, especially among college students. In part, it may have mobilized their guilt at being co-opted by the white establishment and led to abandon their poorer brothers in the ghettoes. In part, it may have made them aware of the fact that they still shared a common fate with poor Negroes, that despite their advantages they were still black and by no means fully accepted by white America. Above all, the middle-class Negroes' newly aroused consciousness of their blackness caused them to believe that whatever they had achieved in white society was at the price of their Negro identity. They became more fully aware that it is not only the poor Negro who has been excluded from the benefits of American society, but that the Negro as a group has been systematically excluded from American culture and history. They saw that they had adopted the image of the Negro that is built into the American educational system and communication media, and that they had thus been deprived of their own group pride and self-awareness. It is these sentiments, it seems to me, that have led middle-class Negroes, particularly though not exclusively in the younger generation, to seek confrontations. They too feel that white America has no conception of the enormity of what it has done to the Negro, that only a fundamental reorientation can bring about the necessary changes, and that whites must be forced to listen.

Such confrontations have been and continue to be necessary, both to force whites to listen and to induce them to share the power they now hold. Even white liberals have been slow to recognize that millions of poor people are living out their lives in misery at the fringes of this affluent society and passing on this misery to their children as their sole inheritance. Only now is it being publicly acknowledged that racism is so thoroughly built into our institutions that it locks the lower-class Negro into a pattern of inequality from which he cannot extricate himself and that it even robs the middle-class Negro of a stable sense of identity. So deeply ingrained are the effects of systematic exclusion that even men of good will, including many Negroes, have failed to notice and to understand them. There is thus a need to find dramatic ways of communicating that the situation is serious and that radical changes are called for.

Once whites can be made to understand what changes are required, however, they may still resist them because of the major redistribution of power these changes represent. Resistance is likely even where whites are committed to change in principle, because every change in power relationships requires them to give up some advantage or at least some way of looking at things to which they have become accustomed. It is particularly likely, however, because many whites, including many of those who are in control of major institutions, are not at all prepared to share their power. Since the system does not make established channels available to Negroes for the achievement of power without the active support of whites, they are required at times to work outside established channels. They have to resort to the tactics of confrontation and, under special circumstances, to acts of civil disobedience in order to persuade a reluctant white community that the current American crisis makes a fundamental realignment of power essential.

◿ OPENING THE SYSTEM ◺

To be effective in the long run, changes in power relationships must be of such a nature as to increase the openness of the system to the full participation of Negroes and other excluded groups, so that they will have the power within the system to which they are entitled. I take the view that the task is not to overturn the political and legal structure of the society, but to make it function properly, in a way that is consistent with its basic values and procedures. In this view, the underlying structure of the United States, despite its many shortcomings, is built on sound democratic procedures and values. These could, if we were prepared to live up to them, serve as a foundation for a free, just, and decent social order. As it stands now, a large proportion of the population—perhaps three quarters or even more—is well integrated into the system, has meaningful roles within it, and accepts the regime as representative and legitimate. What is wrong is that there are some segments of the population, including most of its Negroes, who have been systematically and permanently excluded from the system through institutional mechanisms built up over decades. If these groups are to acquire their rightful share of power, we must develop new institutional mechanisms that will guarantee their systematic and permanent inclusion in the life of the society.

Such institutional changes, if they are to be extensive and sustained, cannot be achieved without the active cooperation of important segments of the white population. This cooperation, in turn, is more likely to be forthcoming if whites are forced to recognize their own responsibility for the current state of affairs and its inconsistency with their values and beliefs, and to take a critical look at themselves and their society. Thus, to be effective in the long run, confrontations must be designed not merely to extract specific concessions, but to set into motion, among white Americans, a process of re-examining their attitudes.

In stressing white attitudes, I am not proposing that social change must await a change of heart in the majority of whites. Social-psychological research indicates that attitude change is far more likely to follow rather than precede institutional changes. But at least some influential whites must be sufficiently committed to these institutional changes in order to help bring them about. Moreover, the new institutional mechanisms can be maintained and can eventually gain wide acceptance only if they are created under conditions that permit and encourage a reassessment of related attitudes.

Some black nationalists may be impatient with this emphasis on white attitude change. They feel that they are demanding only what is theirs by right and that they cannot be expected to wait until whites have been persuaded to give it to them out of the goodness of their hearts. But the attitude changes I have in mind refer, precisely, to a new awareness of the way in which Negroes are being deprived of their rights and of the institutional patterns that are needed to assure these rights. Efforts at attitude change are designed to gain the cooperation of whites by arousing, not their sense of charity, but their sense of justice.

I am, of course, assuming that such attitude changes are not only necessary but possible. Here, again, some black nationalists may disagree. If we are to take them literally, they are convinced that all white Americans are racist to the core, bent on genocide, and beyond redemption. Such a position is not only self-defeating, in that it denies the possibility of change, but also has elements of a self-fulfilling prophecy. It is neither realistic nor profitable to assume that all whites are alike and that none is open to change. To be sure, there are numerous racists in our midst whose attitudes can be changed only through a profound therapeutic or conversion experience, and there are groups in this society whose own status is so insecure that they will bitterly oppose any move to include Negroes. But there are wide segments of white America capable of change, whether it is because their conscience has been pricked, or because their self-interest has been redefined, or because they have acquired a new view of what is socially expected. It may be true that there is a taint of racism in every white American, since he has grown up, lived in, and benefited from a society whose Negro members are denied their rights. But this is beside the point, for the issue is not the moral purity of white Americans, but their potential openness to new policies.

In this connection, I think it is a serious mistake to single out the "white liberal" as the principal target for contempt and attack. There is good reason to feel angry and disappointed at those white liberals who enthusiastically favored change as long as it did not touch their personal lives, but who withdrew their support of the movement when it began to demand a realignment of power relationships. There is, understandably, a special bitterness reserved for those who pretend to be friends and fail to come through, those who ought to understand and fail to do so. To heap venom on the white liberal, however, is largely an act of self-indulgence, for the fact remains that he is not the main enemy. He is, rather, a potential ally—even if not an entirely reliable one—in the real battle that is now before us, the battle against those who favor ruthless repression as a response to the current crisis. It is the white liberals who, by and large, have been opposing the efforts at massive repression and have asked instead for an attack on the causes of riots. It is white liberals (and a few middle-class Negroes) who issued the report of the National Commission on Civil Disorders, which begins to show an understanding of white society's responsibility for the conditions in the black ghetto. The white liberal has a tradition of supporting social reforms; he has a self-image as one who is open to change; he has a reservoir of guilt about social injustices. There is a need for confrontations that capitalize on these dispositions and mobilize his support.

THE DILEMMA OF CONFRONTATION TACTICS

I have argued that the current situation calls for tactics of confrontation, but that such confrontations can create meaningful and lasting changes only if they induce white Americans to re-examine their attitudes and to open up the system to full Negro participation. Here we find ourselves in the face of an inherent dilemma. Confrontations often tend to sharpen the lines of division between conflicting groups and to harden their positions. Thus, far from creating the conditions for a re-examination of attitudes, they may reinforce existing attitudes of distance, hostility, and distrust. Demands for power by an excluded group are threatening to those who now hold power, and particularly to those groups whose own power is precarious. Their defensive reaction, far from opening up the system to those who are now excluded, may have the effect of strengthening the barriers to wider participation.

These effects are particularly likely to occur when the confrontation uses violence or the threat of violence, and is directed not just at the acts of the adversary, but at his person. There are a number of ways in which violent or hostile confrontations by Negroes militate against positive attitude change among whites: (1) they reinforce whatever negative attitudes toward Negroes are present in the white population, including the attitude that Negroes are threatening and dangerous and that they cannot be trusted; (2) they arouse defensiveness among whites, causing them to focus their attention on the dangers to which Negroes are exposing them rather than on the grievances that Negroes are trying to communicate; (3) they tend to reduce whatever guilt may exist among whites for discrimination against Negroes, because isolation of Negroes and hostility against them are now fully justified; (4) they create an atmosphere of polarized opposing camps, which is inconsistent with the exploration and discovery of common interests and mutually advantageous solutions; and (5) they tend to unify the different segments within the white population, strengthening the hands of the racists and effectively silencing pro-Negro elements.

It is quite likely that violent confrontations will not only discourage attitude changes conducive to an opening up of the system, but will actually constrict Negroes' opportunities for meaningful participation in the system. A very probable outcome of the repeated eruption of violence in black ghettoes is a resort to ruthless repression of the ghetto population. Those who favor repression can play on the fears of the white community and can apply effective pressures on governmental officials to deal firmly with what they can describe as threats to the basic integrity of the system. Officials, in turn, may feel compelled and justified to use any means at their disposal to "stop the violence." The signs of such repression are already evident in the responses to the recent riots: the massive arming of some city police forces, the "deputization" of citizens in Chicago coupled with incitement to repressive violence by that city's mayor, the proposals in Congress for the use of detention camps and the requirement of identification passes for all ghetto dwellers. There is every reason to believe that the authorities have the physical capacity to organize such repression; and I have no doubt that they also have the psychological capacity to use it, given an atmosphere of mass hysteria. The garrison state thus ushered in would erect barriers to black participation in society far more impenetrable than those of today.

A less extreme response to violent confrontations may be a partial yielding, with whites abandoning the inner cities entirely to Negroes and permitting them "self-determination" within their own communities. These communities, however, would be cut off economically from the rest of the society and under constant surveillance against any attempts to push out beyond their walls. At best they would resemble our Indian reservations, at worst the African townships in Rhodesia and South Africa.

Perhaps the least extreme response of the authorities might be a pattern of alternating between yielding to demands and resorting to suppression. Periodic eruptions of violence would be accepted as a way of life, accompanied, on the one hand, by increased reliance on the coercive power of the police and, on the other, by a corruption of legal processes. Such a solution would undermine the stability and legitimacy of the regime and weaken the political structure. Perhaps the system might be more open to Negro participation, but participation as such would diminish in value under these conditions.

Violent confrontations are not necessarily and totally ineffective in producing attitude change. For example, the riots in the ghettoes—though they have instigated strong repressive measures—did induce some whites to reappraise their attitudes. The chances are, however, that as such tactics continue to be used, their potential of frightening white Americans will far outweigh their potential of challenging white attitudes. This is particularly likely if the object of rioting were to shift from the ghetto itself to the white neighborhoods. In short, it is to be expected that as violent confrontations continue, more and more segments of the white population will become alienated from Negro efforts to foster social change and will support a repressive approach.

Thus, if our goal is to bring about a thorough re-examination of white attitudes and to open the society to full participation of those who are now excluded, we cannot rely on the tactics of violence. We must find techniques of confrontation that minimize the alienation of whites, and ways of challenging existing power relationships that protect the integrity of the system. It is part of the genius of nonviolent action that it provides precisely such techniques.

THE UNIQUE POTENTIAL OF NONVIOLENT ACTION

It would be unrealistic to maintain that nonviolent confrontations completely avoid alienating the adversary. They do, after all, contain a degree of force and threat; they are often disruptive and inevitably contribute to an atmosphere of tension. Relative to violent confrontations, however, they are far more likely to create the conditions for lasting attitude changes, as well as for a restructuring of social institutions and a realignment of power relationships. What is particularly important is that the effectiveness of nonviolent tactics in generating change is likely to increase with time, whereas, as I have pointed out, the opposite is likely to occur when violent tactics are used.[4]

What are the characteristics of nonviolent action that account for its unique potential in producing durable and cumulative changes, both at the level of individual attitudes and at the level of institutional patterns? Let me suggest some possibilities, looking first at mechanisms of attitude change and then at sources of institutional change.

Attitude change. Two features of nonviolent action contribute to its unique capacity for producing lasting changes in

---

[4] The relative advantage of nonviolence is likely to be especially great now that the nation has had repeated experiences of violent civil strife. Because of the contrast, nonviolent confrontations should be perceived as even less threatening and hostile than they were in the past. It is also probably true that whites may be more inclined now to respond to nonviolent action because they see it as an alternative to violence and as offering the hope of averting further violence. This raises the question whether the effectiveness of nonviolence actually depends on the existence of violence with which it can be contrasted and for which it can be substituted. Whatever implications this possibility might have for the general theory of nonviolence, it does not in any way reduce—if anything, it enhances—the relevance of nonviolence to the present situation.

attitude. It provides important new information about the non-violent actor to the adversary and to relevant bystanders. At the same time, it induces them to take some form of reciprocal positive action toward him (or, in the case of bystanders, to engage in some supportive behavior). Both of these conditions facilitate change, but it is their combination that makes nonviolent action especially powerful.

When Negroes confront white America nonviolently, they provide new information, not only about their concerns and intentions, but also about their underlying character. Their militancy, because it is combined with an open and conciliatory attitude, communicates a serious commitment to changing their situation, rather than a desire to threaten or destroy whites. Their nonviolence, because it is combined with a strong determination and an obvious willingness to make sacrifices, communicates a readiness to work out mutually satisfactory resolutions, rather than a posture of weakness and a passive acceptance of white oppression. Militant nonviolence, moreover, enhances Negroes' own self-respect and thus communicates their expectation of respect from the white community. Because of the generally reduced level of tension and threat perception in a nonviolent (as compared to a violent) confrontation, whites are more likely to be attentive to these new items of information transmitted by Negroes. The information, in turn, if properly perceived, may lead whites to re-examine their image of Negroes, and to perceive them in a new light.

Nonviolent actions, however, affect not only the antagonist's perceptions, but also his own actions. What the nonviolent actor does makes certain responses by the adversary possible or necessary, and others impossible or unnecessary. Nonviolent action tends to tie the adversary's hands. He cannot respond to it as violently and as ruthlessly as he would to violent action. Instead, a nonviolent strategy often forces the adversary to reciprocate with nonviolence, just as a violent strategy invites a violent rejoinder. There are various reasons for this. Some are related to the existence of a norm of reciprocity (see Gouldner, 1960); even if the adversary himself is prepared to violate that norm, he often has to take account of the reactions of third parties. There is also a tendency, in much of social interaction, for B's actions to come to resemble A's expectations—that is, for B to enact the role into which A casts him. Thus, if Negroes, pursuing a nonviolent strategy, treat whites as if they were friendly, trustworthy, and honorable, then they may force them actually to become friendly, trustworthy, and honorable. Finally, internal processes within the opposing group, set into motion by the nonviolent confrontation, may bring about reciprocal action. That is, the nonviolent action may challenge some elements within the white community—notably the white liberals—in terms of their own value system and mobilize supportive action on their part. It may move them from a neutral or indifferent posture into an active alliance with Negroes, with efforts to pressure the white leadership to reciprocate the nonviolent action. This is particularly likely to happen if the initial white response to the nonviolence was one of violent suppression.

As the adversary reciprocates by engaging in positive, supporting, and conciliatory actions toward those who initiated nonviolent moves, strong forces toward attitude change are likely to be mobilized in him. Positive actions by the adversary commit him to an increasingly friendly relationship with the nonviolent actors, which tends to generalize to his underlying attitudes toward them. What is crucial here is that B's observation of his own friendly actions toward A produces attitude change in a favorable direction. It is often true that our observations of our own treatment of an object exert a greater influence on our attitudes than do the characteristics of the object itself. There are various reasons why one would expect attitudes to fall into line with the actions that one has taken (see Kelman, 1962b). One, which has been explored in a number of social-psychological studies, is the need to justify our actions to ourselves. Another and perhaps more basic one is our tendency to define people and things largely in terms of our own actions toward them (a tendency that is nicely captured in the book of children's definitions entitled *A Hole Is To Dig*). In fine, to the extent to which nonviolent action can force the adversary to reciprocate in kind, it is likely to lead to increasingly friendly attitudes, just as the reciprocation of violent action is likely to lead to increasing hostility.

The unique power of a nonviolent strategy is that it provides for the *joint occurrence* of genuinely new information about those who undertake the action and friendly behavior toward them on the part of the antogonist. New information itself may be an insufficient basis for attitude change because the recipient may lack the motivation to consider it actively and seriously. Thus, for example, an educational campaign designed to communicate the mood of the Negro population may not have much impact because whites, even if forced to expose themselves to it, may choose not to listen. Involvement in positive action toward the other group does create the motivation for re-examining one's attitudes, but it too may fail to produce relevant attitude change if it provides no truly new information to be taken into account. Thus, for example, white assistance to poor Negroes may generate friendly feelings toward the recipients, but would provide no new inputs about the actual mood of the Negro population. (As a result, those who give such assistance are often shocked to find that the recipients are not "grateful" for it.) Someone's attitudes are most likely to be restructured when he is dramatically confronted with challenging new information about another group, in a context in which he is open and receptive to it, that is, when he himself is engaged in friendly actions (or actions that imply friendliness) toward that group (see Kelman, 1962a).

Nonviolent confrontation has the potential of communicating relevant new information dramatically and, at the same time, forcing representatives of white society into negotiation, discussion, and reciprocal action. As whites engage in these positive interactions, forces toward re-examining their attitudes are set into motion. They become more open to the new information about the Negro and his condition, more inclined to examine the issue and its implications for their own values, and more willing to look into themselves and their society. In short, their own inner forces are mobilized toward change. Change is more likely to occur, therefore, and to be sustained.

Institutional change. Nonviolent action has a unique capacity for producing changes in social patterns that are thoroughly built into institutional structures because it makes maximum use of the potential for change present *within* the system. It challenges forcefully the ways in which power is allocated and used, while at the same time expressing a firm commitment to the underlying values and procedures of the system.

Nonviolent action is directed at practices that are considered illegitimate, in the sense that they deny or fail to uphold the rights of a segment of the population and thus violate some of the system's basic assumptions. These may be laws or social patterns that have the effect of excluding that group, of discriminating against it, and of putting it at a disadvantage; or they may be policies that fail to provide some of the group's vital needs or to assure the representation, the protection, the benefits, and the opportunities to which its members are entitled. Nonviolent action does not hesitate to challenge "law and order," when they are used as a cover for practices that are unjust and hence illegitimate. It involves agitation and encourages controversy. At times it calls for civil disobedience, to test a law that is unjust or even to dramatize a protest action. Nevertheless, all of these activities, unlike those involved in violent action, uphold and in fact enhance the integrity of the system, even as they present challenges to it.

Two features of nonviolent action account for this phenomenon. First, nonviolent action is disciplined and restrained. Its purpose is never to create disorder or disruption per se, but to make a specific point and produce a specific effect. In refraining from violence, even under provocation, participants make very evident both their restraint and their commitment to those values on which any decent society is built. Violations of law are always of a very specific nature and usually based on the belief, often tested in court, that the law in question is invalid or unconstitutional. Those who break laws do so openly and are prepared to pay the price for their actions. In short, though nonviolent action involves a departure from normal politics and established channels (because these have failed to offer relief), it demonstrates a profound respect for law, for orderly processes, for the welfare of others, and for the basic human purposes that societies are designed to serve. It not only upholds the system, but actually strengthens it by attempting to restore to law and order the functions for which they were intended and thus their legitimacy.

Secondly, through the direct or symbolic enactment of an alternative pattern that corresponds to the desired state of affairs, nonviolent action provides a model of how the system might ideally work. The action is not designed to destroy the system, so

that a new one can be built in its place, but to push to the limits
its potential for change. Participants in sit-ins and Freedom Rides
acted *as if* facilities were integrated. Participants in voter regis-
tration drives acted *as if* the Constitution applied to them. Participants in the Poor People's Campaign are acting *as if* they had
access to the seats of power. Insofar as these assumptions do not
hold, the action presents a challenge to the system and may even
be technically illegal—as it was in the Freedom Rides and may
become in the Poor People's Campaign if participants push their
assumption to the point of sitting-in at Congressional offices. But
the challenge is one that affirms the integrity of the system by
forcing it to live up to its basic values.

In affirming the integrity of the system, nonviolent action
strengthens those forces within the system that are supportive of
the desired changes and, at the same time, reduces the forces of
repression. Thus it becomes easier not only to introduce new
patterns, but also to institutionalize them, to embed them in the
societal structure. Since the new patterns are, in significant ways,
continuous with the existing structure, they are more readily ab-
sorbed and maintained. Continuity is further enhanced by the
fact that nonviolent efforts toward change themselves anticipate
the new patterns they are designed to produce, so that new institutional arrangements can be built directly upon them.

In sum, nonviolent action mobilizes internal forces within
the social system, as well as within individual antagonists and bystanders, toward the acceptance and support of change. Moreover,
it sets into motion psychological and societal processes that facilitate the integration of new patterns, making changes both lasting
and cumulative. By its use of tactics that emphasize concern for
the adversary as a human being and by its choice of actions that
exemplify the desired state of affairs, nonviolence manifests here
and now the social conditions that it hopes to create for the future
and thus avoids the usual split between means and ends. The continuity between means and ends, between present and future,
makes possible the kinds of changes that our current racial crisis
calls for: changes that are built into the structure of individual
attitudes and of institutional arrangements.

CHAPTER 10

❧❧❧❧❧❧❧❧❧❧❧❧❧❧❧❧❧❧❧❧

INTRODUCTION

In this next chapter I turn to some problems relating to the context of social action. Specifically, I examine some of the social-psychological factors that inhibit political dissent in an atmosphere of national crisis brought on by international tensions. The studies and experiences on which I draw are mainly from the 1950s—from the years identified with the name of Senator Joseph McCarthy.

The atmosphere today is clearly very different from what it was in the McCarthy years. Yet the lessons taught by that period are by no means irrelevant. I argue that the legacy of the McCarthy era is still with us; though greatly attenuated, it is incorporated in our institutional mechanisms and habits of mind. Moreover, the Vietnam war and the dissent from it have created the atmosphere for reactivating repressive tactics. That there have been strong pressures to discredit and silence dissenters is beyond dispute; what is so different today, as compared to the 1950s, is that dissenters have refused to be intimidated.

Parts of this essay are based on a talk presented to the League of Women Voters of Menlo Park, California, in May 1955, under the title "Individual liberties in an atmosphere of conformity." The section on "The academic response to Mc-Carthyism" is a slightly edited version of a review-article on The Academic Mind, *entitled "Apprehension and academic freedom" and published in the* Public Opinion Quarterly, *1959, 23, 181–188. It is reprinted here by permission of the editor. Finally, I have drawn on a deposition I gave to an attorney of the American Civil Liberties Union in August 1966 in connection with the ACLU's action in the Federal Court in the District of Columbia, challenging the constitutionality of the House Committee on Un-American Activities.*

I have tried to bring these earlier materials together in a way that would highlight their relevance to the changed situation of today. However, even in the few months that have elapsed since the completion of Chapter Ten (in November 1967), the atmosphere has changed and some of my remarks do not sound quite as "current" as they might. The initiative of another Senator Mc-Carthy—Eugene of Minnesota—has helped to legitimize dissent from the Vietnam war. With President Johnson's decision not to seek re-election, with the restriction on bombing of North Vietnam, and with the initiation of the Paris peace talks, some of the demands of the dissenters have become established policy. As I write these prefatory lines, the negotiations in Paris are making no noticeable progress, and it is clear that there is still quite a distance between the Administration's Vietnam policy and that sought by its critics. Nevertheless, criticism of Administration policy is too widespread and institutionalized to be regarded as an act of treason.

While pressures against dissenters who merely advocate a change in policy have lost their bite, pressures against those dissenters who advocate resistance continue unabated. Only a few days ago, Benjamin Spock and three of his four codefendants were convicted of conspiracy to counsel draft evasion in a trial that represents a direct threat to the freedom to dissent. Moreover, there is a prevalent mood in favor of repressive tactics in response to those protests—in the ghettoes, at the universities—that are outgrowths of the Vietnam war, though not explicitly directed at it. Thus, despite the political developments of the last few months, the crisis atmosphere and the pressures against dissent cannot be ignored. In this context, it is still worth our while to examine the implications of the McCarthy years.

Pondering these implications may be particularly useful for some of the young radicals of today. One of their great strengths is that, having grown up in the post-McCarthy years, they have never acquired the debilitating pattern of caution that characterized the preceding generation. They have therefore had a valuable and refreshing influence on the renewal of activism. Their psychological distance from the McCarthy experience, however, may also have two negative effects.

First, they may have the false sense of assurance that it could never happen to them. I suspect that they are partly right, in that they have been socialized differently and have developed their political consciousness under a different set of circumstances. Nevertheless, under the appropriate social conditions, they too may be induced to yield to the powerful pressures exerted against dissenters, and an awareness of these social conditions is the best form of immunization.

Secondly, some of the young radicals display an intolerance toward their opponents that is disturbingly reminiscent of McCarthyist tactics. I agree with their feeling that the right to life of Vietnamese or of Negro ghetto children is a higher value than the freedom of speech or movement of government or university officials. Their position becomes dangerous, however, when it becomes so broadly extended that anything their opponents do or even say is by definition murder of innocent children and anything they themselves do is by definition defense of these children. This is the same logic that allowed McCarthyists to equate the dissent of others with acts of treason and their own repression of dissent with saving the country from destruction. Some young radicals are impatient with the stress on civil liberties and free-

*dom of speech as ends in their own right. Perhaps if they pondered
the implications of the McCarthy years, though they seem so re-
mote from their own experience, they might conclude that those
of us who question the status quo have a greater stake than anyone else in maintaining the integrity of civil-libertarian principles.*

Political Dissent in a
Crisis Atmosphere

In September 1967 the newspapers reported that the National Science Foundation had turned down a request for renewal
of a research grant by Stephen Smale, a brilliant young mathe-
matician at the University of California, Berkeley, and recipient
of the international Fields Prize in 1966. The request was not rejected outright but, according to the letter announcing the action,
was turned down "in its present form," in light of Smale's administration of his existing NSF grant. The case aroused attention
because Smale is an outspoken critic of U.S. policy in Vietnam
and one of the founders of the Vietnam Day Committee. In 1966,
while attending the International Congress of Mathematicians in
Moscow, he made the headlines by giving a press conference on
the steps of Moscow University in which he condemned U.S. involvement in Vietnam, comparing it to Soviet suppression of the
Hungarian uprising in 1956. In the course of his remarks, incidentally, he also criticized the lack of opportunities for dissent in
the Soviet Union.

Smale's actions at the Congress came under severe attack

in various quarters in Washington, particularly since his travel to Moscow was funded by an NSF grant. One of his most persistent opponents was Rep. Richard L. Roudebush, a Republican Congressman from Indiana and a member of both the House Committee on Science and Astronautics and the House Committee on Un-American Activities. Congressman Roudebush was apparently determined that Smale should not receive another grant from NSF and exerted influence in that direction. One of his aides was quoted as saying that "undoubtedly Smale's political activities had an effect on the decision not to approve the grant" and that "the NSF has been totally co-operative in this matter." A spokesman for NSF, though admitting that the agency had received several letters from the Congressman opposing Smale's application, insisted that "the action by NSF was not taken as a result of any political activity or pressures." There is little doubt that political pressures were exerted, but it is not clear to what extent they actually determined NSF action.

That times have changed since the era of Joseph McCarthy is evident from the reactions to the Smale case. It created a considerable stir in the scientific community and numerous letters of inquiry and protest reached the NSF office. By the end of September, the Foundation had apparently reversed its position and indicated a willingness to negotiate a renewal of Smale's grant along the lines of the existing arrangement (D. S. Greenberg, 1967a). As of November 1967, however, it had offered no public explanation of the original action and no evidence to support the allegations that Smale's administrative performance on his current grant was unsatisfactory or improper. In fact, according to D. S. Greenberg (1967b), who has covered the Smale case for *Science,* "at the time NSF made these allegations, it was in possession of documentary evidence which either clearly contradicted the allegations, or showed them to be based on trivial and technical departures from ambiguous regulations" (p. 618). Thus, despite the seemingly happy ending, the outlines of this case arouse a distinct sense of *déjà vu* in those of us old enough to remember the 1950s.

The Smale case is not an isolated incident. The pressures against dissenters have mounted as the American involvement in Vietnam has become more intense and more desperate and as dissent, in turn, has become more vociferous and widespread. In the summer of 1965, the Senate Subcommittee on Internal Security launched an investigation of the protest movement against the war in Vietnam; the resulting report, in the nature of its accusations and its "evidence"—though fortunately not in its effects—had all the earmarks of a document out of the McCarthy period (see Finman and Macaulay, 1966). In the summer of 1966, the House Committee on Un-American Activities, in its investigation of the antiwar movement, issued subpoenas to two leading universities to obtain the membership lists of campus organizations known to oppose U.S. policy in Vietnam; the university administrations complied immediately and without protest—though not without subsequent repercussions. In 1967, "General Westmoreland has said that dissent threatens military morale and encourages North VietNam. Rep. Mendel Rivers has accused the Justice Department and certain federal judges of 'conspiracy' in preventing prosecution of those who advocate defiance of the draft. Police in many cities have photographed or checked the license plates of participants in anti-war demonstrations. Professors who have called for an end to the war have been denied promotions. Muhammad Ali has been stripped of his boxing title for refusing, on grounds of conscience and erroneous classification, to be inducted into the Army" (Dissent in wartime, 1967). Most recently, the Senate Internal Security Subcommittee unanimously authorized its staff to conduct "a full and complete investigation of the activities of the National Conference for New Politics and any organizations and individuals affiliated or associated therewith" (New York Times, October 21, 1967). With 367 organizations represented at the Chicago convention of the National Conference for New Politics in September, this authorization, according to the Times, "amounts to a license to hunt for subversion in practically every organization of dissent now in existence."

The mood today is certainly different from that prevailing in the McCarthy period. Both government and university officials are sensitive to any criticism that they are stifling dissent or encroaching on academic freedom. In contrast to the McCarthy days, they are now responsive to pressures from both sides—not only to the pressures from superpatriots, but also to those from civil libertarians. Thus, Administration spokesmen have tried to discredit the opposition to the Vietnam war, but not to suppress it; similarly, some academic institutions have found ways of making political dissenters feel unwelcome, but they have been careful not to fire them. More than anything else, the present situation differs from the McCarthy period in that critics of existing policy have, for reasons that I shall discuss in the next chapter, by and large refused to yield to pressure and continued to exercise their freedom to speak out.

So far, then, the indications are that both potential dissenters and leaders of various establishments have learned some lessons from recent American history. But will these lessons be sufficient to withstand the increased pressures toward conformity that are bound to arise as the crisis in American society deepens— as our Southeast Asian involvement becomes more hopeless, as our national leadership becomes more distrusted and discredited, as internal cleavages become more pronounced, as the black revolution becomes more bitter and more violent? The continuation of present trends may well create a climate for the suppression of dissent at once more ruthless and more subtle than anything we knew in the McCarthy days. It would be foolhardy to assume, despite the current activism, that the hysteria and acquiescence that marked the early 1950s could not be repeated in the late 1960s. It might be useful, therefore, to recall some of the lessons learned during the McCarthy era and to note some of the principles established in that era which have survived its demise.

THE LEGACY OF McCARTHYISM

The underlying assumption of the loyalty and security programs developed in the early 1950s was the applicability of political criteria to all areas of life. A person's political beliefs and associations were deemed adequate bases for determining his suitability for a variety of jobs, and his right to public housing, tax exemption, or the guarantees of contracts. In order to partake of their rights and privileges as citizens, it became necessary for individuals to establish and avow their political loyalty. Those who failed the political test or did not wish to subject themselves to it (by refusing, for example, to sign a loyalty oath) were effectively excluded from the system. This propensity to impose political criteria on all aspects of life is characteristic of totalitarian states but completely alien to libertarian societies, in which most areas of life are allowed to operate independently and insulated from political interference.

Justification for the widespread use of political criteria supposedly lay in the need to protect the country from subversion. Taking the government's legitimate right to enforce the laws against espionage and sabotage as its starting point, the philosophy of the loyalty program distorted it by the use of two entirely illegitimate equations. First, it equated deviant political beliefs and associations with violations of national security and acts of treason, thus in effect abrogatng the principle that political expression can be curtailed only in the face of a clear and present danger. Secondly, it equated all areas of life with areas involving national security. Thus, tests of political loyalty, which—being based on belief rather than action—were of dubious validity even in sensitive domains, came to be applied indiscriminately in domains to which questions of national security had no conceivable relevance. Prime examples of the extension of political tests into clearly nonsensitive domains were the blacklisting of entertainers and writers with "questionable" political credentials by the film and broadcasting industries, and the exclusion of Communists from college teaching because of their political affiliation without any evidence of incompetence or improper behavior.

It took a long time, even after the supposed death of McCarthyism, before the use of political tests in such areas as college teaching and the entertainment industry began to be challenged effectively. For example, it was not until September 10, 1967, that Pete Seeger, the famous folksinger, after seventeen years on the broadcasting industry's blacklist, first appeared on network television. The discovery of a Communist teacher—and sometimes even of a Communist speaker—on a college campus still arouses passion in most state legislatures. By now, of course, the impropriety of political tests in these domains is widely though by no means universally recognized. For many years, however, the assumptions underlying the loyalty program were accepted extensively and without question throughout our society. They were so pervasive that even the critics of loyalty procedures during the

1950s generally shared them. Most of the early criticism was directed at the excesses of the loyalty program, not at its basic assumptions. Many critics objected to the indiscriminate, ungentlemanly, and stupid fashion in which loyalty procedures were applied and to the frequent disregard of due process of law and the rules of fair play. They complained that, in the atmosphere of hysteria created by McCarthyism, innocent, loyal citizens were being harassed, falsely accused of unorthodox beliefs and associations, and branded disloyal and subversive. They did not, however, question the basic legitimacy of procedures that required citizens to establish their political loyalty as a condition for participating in the life of their society.

One of my favorite illustrations of the extent to which even some of the most eloquent critics of the loyalty program were caught up in its framework of assumptions is the following excerpt from a speech by Kenneth Johnson (1954), Dean of the New York School of Social Work:

On June 22, 1954—after some oral discussion of several weeks—I received an invitation to go to Washington on the evening of November 19 next to speak to the Medical Service Corps Monthly Meeting at the Sternberg Auditorium of the Walter Reed Hospital. This is a program of the Office of the Surgeon General, Department of the Army.

I gladly accepted and willingly filled out some forms—*in triplicate*—so that I could be appointed Civilian Consultant for the month of November. (Remember my commitment is for *one* evening meeting at eight o'clock.) I am fully informed about travel, dinner, honorarium, publicity, and proceed to get material together for this anticipated engagement. I honestly think a contribution can be made in an effort to bring medicine and social work into a better and closer relationship.

On July 8, 1954, E. W. LaCross of Personnel Division, Office of the Surgeon General, Department of the Army (MEDCM—CP) wrote me as follows:

Dear Mr. Johnson:
The Medical Service Corps Division of this office has proposed your appointment as Consultant to the Surgeon General. Prior to your appointment, however, regulations require that certain forms be pro-

cessed. It is requested that the following forms be completed and returned to this office as soon as possible:

SF-85, Request for Report of Loyalty on Applicants and Appointees

SF-87, Fingerprint Chart

DA-1111, Certificate of Nonaffiliation with Certain Organizations

It is important that your fingerprints be legible. The entire first joint of each finger should be entirely inked and rolled. We suggest that two Fingerprint Charts be taken, so as to avoid loss of time in the event one is unclassifiable. Your fingerprints may be properly taken in the Civilian Personnel Office of the nearest Army installation, or if this is impractical, at your local police station.

For your convenience in returning these forms as soon as possible, a self-addressed envelope which requires no postage is also inclosed.

Sincerely yours,
E. W. LaCross
Personnel Division

On July 16, 1954, I wrote E. W. LaCross this letter:

Dear Mr. LaCross:

Your letter of July 8 distresses me. I do not blame you, but I am bound to blame those who are responsible for a policy that forces you to write such a letter.

I agreed with Colonel Black (MSC) to participate in the Surgeon General's Monthly Medical Meeting Series on the evening of November 19 next. I like the idea of this session and am anticipating preparing what I trust will be a genuine contribution.

Then you come along with: (1) request for report of loyalty data; (2) fingerprint chart; (3) certificate of nonaffiliation with certain organizations. You put great stress on the fingerprint business and suggest I go to a police station to have my fingerprints "properly taken."

Please, Mr. LaCross, how foolish can we get? How much more of this nonsense do we have to take?

Remember I was a member of the President's Employee Loyalty Board in 1946–47 and was chairman of the National Security Resources Board Loyalty Board 1947–49. Furthermore from 1949 to

1952, I served as a consultant to the Office of the Secretary of the Army on Employee Loyalty Problems which finally had to be resolved by the Secretary himself.

You just cannot expect decent, dignified citizens to take this sort of abuse.

Because of what you require of me, I must cancel my plan to come to Washington on November 19. Human dignity, self-respect and just plain commonsense, tell me to stay away—this I will do.

Maybe some day "we the people" will have recorded what is so heavily and so sorely on our hearts and our minds.

Sincerely yours,
Kenneth D. Johnson (pp. 446–447).[1]

This eloquent and admirable statement, by bringing out clearly and effectively the writer's objections to the foolish excesses of the loyalty system, probably made a significant contribution to the transition from the extremes of McCarthyism to a saner and less hysterical atmosphere. It is ironical, however, that the writer himself had served on a number of loyalty boards and that he featured this fact in his critique. He showed no awareness of the relationship between the principle underlying the loyalty boards on which he had served and the excesses of the loyalty program which he so rightly deplored. His statement, forthright and valuable though it is, did not attack or even question the basic assumptions behind the loyalty procedures, but merely their application to decent citizens like himself.

The execution of the loyalty program continued to produce many serious violations of individual rights throughout the 1950s and even beyond. But at least it became possible, during the second half of the decade, to fight these violations more effectively and to mount some defense against arbitrary procedures and unsubstantiated charges (see Kelman, 1957). More generally, this period saw a distinct change in atmosphere and a turning away from some of the excesses to which critics like Kenneth Johnson

---

[1] Reprinted from the *Social Service Review* by permission of the University of Chicago Press. Copyright 1954 by the University of Chicago.

had addressed themselves. It took much longer, however, before effective criticism was directed at the basic assumptions of the loyalty program and the legitimacy of its procedures. Such criticisms have emerged only gradually and slowly over the years and, though they have finally brought about some changes in attitude and practice, they have by no means eliminated the legacy of McCarthyism.

Many of the mechanisms and procedures for determining and controlling the loyalty of citizens, instituted at the height of the McCarthy era, survive to this day, despite concerted attacks against them and despite Supreme Court rulings that have narrowed their effective range. Loyalty procedures have become institutionalized throughout the government, even in nonsensitive agencies; though they may be used more wisely and responsibly than in the past, they continue to set criteria for federal employment. Loyalty oaths are repeatedly written into new pieces of legislation—most recently, for example, as an eligibility requirement under the Medicare Act—even though the Supreme Court has now declared some of the state loyalty oaths unconstitutional. The House Committee on Un-American Activities continues its operations, even though it is widely held that it has no legitimate function. The Subversive Activities Control Board, established under the Subversive Activities Control Act of 1950, has been reactivated by Congress, even though federal court decisions on the SACA have eliminated the Board's major powers and it has had no assignments for the past two years.

These mechanisms and procedures maintain and renew themselves because a minority of officials and legislators want them and a majority are afraid to oppose them. They remain slaves to the habits of caution and fear acquired in the McCarthy era. Most personnel officers would rather not take the chance of hiring a man who might turn out to be a Communist; and most Congressmen would rather not be publicly identified with the sacrilegious act of voting against a loyalty oath or against appropriations for the guardians of loyalty. And so the loyalty framework and its institutional bases remain intact. Although the assumptions underlying the loyalty system have by now been effectively challenged, the institutions—and the habits—built on these assumptions linger on, ready to be revived as a new crisis develops.

The Smale case, with which this chapter opened, is a good illustration of the fragility of the new attitudes that have, supposedly, replaced the loyalty framework of the McCarthy era. In the area of government support of scientific research, an important challenge to the use of political criteria was offered relatively early. It came in the report of the Committee on Loyalty in Relation to Government Support of Unclassified Research, issued early in 1956. The Committee was set up by the National Academy of Sciences, in response to a request by Sherman Adams, Special Assistant to President Eisenhower. In a letter addressed to Detlev Bronk, President of the National Academy of Sciences, and dated January 11, 1955, Mr. Adams sought the Academy's advice on ways of handling the problem of loyalty for recipients of government contracts or grants. The request was prompted by the concern that "governmental procedures must be designed to protect the reputation and standing in the community of innocent people." Mr. Adams made it clear, however, that he fully accepted the assumptions underlying loyalty procedures when he wrote: "No one will question the fundamental principle that only those who are loyal to our Government should be beneficiaries of Government grants-in-aid or contracts" (National Academy of Sciences, 1956, pp. 7–8).

The Committee appointed by Dr. Bronk did, however, question this fundamental principle. Its report concluded that support of unclassified research should be based entirely on considerations of scientific competence and that there is no reason for the application of loyalty requirements to such research. The report continued as follows:

The primary objective of a national research program is to serve the public interest by advancing knowledge in science as rapidly as possible. The only conceivable way by which a disloyal scientist doing unclassified research could sabotage this objective is by destruction of the scientific integrity of his own work. But the surest protection of the public interest against this kind of risk is the very process by which science protects itself from lack of objectivity. This process is the continuing scrutiny of the work of a scientist by his colleagues, in his own institution, his professional societies, the editorial boards of the journals in which he

seeks to record his findings, and also in the reviewing
bodies that examine both his past accomplishments and
his proposed program if he is to be considered for a
grant or contract. This critical scrutiny is well designed
to assess the competence of the individual and to detect
lack of scientific objectivity or integrity whatever may
be the cause (National Academy of Sciences, 1956, p. 6).

Elsewhere the report pointed out that "a fundamental contribution leading ultimately to the cure of cancer, providing it were
made generally available, would be no less beneficial to all humanity for having been made by a communist" (p. 4).

More than a decade has passed since this report was issued
and the political atmosphere in the United States has changed
markedly. But the Smale case raises the question whether a new
round is about to begin, in which political criteria will once again
be applied in areas to which they are entirely irrelevant, such as
decisions about a scientist's eligibility for research support. The
ingredients for such a revival are clearly present today. On the one
hand, as we have seen, the legacy of McCarthyism has not yet been
dissipated: The institutional mechanisms established in the early
1950s have not been dismantled, nor have the habits of thought
formed in those days been unlearned. On the other hand, we find
ourselves once more in an atmosphere of crisis, which character-
istically generates pressures toward conformity and the suppression of dissent.

✑ PRESSURES TOWARD CONFORMITY ✑

Strong pressures toward political conformity coupled with
infringements on civil liberties are most likely to arise at times of
national crisis and international tension. It is no mere happen-
stance that Joseph McCarthy's rise coincided with the Korean
War and that his personal power began to wane after that war
had come to an end. More generally, the loyalty program with its
violations of freedom of speech and of individual rights was very
much a product of the Cold War. The gradual improvement in
the civil liberties situation, starting around 1955, can be traced,
in large part, to the relaxation of Cold War tensions. And, of

course, the recent resurgence of pressures against dissent in the United States is directly related to the Vietnam crisis.

The dynamic connection between a crisis atmosphere and the suppression of individual freedoms is not difficult to understand. In a situation defined as critical for national survival, the leadership expects citizens to sacrifice their personal preferences and to forget their differences in the interest of national unity. Deviations are not tolerated. There is wide acceptance of the necessity to stand as one man—typically in the face of a common enemy—even if this has to be accomplished at the expense of the nonconformist. Individual freedoms and the right to dissent are regarded as luxuries that any decent citizen must be prepared to forego for the duration of the crisis.

There is the presumption, in a democratic society, that such a crisis is a temporary event, usually coterminous with a state of war. Restrictions on civil liberties are thus seen as temporary phenomena, made necessary along with other wartime sacrifices by the struggle for national survival. National crisis may, however, become a way of life. The exploitation or manufacture of crisis situations has always been the mainstay of authoritarian regimes, and a state of permanent crisis has allowed them to impose permanent restrictions on civil liberties. There is some basis for fearing that the Cold War is creating a similar philosophy of permanent crisis in our country. Though it has had its ups and downs, the Cold War has brought with it a constant obsession with the threat of Communism, a constant awareness of the danger of war and the possibility of nuclear confrontation, a constant emphasis on military needs and the requirements of weapons superiority. As the Cold War—punctuated by periodic hot wars—turns increasingly into a state of permanent crisis, the infringements on individual liberties and the pressures toward political conformity that it generates may well become a permanent part of the fabric of American life.

The inhibiting effects of a crisis atmosphere on individual liberties and the expression of dissent are mediated through various segments of the society. Superpatriots and right-wing activists are able to exercise far greater influence in a situation of perceived national crisis than in calmer periods; the established leadership, even if moderate in character, becomes inclined to seek or at least accept limitations on individual liberties; the general public, in a state of heightened anxiety, becomes willing and often eager to quash the nonconformist; and, finally, the potential dissenters themselves become cautious and helpless in the face of the pressures exerted upon them. Let us look at these four groupings in order.

For superpatriots, the crisis atmosphere offers a very special opportunity. In periods of relative calm, those who espouse extreme right-wing doctrines may be on the fringes of society, ignored or even ridiculed and written off as "crackpots." In periods of crisis, however, they are in a position to make issues that they can use for the advancement of their own power and ideology. They tend to exploit the crisis to the fullest by taking advantage of the fact that a real threat exists and that there is natural anxiety about this threat. Under these circumstances, both the established leadership and the population at large are more likely to pay attention to hysterical denunciations by these groups, which they might otherwise ignore. They are not only afraid to oppose them, lest they be accused of neglecting the need for national security and unity, but they are also more inclined to accept the validity of their point of view. Thus, by playing on the fears of the population and on the tensions of the leadership, extreme right-wing activists manage to have a decisive impact on policymaking and to dominate the body politic.

From their newly achieved positions of power and respectability, the superpatriots are able to hunt for heresies and to root out political deviance. One of their most effective weapons in this effort is the use of ambiguity. They apply the terms that characterize their enemy, whoever he may be, in a completely flexible way. Such epithets as Communist, subversive, or un-American have no specific, concrete meaning for them, but are used arbitrarily against anyone to whom they happen to object, regardless of his personal history. Thus, by the very simple verbal manipulation of equating political dissent with treason, they can transform the generally accepted demand for punishing traitors into a call for stamping out all nonconformity. In a crisis situation in which everyone is concerned about the survival of society, their verbal magic meets with little resistance.

The established leaders find it so difficult to resist super-patriotic excesses in a time of crisis because they themselves are preoccupied with the need for unbroken national unity and the danger of subversion. During a period of hot or cold war, the government finds it necessary to take strict security measures as protection against espionage and sabotage; and to discourage dissent lest it undermine the nation's image of militancy and determination. To accomplish these ends, it feels justified in imposing certain restrictions on the traditional liberties of the population. Moderate leaders of the establishment may find the style and methods of the extreme right wing distasteful, but they agree with its goals and believe that the extremists are only advocating steps that must, after all, be taken. They are, therefore, unable or unwilling to oppose the extremists and are inclined, in fact, to encourage them at first and to use them for their own purposes. Eventually, of course, they may discover that they have become the captives of the extreme right wing by legitimizing its goals, methods, and spokesmen, and that they cannot terminate the symbiosis at will. Such a discovery was finally made, for example, by the moderate Republican leadership, whose active or tacit support contributed importantly to McCarthy's power (see Rogin, 1967, especially p. 253ff.).

The established leadership may also contribute to the erosion of civil liberties—even if, in principle, it is committed to their maintenance—by its communications to the general public. In their efforts to mobilize the population in response to the crisis, officials are likely to stress the existence of an internal threat and the illegitimacy of dissent. As a result, they help to create an atmosphere of anxiety, suspicion, and intolerance, which further reinforces restrictions of individual freedoms. These restrictions may go further than they had intended, but the leaders' hands are often tied by the public moods that they themselves had brought into being.

In the general public, a crisis situation engenders concern about real threats to the social order. It also enhances the average citizen's suceptibility to propaganda that preaches intolerance and prejudice and his readiness for heresy hunting. The psychological dynamics of these reactions are similar to those found in studies of racial and religious prejudice. In the general atmosphere of anxiety created by the crisis situation, individuals feel threatened and inadequate. Many Americans today, for example, are afraid of what they perceive as the aggressive expansionism of the Communist world and are not convinced that the West will be capable of resisting these forces. Many of the needs that arise in such a situation of anxiety and doubt can be satisfied by the creation of a devil in the shape of the political deviate.

Thus, for example, the frustrations produced by a crisis situation create hostility for which the individual needs an outlet. The deviate can serve as a convenient scapegoat. The crisis situation also is likely to produce a need for a simple, understandable explanation of the society's problems. The deviate can provide this explanation. He can become a focus for anxieties whose origin has previously been vague, and he represents a clearly visible enemy who can be made responsible for everything. Rooting out the "internal enemy" also satisfies the need for getting something done, for feeling that the situation is being dealt with in an active way. It represents a concrete, noticeable accomplishment, even if it does not deal with the real issue. Finally, a situation of crisis creates a strong need for unity; fighting the deviate satisfies this need, both by eliminating a possible source of disunity and by clearly separating those who are "with us" from those who are "against us." A group's feeling of unity is increased when its members know whom they are united against. In short, then, on the level of what we might call the worried citizenry, a crisis situation is likely to create a variety of personal needs that are satisfied by intolerance and hatred of the nonconformist. These needs, together with the increased perception of threats, make the average citizen more susceptible to extremist propaganda and more favorable to the stifling of dissent.

The actions of the extreme right wing, the established leadership, and the worried citizenry in a crisis situation combine to exert enormous pressures on the potential dissenters, on those individuals who, in one or another area of their lives, may have ideas differing from those commonly held. Potential dissenters may be found in all segments of the population, though they are particularly likely to emerge from the intellectuals and the educated. The pressures on these individuals, generated in a crisis situation, inhibit dissent by discouraging them from developing independent opinions or engaging in independent actions with respect to political and social issues.

We can learn a great deal about the impact of such pressures on potential dissenters by examining the response of the academic community to the inroads of McCarthyism. To this end, let me review in some detail *The Academic Mind* by Lazarsfeld and Thielens (1958), which reports the major piece of social-psychological research on the effects of that period in American history.

THE ACADEMIC RESPONSE TO McCARTHYISM

In the spring of 1955 an extensive survey of academic people was conducted by the Bureau of Applied Social Research at Columbia University under the sponsorship of the Fund for the Republic. The purpose of the survey was to get some indication of the ways in which college professors were affected by the events of the preceding decade—"the difficult years," as the authors call them—a period characterized in the country at large by an overwhelming interest in loyalty and a concomitant concern with the political opinions and associations of college teachers. The sample was limited to college teachers in the social sciences, of whom 2,451 were interviewed in 165 colleges. The content was limited to attitudinal material—to the effects of the difficult years on the feelings, subjective experiences, and expectations of the social scientists (as distinguished from their possible effects on such objective criteria as the kinds of course taught and the kinds of research undertaken, which can best be studied by an analysis of various documents). *The Academic Mind* reports the findings of this survey.

The key analytical tool of the report is an *index of apprehension*, which is based on respondents' answers to two sets of items. The first set indicated the extent to which a respondent had "worried" about his political views, for example, about the possibility that they might be misrepresented by his students, or about the effect they might have on his career. The second set measured "caution," the extent to which a respondent reported that he had engaged in precautionary behavior, such as toning down his writing, in order to avoid controversial issues. The percentage of respondents who indicated apprehension varied considerably from item to item. Thus, 40 per cent said they had worried "about the possibility that some students might inadvertently pass on a warped version" of what they had said and lead to false ideas about their political views. But "only" 9 per cent said they had toned down something they had written lately because they "were worried that it might cause too much controversy."

The absolute percentages in and of themselves, of course, are very difficult to interpret. For one thing, as the authors point out repeatedly, there are no comparable data from earlier periods which would allow us to determine whether these percentages represent an increase or decrease in the level of apprehension. For another thing, it is quite possible that responses to these items are sometimes affected by distortions, committed with varying degrees of consciousness. This possibility allows the reader to reinterpret the absolute percentages according to which ax he happens to be grinding. Thus, several reviewers of *The Academic Mind,* who believed that the threats to academic freedom in the 1950s had been greatly exaggerated, argued that the percentages obtained overestimate the actual level of apprehension. Respondents, they said, may have magnified their anxiety about the danger they had experienced in order to magnify their own heroism in the face of such dangers. Let us accept this possibility of a "self-flattering disposition to engage in heroics." What these reviewers completely ignored, however, was that this very disposition, which would presumably have led to an upward distortion of the amount of "worry," should by the same token have led to a downward distortion of the amount of "caution" reported. In other words, people who like to think of themselves as heroes would be less likely to report that they modified their behavior in response to external threats. All in all, these two tendencies should have canceled each other out when the index of apprehension was computed.

The interviews themselves did not provide much basis for evaluating how much and what kind of distortion was likely to have entered into replies to specific questions. To obtain such information would have required a kind of probing into the implications of various responses and the motivations and defenses that lay behind them that was impossible (and probably not quite necessary) for a survey of this sort. Some relevant information on this point, however, can be found in David Riesman's field report, which is included in the book. Professor Riesman, himself a subject in the original survey, probed—with the use of interviews or mail questionnaires—the reactions of nearly 600 of the respondents to the interview experience. This Quaker Oats box approach—social scientists looking at social scientists who were looking at social scientists—produced some intriguing findings. There appear to have been a variety of problems with the interviews, at least in the best and the poorest colleges, and some 10 per cent of the respondents voiced rather serious complaints. When all is said and done, however, Riesman concludes that the interviews generally yielded an accurate picture of the respondents' feelings. Some respondents were unhappy because the interview did not give them the opportunity to present the nuances of their positions, and the complex rationales and rationalizations that lay behind their actions and beliefs. This does not mean, however, that the interview failed to give the study directors the opportunity to get adequate information on what they were interested in, the relative level of apprehension of each respondent.

If we assume, as I am inclined to do, that the reported percentages do represent a fair picture of the state of apprehension in the academic community, what conclusion can we draw? That, of course, is a completely subjective matter, depending on our level of aspiration. When I first read that "only" 9 per cent of the respondents reported that they toned down their writings, and "only" 12 per cent reported that they were more careful in recommending reference material to students lest it be criticized later for being too controversial, I felt pretty encouraged. My feelings changed, however, when I read the later chapters on "Patterns of Caution" in which concrete illustrations are given of the types of precautionary behavior that professors reported. From the point of view of my own value assumptions, the picture is gloomy when "as many as" a tenth of the respondents reported behavior of this type. My own feeling is that the percentages expressing worry and caution and the qualitative data on patterns of caution are enough to indicate that we are not dealing with an isolated phenomenon blown up out of proportion, but with a real corrosion of the academic atmosphere. This feeling becomes reinforced when one looks at the number and nature of "incidents"—attacks against the college or an individual teacher—reported by the respondents. There are 990 separate incidents reported at the 165 schools in the sample, many resulting in the firing, forced resignation, or failure to promote the teacher involved. Many of these incidents, it should be added, were corroborated, that is, reported by two or more respondents. As for the uncorroborated incidents, the authors go to great lengths to show, by a very skillful examination of internal evidence, that these are not likely to be spurious.

While the quantitative and qualitative description of the manifestations of apprehension is of great interest, it is by no means the major purpose of the book. The authors are fully aware of the limitations of the absolute percentages they report, and of the subjective nature of the interpretations that can be placed on them. Thus, in discussing their results on the "caution" items, they say very clearly: ". . . we don't mean to use any of these figures by themselves for describing the social reality. They are part of a larger set of indicators which, when taken together, will permit us to distinguish various levels of apprehension" (p. 79). None of the conclusions of the study is based on findings about the amount of apprehension per se. Rather, the index of apprehension is used as a rough way of dividing the sample into groups with varying degrees of apprehension. With the index of apprehension, then, as their major analytical tool, the authors are able to learn something about the nature of apprehension and about its relationship to a number of other variables. It is this complex of relationships between apprehension and other variables that is the heart of the argument of *The Academic Mind* and that permits us to draw some conclusions about the possible antecedents and consequences of apprehension.

The authors develop their argument with a brilliant display of virtuosity. They take the reader step by step, constructing indices where these become relevant, relating indices to each other, gradually bringing together all the necessary bits of evidence, until everything falls into place and their story is completely told. I found myself following the argument with a feeling of suspense and esthetic enjoyment, and becoming increasingly convinced as I read on. The argument is largely statistical and is developed in numerous figures and tables. Despite the fact, however, that the book is an almost continuous procession of data—the first table appears on the second page of text and the last figure appears only four pages before the end—it is by no means an example of rank empiricism. Data are presented selectively and interpreted fully so that they add up to a coherent picture. There is no explicit theoretical system in terms of which the material is organized, but there certainly are some underlying theoretical notions and a consistent interpretive scheme which give unity to the data.

What, then, is the content of the basic argument *The Academic Mind* develops? In their attempt to tease out the meaning of apprehension, the authors relate it to two sets of variables: characteristics of the individual social scientists, and characteristics of the situations in which they find themselves. As far as the individual teacher is concerned, the pivotal variable turns out to be his "permissiveness." An index of permissiveness is developed, based on a number of items which tap the respondent's willingness to have unorthodox views freely presented on campus. Permissive teachers clearly tended to be more apprehensive. This can be accounted for by a number of factors whose relationship to apprehension the authors have previously demonstrated. (1) Permissive teachers were more likely to be the objects of attack, since they were more likely to have engaged in controversial activities. (2) Permissive teachers were more vulnerable; for example, they were more likely to have belonged to controversial organizations —and hence had more reason to fear for their professional security. (3) Permissive teachers had a greater concern for the state of civil liberties and academic freedom in general. Thus, the concept of permissiveness helps to bring together the various personal determinants of apprehension. At the same time, an analysis of other characteristics that are associated with permissiveness makes it possible to evaluate some of the effects of the "difficult years." Permissiveness emerged as the prevailing norm in the social science profession. Permissive teachers were found to be more productive, more likely to achieve professional distinction, and more strongly oriented toward the profession at large. Thus, the relationship between apprehension and permissiveness would suggest that it was the better teachers, the ones with the greatest scope and involvement in their discipline, who were most affected by the "difficult years" and whose "effective scope" was threatened. One qualification that should be introduced here is that, while productivity was directly related to permissiveness, the relationship between productivity and apprehension was curvilinear. Teachers at a middle level of productivity were most apprehensive. One would guess that the highly productive, even if they were permissive, were less likely to become apprehensive, because they worked at better institutions and because they had a greater sense of professional security.

In the relationship of situational factors to apprehension, the pivotal variable turns out to be the quality of the school. A quality index was developed on the basis of certain objective data, obtained from independent sources. A major finding of the study is that the higher the quality of the school—independent of the size or type of college involved—the more incidents were reported, that is, the greater the number of accusations directed at the school or its professors. This is largely explained by the fact that the higher-quality schools tended to have more permissive, hence more vulnerable, social science faculties. Regardless of the reason, however, the fact remains that it was the high-quality institutions that were particularly under attack in the "difficult years." There was a redeeming factor, though: In schools of high quality, vulnerability and pressure were high, but administrative protectiveness was also high. In schools of low quality, on the other hand, the faculty was less vulnerable and the external pressures were smaller—but the administration was not likely to defend academic freedom if attacks did occur. The resultant level of apprehension was, therefore, almost equal in the two types of school, although its components were different. Level of caution was higher in the low-quality schools, and level of worry was higher in the high-quality schools. It was the faculties in schools of medium quality who were maximally affected by the "difficult years." These were schools that presumably attracted a relatively permissive faculty but were not able to offer them the kind of protection available in the top colleges.

These are the main outlines of the argument presented by

Lazarsfeld and Thielens. The whole complex of relationships they trace provides a good picture of the segments of the academic world that were most subject to attack and that were most likely to be affected by the atmosphere of the "difficult years." The combination of data they are able to bring to bear on the problem also makes it quite clear that the apprehension they found was not just an epiphenomenon but was indeed related to the pressures that the Cold War brought on. The pattern of relationships among apprehension, permissiveness, school quality, and administrative protectiveness would be difficult to understand in other terms. Above all, the very simple finding that, at all levels of permissiveness, the greater the number of incidents at a college the higher the level of apprehension of its faculty clearly suggests that reality factors were involved, some of the reviewers of *The Academic Mind* notwithstanding.

There is one additional finding of the study to which I would like to devote a few comments. The general tendency was for respondents who were more apprehensive to be more "activist," at least in a mild sort of way. They were more likely to indicate an intention to stand up for freedom of expression; they were more likely to belong to controversial organizations and to subscribe to liberal magazines. Thus, by and large, the apprehension was not of a paralyzing nature and there remained some resistance to pressures. This finding is clearly consistent with the general relationship between apprehension and permissiveness, although the authors do not explicitly deal with it in that context. The apprehensive people, being more permissive, were more likely to be concerned with freedom of expression, to belong to controversial groups, and so forth, and thus, despite their apprehension, they manifested these behaviors to a greater extent. The question still remains, however, why apprehensive people, who showed other signs of precautionary behavior, did not also withdraw in *these* respects. To explain this, the authors suggest that the teachers (presumably this would be particularly true for permissive teachers) were subject to cross-pressures from the general community and their own colleagues. This led to a pattern of "cautious activism," which was characterized by public courage (in matters that were largely restricted to the campus and observable by colleagues) and private caution (in matters that were not readily observed by colleagues but might have repercussions in the community at large).

I would like to suggest a somewhat different explanation, not inconsistent with the one the authors present, but putting more emphasis on the subtle psychological manifestations of apprehension, regardless of the overt level of courage a teacher displayed. It seems to me that the main difference between the items that the authors use to indicate "activism" and the items that enter into the apprehension index can be described in terms of a gross-subtle dimension. Despite his apprehension, the permissive teacher may have shown resistance in situations in which the issues were clearly drawn and in which he had to face, in a very gross way, the demands made by his principles. Questions about his intended reaction to encroachments on freedom of expression certainly confronted him directly with the issue. Similarly, dropping his subscriptions to liberal magazines or his membership in controversial organizations would have been so gross a change that he could hardly have avoided its implications. In such situations, involving conscious choice, he may have displayed an "activist" pattern. This may have been partly a response to implicit pressures from colleagues, but it may also have been a genuine manifestation of the courage of his convictions. Some individuals may even have reacted in a "counterphobic" fashion; they may have gone out of their way to engage in defiant behavior. Others may have fluctuated between caution and defiance, in response to the internal conflict they experienced.

Regardless of the amount and kind of courage they displayed, however, these persons may have been very much affected by the "difficult years." They may have worried more about the political implications of everything they said and did for fear of the possible repercussions. They may have lost some of their spontaneity, some of their freedom in expressing ideas. This increased concern about the consequences of their actions may have led to rather subtle changes in behavior—to a tendency, for example, to avoid making statements in class or assigning readings to their students that might cast doubt on their own political orthodoxy. It is these subtle changes, described by Lazarsfeld and Thielens in their chapter on "Patterns of Caution," that were tapped by the "caution" items. Typically, the person would not even have been conscious of the fact that he had changed his behavior. Only gradually, as he looked back upon his own behavior over a period of time, he might have observed that such subtle changes had taken place. Often, it may have been the interview itself that stimulated such introspection and, almost for the first time, made him aware of what had happened to him. For many, courage and cowardice in the simple sense may not have been the issue at all. They may have been courageous where courage was clearly called for, and yet the "difficult years" may have had a corrosive effect on them. In fact, once the issue of bravery has been introduced, we are already caught in a less-than-favorable intellectual atmosphere. If it requires an act of courage—and I mean personal rather than intellectual courage—for a teacher to say what is on his mind or to read what he wishes to read, then we have come uncomfortably close to a politicization of intellectual life that inhibits independent thought.

I place so much emphasis on this last point because it represents one effect of the "difficult years" that survived long after McCarthy had been discredited and the excessive tactics identified with his name had abated. Direct attacks and overt courage in the face of such attacks had ceased to be important issues. But, at least throughout the 1950s, the subtle patterns of caution described in *The Academic Mind* continued to dominate the academic community. Many professors continued to be preoccupied with the political safety of their words and deeds and extremely reluctant to take a public stand on controversial issues. It was not until the emergence of the civil rights movement in the early 1960s that a new pattern began to manifest itself.

THE POTENTIAL DISSENTER

The Academic Mind illustrates the ways in which the pressures generated in a crisis situation may inhibit the overt behavior of potential dissenters by increasing their level of apprehension. Fearful of the consequences of political nonconformity, which, in the crisis atmopshere, is met with severe social disapproval as well as with more specific penalties, such as dismissal from employment and blacklisting, they comply with the pressures that are, directly or indirectly, exerted upon them. They disengage themselves from legitimate activities and associations because others regard these with suspicion, and they limit their involvement in controversial political and social issues to avoid the risk of future damage. It is especially interesting that many of the respondents in the Lazarsfeld-Thielens study, who showed no gross changes in their overt behavior in response to the pressures, were nevertheless affected by them in subtle ways. The resulting pattern of generalized caution and constriction, as we have seen, is particularly likely to maintain itself even after the direct pressures have been reduced.

A further illustration of the inhibiting effects of a crisis atmosphere on overt behavior is provided by another social-psychological study, carried out in 1951 and concerned with the reactions of federal civil servants to the pressures of the McCarthy era (Jahoda and Cook, 1954). A large proportion of the respondents in this study did indeed restrict their political activities in response to these pressures. What is most important, however, is that the restriction extended beyond the specific activities that were directly disapproved. Many of the respondents reported that they were avoiding activities that had never been specifically questioned and that, by no stretch of the imagination, could be considered subversive. The assumption seemed to be that one never knows what might, some time in the future, become questionable and be viewed as subversive or as providing clues of subversion. Thus, these federal employees adopted voluntary restrictions upon their reading matter, ownership of books, subscriptions to periodicals, membership and activity in organizations, and discussion of controversial subjects. For example, one respondent said: "I buy *The Nation* from a newsstand; there is no sense in being on their subscription list." Another said: "I dropped out of the American Veterans Committee; it isn't on the list but it may get there."

Thus, the Jahoda-Cook study points to another possible long-run effect of the restriction in political behavior produced by the pressures of a crisis situation. The habit of compliance may gradually lead to a general attitude of cautiousness, an avoidance of any kind of activity or statement that might possibly be interpreted as subversive, and a tendency to say and do only things that are harmless and conventional. The area of conformity tends to be broadened as individuals voluntarily set up boundaries that are far more restrictive than those imposed from the outside.

There is a second type of reaction to the pressures generated in a crisis situation that goes even deeper than compliance and inhibition in overt behavior—a reaction at the level of political and social *beliefs*. The crisis atmosphere may foster a complete acceptance of the conventional point of view on social and political issues and of the notion that deviation as such is bad. The individual would thus conform not simply out of fear of the consequences of deviation but because he is convinced that his own personal opinions are wrong. This type of reaction was described very well by Tocqueville in a book first published in 1835: "Not only does he mistrust his strength, but he even doubts of his right; and he is very near acknowledging that he is in the wrong, when the greater number of his countrymen assert that he is so. The majority do not need to force him; they convince him" (Tocqueville, 1954, pp. 275–276). This type of reaction is even more dangerous than the compliance reaction because it undermines the basic values of individual responsibility and independent thought. Ultimately, it tends to lead to a complete dependence of the individual's self-esteem on his agreement with majority opinion and his acceptance by others. If he finds himself in disagreement, then—far from insisting on his right to hold nonconformist views—he reacts with guilt and readily takes all the blame upon himself.

That strong pressures toward uniformity may produce such a reaction is quite consistent with what we know about individuals' extreme dependence on social support for the stability of their beliefs. Even a person's beliefs about himself and his basic characteristics are vulnerable when social support for them is lacking or has been removed. Under the appropriate experimental conditions, for example, subjects have manifested changes, not only in their attitudes, but also in their self-images, to bring them into line with the communications of others. Beliefs and actions that have primarily an institutional definition—such as those relating to a person's loyalty to his country or his group and to the quality of his citizenship or group membership—are particularly dependent on social support since, after all, their entire origin is social in nature. Thus, when his fellow citizens, the mass media, and legitimate political agencies question the loyalty of his beliefs and actions, many a potential dissenter is bound to be beset with serious self-doubts. There are very few people who have the conviction that they themselves can define what is American or un-American, what is loyal or disloyal, what is proper or improper behavior for a citizen, with complete disregard of majority opinion and, in particular, of those social and political institutions within whose legitimate domain of operations such judgments are perceived to rest.

The research on thought reform or what is popularly known as "brainwashing" is quite instructive in this connection. There is no reason to assume that the effects produced in such situations have been due to drugs, hypnosis, or torture. They can be understood in terms of general social and psychological processes that "brainwashing" sets into motion. One of the major weapons used in Chinese thought-reform efforts directed at civilian prisoners was the mobilization of the victim's guilt (Lifton, 1961). Given the proper circumstances, guilt feelings can be aroused in almost anyone, since there is no one who has not, on occasion, had doubts about his own actions. But the key element in the "brainwashing" situation, according to many of the social scientists who have studied it, is the deprivation of social support for the individual's own beliefs and values. Typically, this has been accomplished by isolating him from others who share his frame of reference. In the prisoner-of-war camps for Americans in Korea, for example, systematic efforts were made to break up the solidarity of the group and to deprive prisoners of the opportunity for consensual validation of their opinions and beliefs. All of the sources of communication and information were controlled by the prison authorities; prisoners received only specially selected mail from home and no other news from their own country. They were unable to talk freely to others who shared and supported their earlier beliefs and values (Schein, 1961). These conditions were effective in undermining their beliefs in themselves, in their own ideals, and in their own society.

The pressures generated in a crisis situation do not, of course, produce physical isolation in the sense in which it was possible in Chinese prisons or in Korean POW camps. They can be quite effective, however, in producing social and psychological isolation of the potential dissenter. He finds himself surrounded by a consensus that insists there is only one way for normal and decent citizens to view the present reality. Moreover, he finds himself at odds with those official agencies that are perceived to speak with authority about the proper behavior of the loyal citizen. As a result, he begins to doubt and reject himself, becomes confused about his own beliefs and values, and constricts his thinking about social issues. At the height of the McCarthy era, one often heard of extreme reactions in which individuals under attack for actual or alleged political deviance accepted the implication that they were wrong, that they had sinned, and that they deserved punishment. A typical story concerns an individual, who, when notified that his passport application was being held up, immediately assumed that this was due to some questionable activities on his part. Although he had never thought of himself as a subversive before, he began to search in his past and remembered, for example, that at one time he had subscribed to the *New Republic* and that his sister had attended Socialist meetings. By the time he learned that the delay had been due to a minor technical problem, unrelated to security considerations, he had developed strong feelings of guilt and self-rejection for his personal failings and had come close to a psychotic breakdown.

In short, in a crisis atmosphere, not only dissident action but even deviant belief is sharply discouraged. A potential dissenter discovers very quickly and painfully that nonconformity of any kind is socially disapproved and cause for suspicion. In response, he is likely to develop a pattern of withdrawal from political activity and from attention to social issues in general. He may become apathetic in the conviction that the less one does the less likely he is to run into problems. He may develop a philosophy of never rocking the boat, never placing himself in a position where his actions might be questioned, and blandly engaging only in those activities that are clearly noncontroversial by anyone's standards. This overcautiousness and apathy and the resultant constriction in his intellectual horizons and range of activities may eventually cause him to avoid not only the taking of potentially questionable actions, but also the thinking of potentially questionable thoughts. Furthermore, the crisis-generated pressures, by effectively depriving him of social support for his beliefs and values and by throwing into question his quality as a person and as a citizen, may create serious self-doubts in him, undermine the stability of his beliefs, make him confused about his own values, and cause him to accept the reality of his own guilt.

The self-doubt and excessive caution generated in potential dissenters deprives society of the contributions of precisely those individuals on whom a democratic system depends for critical thinking about social issues, for a willingness to entertain new ideas, and for the development of alternatives to existing policies. Once these individuals become more constricted, cautious, and apathetic, they can no longer enact effectively their roles as citizens in a democratic society, roles that require them to think independently, to take positions on public issues, and to act in line with their beliefs. Even those critics of official policy who have not experienced personal attacks may curtail their actions and thoughts, having witnessed the consequences suffered by others. We know from totalitarian societies that a small number of "test cases" may have widespread effects. By making an example of a few dissenters and independent thinkers, such societies manage to create a general atmosphere of political conformity, apprehensive caution, and constricted imagination. Our society is not immune to such forces.

➢ CONCLUSION ➢

If we are to preserve the right to dissent and other individual liberties in the years to come, we must be fully aware of the dynamic connection between infringements of such liberties and the existence of a crisis atmosphere rooted in international tensions. As long as our government is committed to the pursuit of the Cold War and of counterinsurgent adventures abroad, the fate of our political freedoms at home will remain precarious. They can be securely re-established only if we make fundamental changes in our foreign policy and in the national priorities that are dictated by that policy.

This does not mean that efforts to safeguard civil liberties are irrelevant as long as the Cold War continues. It is essential that we insist on these liberties and practice them and that we resist all infringements upon them, if they are to survive the pressures of the crisis atmosphere. At the same time, however, we must concern ourselves with eliminating the state of permanent crisis that creates the long-run conditions for assaults on political freedom. As individuals, we must not only protest the war system and its increasing stranglehold on our society, but we must look for concrete ways of withdrawing our personal support from it.

To take scientists as a case in point, it was extremely important and encouraging that so many protested the threats to Stephen Smale's freedom to dissent. Scientists must also recognize, however, that when they develop the weapons for the Cold War and for Vietnam-type interventions, and when they participate in secret research for military purposes, they are helping to create the conditions for the very violations they are protesting. In offering their scientific skills to destructive purposes and in abandoning the open exchange of findings that is so central to the scientific ethos, they contribute to an atmosphere in which the encroachments of the state on individual liberties and personal values are routinely accepted. Thus, scientists can contribute most effectively to protecting the freedom to dissent by withholding their personal participation in classified research and in the further development of the instruments of warfare.

CHAPTER 11

INTRODUCTION

In Chapter Ten I discussed some of the conditions that inhibit dissent and activism, drawing primarily on the experiences of the Joseph McCarthy era and its aftermath. The end of the 1950s, however, and particularly the past three or four years, have seen a dramatic surge in activism. The freedom to dissent continues to be threatened and is likely to be faced with serious challenges in the years to come, but the atmosphere today is remarkably different from that of ten years ago.

In the final chapter of this volume I address myself to the sources of this new activism. Specifically, I discuss the protest movement in opposition to the war in Vietnam, which represents, in my view, a new departure in social action, both in quantitative and in qualitative terms. Among the innovations of that protest movement were the teach-ins, in which I participated actively from their inception at the University of Michigan early in 1965.

The teach-ins provide an excellent illustration of the substantive *contributions that intellectuals in general, and social scientists in particular, can make to the policy process. The data, the concepts, and the modes of analysis that they can bring to bear are of great potential usefulness in the evaluation of existing policies and in the search for alternatives. Specialized knowledge, of course, is no substitute for moral indignation, nor is critical analysis a substitute for personal commitment in dissent. These are, however, essential components of dissent to which social scientists and other intellectuals have something unique to offer.*

Chapter Eleven, after describing the increase in activism in recent years, examines the context of the new activism and some of the conditions that account for it. In turning specifically to the reasons for the profound concern that the Vietnam war has generated, it presents a substantive analysis of the long-run implications of American action in Vietnam for our foreign policy process. The chapter and the book conclude with a discussion of the functions of dissent—particularly, but not exclusively, on the part of intellectuals—in the face of such national disasters as the Vietnam war.

In writing this chapter, I have drawn on four earlier papers. One is my introductory address at an international conference on "Alternative perspectives on Vietnam," held at the University of Michigan in September 1965. This address, entitled "New departures in social action: The response of intellectuals to the Vietnam conflict," originally appeared in Alternative Perspectives on Vietnam: Report on an International Conference *(see Converse, Kelman, and Vandenberg, 1966). A second paper on which I have drawn is an address presented in Detroit on April 18, 1966, as part of "Focus on Vietnam," an educational series sponsored by the American Friends Service Committee. Thirdly, portions of my "Notes on faculty activism," published in the* Letter to Michigan Alumni, *1966, pp. 2 and 9–11, are reprinted here with the editor's consent. Finally, a slightly expanded version of my contribution to a symposium "On civil disobedience, 1967," published in the* New York Times Magazine, *November 26, 1967, pp. 126–128, is reprinted in the last section of this chapter by permission of the editor.*

Alternative Perspectives on
Foreign Policy:
The Intellectual and the Dissenter

In focusing on student unrest on American campuses (with its counterparts in many other countries), we sometimes tend to ignore the upsurge in activism at the faculty level. Faculty activism is different in character and is, of course, less dramatic and intense than some of the student activities that have captured the headlines. Yet it does represent, in its own right, a new departure in social action. Moreover, while the new faculty activism is to some degree stimulated by and supportive of student activism, it also has independent roots. It is part of a wider movement within the American intellectual community—among scholars and scientists, artists and writers, philosophers and religious leaders— toward greater involvement in the vital issues of the day.

When I speak of activism here, I do not refer to the adoption of a particular set of action techniques, but to the willingness to commit one's self to a definite position on policy issues, to stand up for this position in public, and to enter actively into the policy debate. While there are many variations in degree and kind of activism, they all imply at least some readiness to place commitment above "respectability" as it is popularly defined—by engaging in forms of protest that are more obtrusive than the usual "letter to your congressman" or by taking a stand that represents a break with an apparent national consensus.

My analysis is concerned with only part of the spectrum, with activism that reflects a commitment to the causes of social justice and world peace. In other words, in terms of the common distinction, it is concerned with left-wing rather than right-wing activism. Because of the ambiguity and historical irrelevancy of the left-right dichotomy, I prefer to distinguish between orientations based on an *inclusive* definition of national and international society and those based on an *exclusive* definition. Thus, the kind of activism that I refer to is concerned, domestically, with bringing into full participation in American society those elements that have heretofore been excluded from its benefits and even its protection; and, internationally, with the establishment of a world community whose members collaborate on efforts to maintain security and to reduce the disparity between rich and poor nations.

To establish the fact that there has indeed been an increase in this kind of activism among American intellectuals would require comparison between the present and earlier historical periods. Such comparisons are difficult to make, since comparable data on the level of activism in different periods are not readily available, and since the nature of the response depends so much on the types of issues to which it is addressed and on the types of communication media through which it is expressed. If we restrict ourselves to recent history, however, there seems to be little doubt that there has been a marked increase in activism, in the willingness to become involved and to take a stand, since the early years of the Cold War. In recent years we have seen ever more active participation of intellectuals in the civil rights struggle, mobilization of a considerable segment of the academic community in opposition to civil defense and in support of a test-ban treaty, and resistance to infringements on freedom of speech and the right to dissent. Perhaps a new level of activism has been achieved with the response of academic people and other intellectuals to the war in Vietnam. It seems fair to propose that we have embarked on a new phase of participation in foreign policy issues by the intellectual community, qualitatively different from the type of participation that we have known in the past.

Many intellectuals have, of course, been involved over the years in various aspects of the peace movement—in activities oriented toward a sane nuclear policy, extension of disarmament, reduction of international tensions, and establishment of patterns of international security and international cooperation. Activities along these lines have shown a marked increase in scope since the time of the Berlin crisis in 1961, and have received further impetus through such events as the proposal for a massive civil defense program and the Cuban missile crisis. Many intellectuals have not only participated in these activities as citizens, but have entered into the policy debate from the vantage of their areas of speciali- zation. They have tried to apply their special knowledge and intellectual approach to the analysis of policy issues and to the development of proposals for policy alternatives.

At the same time, there has been a steady development of peace research as an area of systematic theoretical and empirical investigation, which has also shown a marked increase in scope during the past decade. It is not possible to draw sharp bound- aries that would define the area of peace research, but peace research certainly includes or utilizes studies of the properties of international systems, of conflict and conflict resolution, of foreign policy decision-making, of international attitudes and public opinion in the foreign policy process, of political ideologies and loyalties, of international organization and cooperation, of the conditions for and consequences of disarmament, of political and social change in the developing world, and of processes of negotiation and bargaining. Peace research does not differ—and rightly so—from any other research on international relations or political behavior, in terms of the criteria for scientific objectivity and validity that it tries to meet, just as cancer research does not differ in these respects from any other biochemical or microbio- logical investigations. Yet the selection of the problems to which the peace researcher addresses himself is based, at least in part, on his desire to contribute to a peaceful world order.

Concern with policy issues on the part of American scholars and efforts to apply their specialized knowledge to analysis of these issues are, thus, by no means an entirely new phenomenon. Yet the activities that were inaugurated with the "teach-in move- ment" of 1965 strike me as a new departure in the involvement of intellectuals in the debate of foreign policy issues. The magni- tude of the response that the Vietnam crisis has elicited is un- precedented, both in terms of the number of individuals who have become activated and in terms of the amount of energy that they have been willing to invest in the movement. These indi- viduals vary considerably in their political views, in their concep- tions of social action, and in the alternative Vietnam policies that they favor, but they share a deep concern about the direction and implications of our Vietnam policy and a commitment to the search for alternative solutions.

The teach-in movement, in bringing together thoughtful analysis and debate of policy issues with deep concern about fundamental value questions, introduced a form of social action uniquely appropriate for the intellectual and specifically designed to use the resources available to him. It brought into active and concerned participation in policy debates not only the directly relevant specialists within the intellectual community, but the entire range of scholars and intellectuals, many of whom had had no prior history of political involvement. Thus, the teach-ins helped to forge the combination of policy analysis with value concern into a vigorous protest movement.

In the early days of the teach-in, there was some discussion about whether the movement represented debate *or* protest. This discussion missed, in my opinion, the central meaning of the whole movement to its participants: Study, analysis, and debate *were* their way of protesting, of expressing the depth of their concern about existing policies, and of beginning the search for alternatives. Since these early days, of course, activism among intellectuals has clearly moved beyond debate. On the one hand, debate seemed to have reached the limit of what it was able to accomplish. On the other hand, the draft became an increasingly pressing issue and many older activists turned their attention to supporting the growing number of draft resisters. In 1967, for example, these developments led thousands to sign the "Call to Resist Illegitimate Authority," which figured so prominently in the conspiracy trial of Benjamin Spock and his codefendants. In 1968, in response to the Spock indictment, many thousands again signed complicity statements. In short, the protest movement that began with the teach-ins proved to be more than a temporary spurt of activism. It adapted itself to the changing circumstances and continued to involve large segments of the intellectual community.

⊰ THE CONTEXT OF THE NEW ACTIVISM ⊱

If I am correct in my assumption that we are witnessing a new and qualitatively different type of involvement on the part of intellectuals in foreign and other policy issues, how can we account for this phenomenon? Let me speculate, first, about some of the experiences that have produced a generally more favorable atmosphere for activism in the 1960s, and then turn more specifically to the sources of the intense concern that the Vietnam war has generated. The conduciveness of the general atmosphere to greater activism in recent years can be traced to three sets of factors: the weakening of the barriers against speaking out that were so powerful in the early 1950s; the increased salience of the inevitable interplay between knowledge and values; and the heightened sense of urgency about the shape of current events.

Weakened barriers against activism. In the preceding chapter I described the changes in the climate for political dissent that have marked the ending of the McCarthy era. Not only have the McCarthyist forces been discredited and the apprehensions of the academic community been reduced, but there has also been a revulsion against the passive and unprincipled response of so many elements in the universities and throughout our society to the challenge of the McCarthy era. A new generation of students, who had not personally experienced McCarthyism at its height and who could not understand the calculating cautiousness that had become second nature to the generation that preceded them, provided the impetus for a newly awakened activism that eventually spread to their elders.

The specific issue responsible for the re-emergence of dissent in the wake of the McCarthy era was provided by the civil rights movement. Civil rights activism, though it used unorthodox methods, was less controversial and less vulnerable to attack than, for example, peace activism, since it was so clearly consistent with basic American values and with national policy. Thus, the civil rights movement helped to revive the habit of speaking out, which gradually spilled over to issues of foreign policy. Civil rights action served as the necessary bridge from the apprehensive silence of intellectuals during the 1950s to their current activism on a number of different fronts.

In this connection, let me point out that there is also a close substantive connection between the struggle for racial justice in the United States and the opposition to the war in Vietnam. The struggle of Negro Americans is part of the worldwide human rights revolution that is gripping developing countries like Vietnam. The American civil rights movement, in fact, was spurred on several years ago by the emergence of independent African nation-states. Now it, in turn, is fostering a greater awareness and understanding among Americans of the social revolutions in developing countries. American intellectuals who have been sensitized by the civil rights movement to the problem of a Negro community with a history of almost total exclusion from the larger society can respond more readily to the needs of populations with a history of almost total exclusion from the benefits of the modern world. The deep concern and moral indignation generated by our Vietnam policy are continuous with those generated by the plight of the American Negro.

Barriers against activism were further weakened by the détente in Soviet-American relations, which reduced the crisis atmosphere in the country and the strong preference for thinking of things in terms of black and white. The Vietnam crisis, of course, has again brought pressures against dissent and the familiar tactic of equating it with disloyalty. One wonders whether we will have a full-scale revival of McCarthyism as the Vietnam war ends with something less than American victory and as we continue to re-enact, in our relations with China, the unrelieved Cold War approach that we have abandoned in our relations with the Soviet Union, an approach based on an undifferentiated image of a totally evil (yet highly rational) enemy. If this happens, there is the danger—which I discussed in Chapter Ten—that activism will again be inhibited. Though this is a possibility that we must actively confront, I tend to believe that the response of intellectuals will be more militant than it was the last time. It seems that some lessons have been learned and that the habit of speaking out has become more firmly established.

Barriers against activism arise not only out of apprehension, but also out of alienation from the sources of power, out of the feeling that one's action is unlikely to have any impact on policy. With the beginning of the Kennedy Administration, this particular barrier to action was also weakened. There was a widespread feeling in the academic community that the Kennedy Administration was interested in and responsive to the ideas of intellectuals and there was indeed evidence that some of these ideas were being adopted. Thus, a new sense of the relevance of their own actions began to develop among intellectuals. Action often took the form of encouraging and supporting certain Administration moves (such as the negotiation of the test-ban treaty), but it also took the form of dissent and opposition to certain Administration policies (such as the creation of a massive civil defense system). This fairly recent experience of relevance has probably contributed to the continuing activism among intellectuals, even though the Johnson Administration has clearly been unresponsive to their ideas. As a matter of fact, it is reasonable to suppose that members of the academic community have found it particularly frustrating to have their contributions ignored, since they have become accustomed to at least a sympathetic hearing; and that this frustration has given added strength to their criticism of policies from which they dissent.

The interplay between knowledge and values. The teach-in movement, as I have described it, represented a bringing together of certain kinds of specialized knowledge with a sensitivity to value questions in social life. The nature of their work, of course, often brings scholars and intellectuals to the intersection between knowledge and values, but only recently has this relationship become a deliberate focus for political protest. What has happened, it seems to me, is that the inevitable interplay between knowledge and values has become more salient and that members of the academic community, in particular, have been more sharply confronted by it.

In recent years the scholar and scientist have become increasingly involved in the execution of policies at all levels of government. The image of the university as an ivory tower is clearly a thing of the past. University professors serve as consultants and as members of study commissions; they carry out projects under contract with government agencies; many of them commute regularly between Washington and their campuses; others take leaves of absence from their university duties to accept assignments in one or another government office. Because of the heavy involvement of the academic community in the policy process, many university people have acquired a stronger sense of responsibility for the nature of the policies that the government pursues. They are uncomfortable with being "mere technicians." They recognize more sharply that they cannot simply contribute their knowledge without asking questions about the uses to which this knowledge will be put, that active participation in the execution of policy must be accompanied by an active concern with the formulation of policy.

The Vietnam war has helped to remind us forcefully that the universities themselves are deeply involved in the war system. They carry out military research, much of it classified and thus directly contradictory to the university's basic values, and some of it contributing to biological or chemical warfare. They train military officers. They provide facilities to recruiters for the military agencies, the Central Intelligence Agency, the manufacturers of napalm. They participated, for a while, in the selection of men for military service. They have been known, in some cases, to carry out projects for the CIA. It has become clear that the university is not purely devoted to the neutral pursuit of knowledge but, by virtue of its policies and actions, often takes a stand on one side of a controversial value issue. Professors have become more sensitive, therefore, to the uses to which the university is put and, more generally, the uses to which their own knowledge is harnessed.

Another important factor with which professors have been confronted is the active concern about the interplay of knowledge and values expressed by students. I shall not attempt to analyze here the sources of this concern among students, although it is certainly related to the rapidly changing nature of the world in which the student finds himself. Whatever the sources of their concern, many students—some committed to an activist role, others searching for a basis of commitment—have presented a powerful challenge to the comfortable assumption that the university can deal with facts and theories while ignoring questions of value, questions about the ends that these facts and theories are to serve. Though there is no simple formula for determining the proper place of value questions in a university education, student concern has provided a needed reminder that these questions cannot be ignored.

The teach-ins struck a responsive chord in students, much beyond anyone's expectations, because they were based on the proposition that issues that have profound implications for fundamental human values are not irrelevant to the concerns of the university and ought not to be excluded from the exchange be-

tween professors and their students. They met some of the needs
of students for meaningful communication with their teachers
around issues about which they both cared. The sense of intimacy
and colleagueship between students and professors that characterized teach-in activities is only matched, in my experience, by
student-professor relations in successful small seminars or in joint
work in the laboratory. The relationship between students and
teachers has not, of course, been devoid of conflict, particularly
as the tactics of protest moved from debate to confrontation. But
there is the new understanding, shared by both groups of activists,
that the interplay between knowledge and values is at the heart
of the university's business.

The sense of urgency about current events. In Chapter
Two I spoke about the "triple revolution"—the revolution in
weapons systems, in systems of production, and in human rights—
which holds promise for a better world if we react to it constructively and wisely, but which also seriously threatens our basic
values if we fail to recognize and respond to the challenges it
poses. Again and again we have been required to come to grips
with these new and ever-changing forces, lest our own society and
the entire world order break apart. The confrontations in Berlin
and in Cuba have underscored the danger of a nuclear exchange
and the urgency of establishing mechanisms of international security. The changes in our methods of production have called
attention to the pockets of poverty in this otherwise affluent nation
and have underscored the danger that, as cybernation progresses,
the gap between the rich and the poor might widen, a segment of
the population might become frozen into a pattern of poverty,
and this permanently excluded group might become increasingly
a source of social unrest and disorganization. The dissolution of
the colonial empires, the demands for social justice in the less
developed parts of the world, and—as part of this world-wide
movement—the racial struggle in our own country have dramatized the dangers of maintaining a society, national and international, in which privilege and power are the prerogatives of the
white race.

In the context of these revolutionary forces, many intellectuals have developed a sense of urgency about the search for new
directions in our national and international affairs. They see these

forces as powerful demands for a more inclusive definition of national and international society. Their activism reflects the conviction that, if we fail to respond constructively and sympathetically to the challenges posed by these forces, we will both miss an unusual opportunity for a saner and more just social order and expose ourselves to serious dangers of violent disruptions and global war. The sense of urgency that provided some of the impetus for the new activism was further deepend by the emergence—not surprisingly—of an opposite response to the revolutionary forces of the day: the response of "right-wing" activism, that is, the attempt to meet the challenge of these forces by shoring up and intensifying an *exclusive* (chauvinistic, segregationist, antiwelfare) definition of the national and international systems. As these elements became more vociferous and succeeded, at least for a while, in capturing the Republican Party, those of us who felt the urgent need of a positive response to the triple revolution were more strongly impelled to speak out.

The Vietnam war has greatly added to this sense of urgency. Dissenters have been concerned not only about the sanity and morality of our Vietnam policy itself, but about the broader implications of our actions in Vietnam for American foreign policy in general and for our way of ordering national priorities. The approach to which we have been committed in Vietnam has locked us into a foreign policy that presents grave threats to world peace and to those of our national values that are basic to just and humane relations with other peoples and to the maintenance of a democratic society at home. Activism has been mobilized in response to the desperate need for alternative approaches that would pull us out of the morass in Vietnam, prevent the occurrence of future Vietnams, and help to reverse the general direction in which our foreign policy is moving.

LONG-RUN IMPLICATIONS OF VIETNAM POLICY

The intense opposition that the Vietnam war has generated among intellectuals and increasing numbers of other Americans is rooted in a feeling of moral repulsion. Dissenters see the war as lacking in any moral justification and are deeply concerned about what it does to the Vietnamese people and, in the process, to the American people. They feel a particular sense of urgency because of the implications that our posture in Vietnam has for American foreign policy in the long run. Specifically, they are disturbed about the pattern that Vietnam policy sets for our relationship to China and the rest of the Communist world; for our relationship to the developing nations of Asia, Latin America, and Africa; and for the relationship of the Administration to the American public in the formulation and conduct of foreign policy.

Relationship to China. Our actions in Vietnam have always faced the danger—and that danger is still very real—that they might lead to further escalation, culminating in a massive land war with China, with the possible involvement of the Soviet Union, and perhaps even in the ultimate nuclear exchange. Our attitudes about the possibility that China might enter into the war have been quite unrealistic and contradictory. On the one hand, we have assumed that China is relentlessly aggressive, bent on world conquest, regardless of the consequences. On the other hand, we have assumed that she is completely rational and will not risk a military confrontation with the United States. We take Chinese remarks about fomenting revolution and destroying American capitalism at face value, accepting them as literal truth. Yet we dismiss Chinese threats of coming to the aid of North Vietnam. The clear indications are that China is neither as aggressive nor as rational as our policy-makers assume. The likelihood of her entering the war depends only in part on deliberate calculations. In large part it depends, as it does for all nations, on the reactions of Chinese leaders to certain momentary circumstances and on the extent to which they become caught in an irreversible chain of events. Thus, our stereotyped, unrealistic image of China may lead to very serious miscalculations about the possibility of a major war.

Quite aside, however, from the possibility that the conflict in Vietnam may escalate into a war with China, it sets the pattern for our future relationship with China and the rest of the Communist world. The analytic framework within which our Vietnam policy is embedded is the Cold War philosophy, conceived in its narrowest terms. According to this philosophy, the only distinction on which policy can be based is that between Communism and anti-Communism, which is tantamount to a distinction between evil and good. It does not allow for differentiations, either within a given Communist regime or between Communist regimes. For example, it does not recognize the possibility that some of China's behavior might be accounted for in terms of its historical experiences or its national interests, rather than its Communist ideology; or the possibility that North Vietnam, despite its Communist regime, may have interests and purposes quite distinct from those of China. In line with these absolute images, the Cold War philosophy assumes that any advance of Communism, wherever it occurs and no matter how small or indirect it may be, constitutes a threat to us and must be blocked.

There does exist a genuine conflict of interests and values between the Western and the Communist worlds (or between segments of them, since neither one of these "worlds" is monolithic) and there are valid reasons for pursuing peaceful competition between them. The Cold War framework, however, dwells on the East-West conflict to the exclusion of everything else. Foreign policy is determined entirely by the desire to contain Communism. Those who share this desire gain our support, regardless of their other qualifications; those who are not prepared to join this enterprise are automatically suspect. The Cold War framework is oblivious to realities and indifferent to values that are unrelated to the East-West conflict. Furthermore, since the containment of Communism is based primarily on military means, a corollary of the Cold War philosophy is the requirement to maintain American military power, almost everywhere and at almost any cost. Military predominance thus achieves priority among our national goals.

Fortunately, during the years since John Foster Dulles, we have gradually moved away from this kind of narrow and exclusive Cold War approach. As a result, in our relations with countries that are not directly touched by the East-West conflict —particularly, I believe, in our relations with Africa—we have been able to develop policies that are relatively independent of the Cold War framework. Moreover, in our relations with the Soviet Union, we have been able to recognize the existence of mutual interests and to develop a policy based on the reduction of tension, on increased cooperation, and on the exploration of steps toward disarmament.

However, in our relations with China—who has become our primary adversary—we are now repeating exactly the same pattern that we have finally learned to abandon in our relations with the Soviet Union. Dean Rusk's pronouncements about China contain unmistakable echoes of the words of John Foster Dulles. If anything, the images that we have of China (and, by the same token, that China has of us) are even more stereotyped, undifferentiated, and hopelessly unrealistic than our images of the Soviet Union used to be, since the United States and China have chosen to isolate themselves from any valid information about each other. The debate on Vietnam and the resulting anxiety about our deteriorating relationship with China have brought some movement toward a more realistic China policy. The new policy, epitomized by the concept of "containment without isolation," represents a step in the right direction. The emphasis on containment, however, with the clear implication of reliance on military power to achieve such containment, indicates that we are still wedded to the basic assumptions of the Cold War framework.

The main effect of our Vietnam policy is to lock us ever more firmly into a relationship with China based entirely on Cold War assumptions. Even if we manage to avoid a war with China in the near future, the type of policy we are pursuing, based on maintaining a strong military presence in Southeast Asia and on blocking by military means anything that looks like a Communist advance, presents the constant danger of a major confrontation with China. It interferes with possible efforts to discover common interests with China and to negotiate arms control and disarmament agreements. It reduces the likelihood that the region will achieve stability through the development of neutral and independent regimes that are politically legitimate and meet the needs of their populations. And, finally, it threatens the détente that has been achieved, after so much effort, between the West and the Soviet bloc.

Relationship to the developing nations. The implications of our Vietnam policy for our relations with China and the Communist world are of deep concern because of their direct relevance to world peace. But perhaps even deeper is the concern aroused by the implications of our Vietnam policy for America's relations to smaller and weaker nations—to Vietnam in particular, and to developing countries in general. If the former set of implications raises questions about the sanity of our foreign policy, the latter raises questions about its basic morality.

The strongest reactions of the dissenters from Administration policy focus on the nature of the role that we are taking in Southeast Asia and on what we are doing to the Vietnamese people in the process. We are bombing, killing, and destroying the homes and the livelihoods of the very people we are supposedly protecting. We are committing or supporting acts of cruelty and torture of which innocent civilians are often the victims, acts in no sense mitigated by the use of cruelty and torture by "the other side." We claim to be fighting for the preservation of the freedom and national independence of the South Vietnamese people, when it is apparent that the government of South Vietnam does not have the support of the majority of the people and shows little concern for their freedom and democratic rights. We claim to be defending the South Vietnamese people against external aggression—a claim on whose basis we have taken the war to the North —when it is clear that, whatever else may be true, this war is primarily part of an internal conflict and the product of a social revolution. In short, our government is conducting a war that causes extreme suffering to the Vietnamese people without any convincing indication that this war is in any sense related to the interests of these people—that it protects them against aggression, or advances their freedom and independence, or meets their real human needs.

The apparent meaning of this war to the Vietnamese people—what it does to them and fails to do for them—has created profound misgivings about the moral basis of our Vietnam policy in the minds of many Americans. Such widespread concern about the morality of our foreign policy represents a new phenomenon. Many of us have questioned the wisdom of American policy in relation to the Soviet Union and to the conduct of the Cold War, but very few have questioned its basic morality. Even those who have felt strongly the need to find a way out of the Cold War and to respond to the dangers of the modern revolution in weapons systems by exploring more innovative steps toward disarmament and mechanisms for international security than we have been prepared to do so far, have not thought of the United States as an aggressor in its relations with other nations. We may have criticized American foreign policy for lack of imagination and insight, for overreliance on military solutions, for excessive brinkmanship in its approach to military confrontations coupled with excessive cautiousness in its approach to disarmament—but not for the pursuit of an aggressive course designed to impose our power on the rest of the world. The implication of our actions in Vietnam, however, is that our government is indeed engaged in an aggressive policy of imposing its will on smaller and weaker nations, regardless of what motivations may underlie such a policy.

These implications immediately bring into play larger questions about the pattern for our relationship with the developing world in general that is set by our policy in Vietnam. Again, our Vietnam policy—and the attitude toward other developing countries in Asia, Latin America, and Africa that it reflects and foreshadows—are embedded in a narrow Cold War framework. Our approach to Vietnam is the product of a foreign policy that gives primacy to the containment of Communism, everywhere and at all costs, and to the maintenance of our status as the greatest world power. The pursuit of these goals has blinded us to the social revolutions that are occurring in the developing countries in the wake of the dissolution of the colonial empires—revolutions that are demanding national independence, social justice, and participation in the benefits of the modern world regardless of race or color. We place so much emphasis on the possibility that a social revolution may be captured by the Communists and may represent an act of Communist expansion that we often fail to see the human needs and strivings that underlie this revolution. Instead of responding actively and positively to these needs, in line with our national tradition, we take, in effect, a stand against social revolution, as we are doing in Vietnam and as we have done in the Dominican Republic.

We are so obsessed with the righteousness of our efforts to contain Communism and maintain our military power that we become oblivious of the rights of smaller nations to develop their own way of life and to pursue their own purposes. While remaining convinced of our own nobility, we treat them with contempt, as pawns in our larger global enterprises. In short, the new moral questions that are brought into focus by the Vietnam crisis, and that were not involved in our conflict with the Soviet Union, are part and parcel of the larger question of America's role vis-à-vis the developing world and the social revolutions occurring within it.

Let me put my argument in other terms. We might distinguish, very broadly, between two kinds of worldwide conflicts: the conflict between East and West, and the conflict, roughly speaking, between North and South, that is, between the industrialized and the developing parts of the world. There have been promising signs that the East-West conflict may be resolved without the outbreak of a world war; both sides seem ready for such a resolution. This does not mean that the possibility of such a war can be dismissed. One of the dangers of the Vietnam crisis has been precisely, as I have indicated, that its escalation might set into motion forces that would inadvertently bring on a war between the United States and the Soviet Union, even though neither side desires it and even though such a war would essentially be an anachronism. But the larger concern raised by the Vietnam crisis relates to the North-South conflict.

If we fail to understand and to respond constructively to the social revolutions in the developing countries, we may be confronted with a war between the poor and the rich parts of the world, divided along racial lines. Our position in Vietnam—and elsewhere in the developing world, such as the Dominican Republic—betokens such a failure to understand. We have interpreted and responded to the demands for social justice and full participation on the part of those populations who have hitherto been excluded from the benefits of the modern world in terms of the clichés of the Cold War. In doing so, we have helped to deepen the racial and economic divisions of the globe and cast our country in the role of the foremost rich, white defender of the status quo. Our policies in Vietnam have increasingly taken on the aspect of a new American imperialism. Though different from the imperialism of earlier centuries, it is nonetheless foreign to our national self-image and deeply disturbing to those of us who want America to participate in the worldwide struggle for the extension of human rights and not to take up arms against it.

Relationship to the American public. The nature of the Vietnam war, the fact that it lacks the kind of apparent moral justification that other wars (whatever else we may think of them) have had, has also produced some disturbing domestic consequences within the United States. There have been deliberate attempts to control information, to withhold it, and even to distort it (as, for example, in the White Paper issued early in 1965). The reports on the procedures of news management in Vietnam and the revelation that the Administration lied about Hanoi's lack of responsiveness to peace feelers (see Schurmann, Scott, and Zelnik, 1966) have created a situation in which the public can no longer believe statements about Vietnam coming out of Washington. Moreover, there have been repeated attempts to discourage and undermine debate and to force a consensus on Congress and the American people.

That governments engage in the control of information and the engineering of consent is, of couse, not new, even in democracies, but these efforts are particularly blatant in relation to Vietnam policy. Communications about Vietnam have been characterized, even more so than foreign policy communications usually are, by Newspeak and mythology. We speak of protection when we mean attack, of external aggression when we mean internal warfare. Our policy-makers have not only communicated these myths, but have actually acted upon them. Since they have felt better able to justify and to fight a war against external aggression than the kind of war that is in fact taking place in Vietnam, they have acted as if this war *were* primarily a war of external aggression—and by doing so they have increasingly made it such. In this atmosphere it has been impossible to review and discuss policies rationally, in keeping with the tenets of an open society.

The Administration has acted with contempt toward Congress, toward the intellectual community, and toward the general public in its formulation and communication of policies on Vietnam. It has taken the attitude that there is no need to inform the public, no need to consult and listen to those who may have different points of view to offer. It has reacted with impatience to any debate or criticism, and has preferred to discourage debate and to dismiss criticism as being based on ignorance of the true facts on the part of those who are not privy to secret knowledge, although, of course, the predictions of the critics have been confirmed far more often than those of the Administration.

This contempt for the opinions of Congress and the public is symptomatic of the new type of foreign policy-making of which our actions in Vietnam are a prime example, namely, foreign policy built on the principle of counterinsurgency. It is in the nature of counterinsurgency that it is carried on by secret bureaucracies whose activities neither can afford nor are required to be exposed to public view. According to Roger Hagan (1964):

> . . . the new stress on counter-insurgency places decisive power in the hands of a bureaucracy almost completely immune to Congressional and public scrutiny: and this is power to do many things—to change the balance of social forces in other societies, to create the image of America that most of the world receives, to give our opponents full pretext to break international law, and to circumscribe the effectiveness of all the other policies and programs we undertake to promote international law and social justice. History will be made by these secret bureaucracies, in ways, and in pursuit of goals, determined with less and less reference to American politics or values, and with almost no sensitivity to minority criticism. If foreign policy has never been directly subject to democratic control, it has been susceptible to surveillance and sensitive to public debate. This will be less so than ever. Even *ex post facto* legislative review and electoral judgment will be difficult, because our role in events will never be clarified (p. 86).

Thus, our Vietnam involvement is likely to strengthen a fundamentally antidemocratic pattern for the relationship between the Administration and the American public in the conduct of foreign policy, to remove foreign policy, with all of its relevance to central national values, from the domain of public discussion.

It is to the everlasting credit of the teach-in movement, of the critics in the universities, in the churches, and in the wider intellectual community, and of a small number of courageous

Senators, that—despite systematic discouragement—debate was carried on and dissent continued to be voiced. The attempts to identify dissent with treason and Communism have, on the whole, been unsuccessful. There has been no inclination on the part of dissenters to fold up in the face of smears, and most though not all responsible Administration officials have shied away from the use of such smears. This does not mean, however, that they have paid much serious attention to the dissenters, although the existence of vociferous dissent has probably slowed down the rate of escalation and has certainly contributed to the opening of the Paris negotiations. The attitude expressed by the Administration has been that dissent is a basic right in a democracy and, though unpleasant and dangerous, must therefore be tolerated as a necessary evil. Dissent has not been viewed as a source of new ideas, new insights, and possible new directions for a bankrupt policy. Instead, while it has been tolerated, every effort has been made to minimize and discredit it, to claim that the dissenters represent a very small proportion of the population, that they lack relevant information, that many of them, though sincere, are dupes, and that in any event they are deficient in patriotism and are aiding the enemy.

Perhaps the most bizarre and at the same time most illuminating reaction to the criticisms of our Vietnam policy has been the oft-repeated statement that such criticisms will cause the enemy to infer a lack of unity and of a will to fight in the United States and to anticipate the imminent collapse of the American effort. There is the clear implication that the critics ought to maintain silence, lest they give the enemy "the wrong idea" and thus prolong the war. In fact, it is highly doubtful that the American protest movement is a major factor in the calculations of Hanoi and Peking, no matter how much they may dwell on it in their propaganda. But, even if it were, the suggestion that criticism ought to be curtailed because it might create "the impression" of a lack of unity points up, among other things, the delusion and self-delusion on which the Administration's Vietnam policy is based.

In the absence of a legal or moral justification for this war, in the absence of a meaningful debate within the United States, and in the absence of genuine support from our allies, the

Administration ultimately bases its action on the consensus of the American people. This consensus does not exist because the conditions for its development have never existed; instead, its existence has been decreed. Having based its policy on this illusory consensus, however, the Administration has then turned around and accused its critics of threatening the policy by creating the impression of a lack of consensus. Instead of recognizing the criticisms as an indication of serious divisions and reviewing policy in the light of this fact, our leaders have disingenuously asked their critics to join in the deception by preserving the appearance of consensus.

We have come full circle. Appearance has been substituted for reality in the process of policy formation, and this is followed by attempts to manufacture a reality conforming to the appearance. The pattern of ignoring facts, of basing our policy on what we would like to believe and then trying to mold reality to conform to our wishes, which has characterized our whole conduct of this war (as illustrated, for instance, in our insistence that the conflict is caused by aggression from an outside power, or that Generals Thieu and Ky are genuine leaders of the Vietnamese people), has thus been repeated in our government's relationship to its own public. The policies of a democratic society derive their strength from the fact that they reflect an actual consensus, worked out through the process of debate and discussion, of examination of criticisms and minority views, of weighing and adjustment of conflicting interests. When the Administration perceives its task as that of creating the appearance of a consensus rather than achieving the reality of one, then our type of democracy is severely threatened. This, however, may well be the pattern of foreign policy-making that is institutionalized in the wake of our Vietnam experience.

⤳ THE FUNCTIONS OF DISSENT ⤶

The Administration's Vietnam policy and the trends in foreign policy-making that it exemplifies and strengthens violate the requirements of a moral and sane response to current realities. It is the nature and the long-run implications of this policy that are of such deep concern to Administration critics and that contribute heavily to the level and intensity of activism today. Critics ask whether a policy can be moral if it places the maintenance of exclusive military power and economic privilege above the extension of social justice and political participation in the hierarchy of national goals; and if it uses destructive, oppressive, and exploitative means in the pursuit of these narrow goals. They ask whether a policy can be sane if it concentrates on ends that cannot be achieved or that can be achieved only at an extreme sacrifice in other values; and if it uses means whose costs and risks are far out of proportion to the probability of their success and to the importance of the goals pursued.

In short, the critics are raising basic questions about the relationship between means and ends in our national policies: Are the means we are using commensurate with the ends we hope to achieve? Are they capable of achieving these ends at all and, if so, at what cost in other values that have to be sacrificed in the process? And, conversely, are the ends that we have chosen to pursue and to which we have assigned priority in our hierarchy of values appropriate, given the nature of the means at our disposal and of the other ends that we have thus chosen to displace? Indeed, it is this kind of questioning of the relationship between means and ends, and the effort to restore the balance between the two, that lies at the heart of the critic's task.

There are three major ways in which dissent can contribute to this process of reassessing the balance between means and ends in our national policies: (1) It can bring new perspectives to bear on the formulation of policy, thus aiding in the search for alternatives in which means and ends are more properly balanced. (2) It can challenge an apparent national consensus, thus demonstrating that existing policy is neither sacred nor self-evident and that the relationship between means and ends remains open to question. (3) It can refuse cooperation with existing policies, thus calling for a testing of these policies against the basic values of the society.

The search for alternative perspectives. Whatever area of national policy we may be considering, the radically changing circumstances of our domestic and international life require a constant infusion of new ideas and perspectives into the policy process and a continuing review of our goals and actions in the light of these. I pointed out in Chapter Four that a regular flow of such new inputs is essential if we are to achieve a proper relationship between means and ends in our foreign policy, but that our policy-making machinery is not equipped to generate these new inputs or to utilize new ideas and data generated elsewhere. Our policy-makers tend to be caught within a limited factual and analytic framework, and to select their ends and means in terms of this framework, thus ignoring new realities and new possibilities that might be quite apparent if they were able to view the problem from a different perspective. The dynamics of the policy-making structure are such that, once a particular framework is adopted, it tends to perpetuate itself and each policy move is likely to strengthen the decision-makers' commitment to it. Even when outside consultants are brought in, they usually contribute in terms of the existing framework, rather than question its assumptions and call for a new perspective.

Clearly this is what has happened to our policy in Vietnam. The difficulty in finding alternative solutions in the Vietnam crisis is caused, at least to a large degree, by the excessively narrow framework within which our policy-makers have approached the problem. Their thinking has been dominated, as I have already argued, by the assumptions of the Cold War and the commitment to contain Communism and maintain American power everywhere and at all costs. These assumptions have led us into a dead end on the issue of Vietnam, and it has proved impossible to develop an acceptable solution within their terms. Yet our policy-makers have been trapped by this pervasive framework, and helplessly pulled by it into actions that are both futile and dangerous. What is desperately needed, then, is a way out of this trap, a way that would cut through the assumptions of the Cold War and permit us to define the problem in terms more accessible to solution. In other words, we need to bring radically new perspectives to bear on the issue, in the hope that these will generate policy alternatives that could not emerge out of the closed system of the Cold War philosophy.

But since new inputs into the policy process, which are so urgently needed, are unlikely to emerge out of the policy-making apparatus itself, it is part of the special role of the dissenter to serve as a source and stimulant of such new inputs. For intellectuals, in particular, the development of new perspectives and the consequent broadening of the range of policy alternatives represents a major challenge. As intellectuals we can and must go to the roots. We must, as I pointed out in Chapter Two, view the existing policy as only one of a range of possibilities, throw into question the assumptions on which it is based, and explore alternative assumptions on which alternative policies can be built.

The new inputs into the policy process that intellectuals can provide may be of different kinds, varying in the extent to which they are based on specialized knowledge. One source of expert inputs into the debate on Vietnam policy has been the work of the area specialists, who are in possession of a great deal of concrete information about the social, political, and economic conditions within Vietnam and within the larger region of which it forms a part. They have thus been able to introduce new facts, ignored by our policy-makers, and new analyses that have challenged some of the assumptions of current policy.[1] A second domain of expertise that can serve as a source of new analytic perspectives is represented by social and political theorists, who are able to suggest new ways of conceptualizing the problem of Vietnam that might yield alternative policy directions. Thus, in the international conference on "Alternative Perspectives on Vietnam" held in Ann Arbor in the fall of 1965 (see Converse, Kelman, and Vandenberg, 1966), we examined the problem of Vietnam from four different theoretical perspectives: the study of international systems, the study of social change and economic development, the study of conflict and conflict resolution, and the study of revolutionary warfare. These various theoretical approaches yield general propositions that can be applied to the

---

[1] An excellent example of the use of this type of specialized knowledge as an input into the policy process is the statement, recommending basic changes in U.S. policy toward China, issued by 198 scholars in the field of Asian affairs on March 21, 1966 (see Foonote 2, Chapter Four). This statement, coming from a group of people who are obviously knowledgeable and prestigious, provided an opening for the reconsideration of our China policy from a long-overdue, new perspective. Such an initiative could not very well come from inside an Administration locked into an anachronistic, unrealistic, and unproductive China policy.

special case of Vietnam. Such attempts may provide new handles for dealing with policy problems that could not have been found in the existing framework and set of assumptions.

It is interesting to note the important role that anthropologists have played in the dissent against the war in Vietnam, particularly since anthropologists as a group have had practically no previous involvement in peace action or peace research. I think it is not entirely a coincidence that anthropologists at the University of Michigan were instrumental in developing the concept of the teach-in, that the first speaker at the first teach-in was an anthropologist, and that the leaders of the teach-in movement on many campuses were anthropologists. Many disciplines have, of course, been actively represented in the movement, but I think there is some symbolic significance to the role of the anthropologists as prime movers on Vietnam. During an earlier phase of peace action in the academic community, it was the atomic scientists who played the key role and symbolized the form of the intellectuals' concern. They felt a special sense of responsibility because of their contribution to the development of nuclear weapons, and because of their knowledge about the nature and effects of these weapons. In similar fashion, I would propose, the anthropologists symbolize the form of the intellectuals' concern today. Some anthropologists, of course, have knowledge of Vietnam and Southeast Asia based on personal observation, and specifically the kind of knowledge that is required for the new analysis that the dissenters have been calling for: knowledge about the needs, values, and ways of life of the Vietnamese people—not just of the elites but especially of the population at large, and not just in the urban centers but especially in the villages. Beyond acquiring special knowledge about a particular area, the anthropologist, as part of his professional training, learns to view and value different cultures in their own terms, and to be sensitive to any indication of ethnocentrism or cultural arrogance. It is in this sense that the anthropologist symbolizes the new concern that has been activated by the Vietnam conflict—for it is fundamentally a concern with the human rights of distant people, who are weaker and poorer than we are, who have cultures and skin colors that differ from ours, but whose needs and values and rights are as important as ours and demand our total respect.

I have mentioned, so far, the new inputs into the policy process that intellectuals can make by virtue of their specialized knowledge and training. There are also, however, vital contributions of a nonspecialized nature that intellectuals and thoughtful citizens, scientists and artists, humanists and religious leaders, can make to the development of alternative perspectives. Until recently, defenders of the Administration policy in Vietnam placed great emphasis on the extent to which the protest movement was (according to them) dominated by nonspecialists. Aside from the fact that they consistently underestimated the representation of Southeast Asia specialists and international relations experts among the critics, and aside from their failure to realize that anthropologists, sociologists, and even some psychologists do indeed have specialized knowledge relevant to Vietnam policy, they failed to understand that the discussion of policy alternatives is a process to which every thoughtful citizen—certainly everyone who regards himself as an intellectual—can and must contribute. Questions about the proper relationship between means and ends in our national policies require the bringing together of specialized knowledge with imaginative, analytic thinking and with a sensitive concern for human values.

Thus, quite aside from specialized inputs, there are certain general contributions that the intellectual community can make to the consideration of policy issues and to the development of policy alternatives. These general contributions, at their best, consist in the ability to think analytically and undogmatically, in the orientation toward evidence and openness to different sides of each issue, in the readiness to abandon preconceived notions from the past and to entertain wide-ranging possibilities for the future, and in the application of knowledge and intelligence to the systematic solution of problems rather than to the formulation of slogans and the scoring of debating points. These intellectual contributions do not presuppose that we avoid feeling strongly about the value questions that a policy brings into focus. They go hand in hand with the raising of basic questions about the ends that our policy pursues and the values that it violates. Such questions must be guided by an evaluative perspective that avoids abstractions—that asks what a given policy alternative means to concrete human beings, to the satisfaction of their needs and the enhancement of their personal dignity. By deliberately addressing ourselves to these questions, we may find solutions that are more consistent with fundamental human values than American policy in Vietnam has been.

The challenge to an apparent consensus. As he raises basic value questions in the search for alternative perspectives, the dissenter also makes a second type of contribution: He challenges what might appear to be a national consensus and demonstrates that it is not universally shared. His mere expression of dissent communicates that the existing policy is neither sacred nor self-evident. He refuses to accept that policy by default and to recognize the official course of action as the only possible course, which is somehow required by the structure of reality. He thus helps to break the spell cast by existing policies by denying them the appearance of legitimacy that comes from an unchallenged consensus. He insists that there are indeed other ways of looking at the situation—both from a moral and from a prudential point of view—and that the relationship between means and ends remains open to question and reconsideration.

The act of challenging the claim of consensus by vigorously expressing dissent is especially important in view of some of the long-range implications of our Vietnam policy that I have discussed. If I am right in proposing that this policy reflects and reinforces a relationship to the smaller and weaker nations of the developing world based on the blatant use of military power and on a callous disregard for their rights, their needs, and their strivings, then it is indeed vital that at least a vociferous minority of Americans disassociate themselves from it. Even if this minority did not succeed in producing changes in national policy, it would provide a human bridge to other parts of the world from which this policy is increasingly isolating our country; it would keep alive certain traditional American values that this policy violates; and it would allow the history books to record that the advent of the new American imperialism did not remain entirely unchallenged.

Challenging the claim of consensus is equally important from the point of view of the domestic implications of our Vietnam policy. I suggested that we are setting a pattern for the process of foreign policy-making in which crucial decisions are made in secret, without consultation or debate by Congress and the public, and then legitimized by creating the appearance of a consensus. We can counteract these tendencies in foreign policy-making to the extent to which we refuse to be caught up in a manufactured consensus and expose its artificial character.

In challenging an apparent consensus, even a small number of dissenters can have a powerful effect. Some interesting leads about the dynamics involved in consensus-breaking come from a series of experiments on group pressure conducted by Asch (1965). Asch asked his subjects to carry out a simple task of perceptual judgment: matching the length of a given line with one of three unequal lines. The correct answer was usually obvious and under normal circumstances (in a control group) there were virtually no errors in judgment. Each experimental subject, however, made his judgments in a group situation in which, without his knowledge, all of the other "subjects" had been instructed beforehand to give the wrong answers on certain critical trials. Under these circumstances, only one fourth of the subjects remained completely independent, refusing to yield to the "group pressure" on all trials. The remainder yielded at least some of the time, with one third accepting the obviously false judgments of the majority on half or more of the trials.

There is one variation of the Asch experiment that is particularly suggestive when it comes to the potential of dissent. In this variation, *all but one* of the experimenter's collaborators were instructed to give false judgments. One group member, however, was instructed to deviate from the consensus and to give the correct answer on each trial. This procedure had a dramatic effect on the behavior of the experimental subjects. Only 5.5 per cent of the judgments in this condition conformed to the false majority, as compared to 32 per cent in the standard experimental condition. In other words, the fact that a single individual dissociated himself from the group consensus provided sufficient support for most subjects to permit them to resist the group pressure. By breaking the unanimity of the consensus, the lone dissenter established the fact that the group's judgment was not beyond question.

This finding, of course, cannot be automatically generalized to all situations. What it suggests is that, under the appropriate conditions, a lone dissenter or small minority may make a considerable difference. In the Asch experiment, the dissenter was, in every other respect, a "typical" group member who could not be readily dismissed, and, most importantly, he gave voice to misgivings that the subject himself felt. The conditions surrounding the dissent from the Vietnam war were comparable and, indeed, by breaking the unanimous consensus in support of Administration policies, the dissenters had a major impact.

Early in 1965 the dissenters were only a small minority of the American population and even of the intellectual community. Neither their numbers nor their credentials, however, were negligible. They succeeded in making the war a matter of debate, in establishing the fact that disagreement with Administration policies was both possible and legitimate. Gradually, with the help, of course, of events in Vietnam and throughout the world, they were joined by wide segments of the opinion leadership in the country and eventually by the majority of the general public.

Actually the evidence shows that public support for the Vietnam war was never wholehearted and that the dissenters were in fact giving voice to widespread misgivings. The Administration and the press had consistently overestimated the public's support for the war. They relied on the findings of commercial opinion polls, which can be quite misleading in this regard. Such polls usually use a single question or a small number of questions, calling for a simple approval or disapproval of existing policy. For example, the Gallup Poll has asked, "Do you approve or disapprove of the way Johnson is handling the situation in Vietnam?" The response to questions of this type is greatly affected by the general tendency to endorse existing policies and to support the President on foreign policy issues. Such questions provide no information on the depth of the support, on the public's possible reservations, or on its openness to various alternative policies. The Administration claimed the distribution of responses to such questions was an indication of support for the war. Moreover, it misread even these limited data to conclude that opposition to the President's handling of the war came mostly from those who favored greater escalation.

How misleading such poll data can be was demonstrated by a more intensive and sophisticated study of public opinion on the war carried out by a group of social scientists at Stanford University, in cooperation with the National Opinion Research Center, in February-March of 1966 (Verba *et al.*, 1967). They repeated the question about approval or disapproval of the President's handling of the situation in Vietnam and confirmed the finding of other polls conducted at that time: 61 per cent of their respondents expressed approval, as did 56 per cent of the respondents in the March 1966 Gallup Poll.[2] They asked many additional questions, however, which allowed them to put this finding in perspective. Thus, their data indicated that the majority of the public favored a negotiated settlement involving a willingness to deal with the Vietcong that went beyond Administration policy at the time. An overwhelming majority (88 per cent) expressed approval of American negotiation with the Vietcong. While the majority opposed American withdrawal, particularly if it was linked with a Communist take-over, they favored a new government with Vietcong participation and free elections in South Vietnam, even if these might lead to a Vietcong victory.[3] The Stanford–NORC Poll

---

[2] Since that time, of course, the proportion of the population expressing approval of the President's handling of the war has declined sharply. By July 1967, for example, only 33 per cent of the respondents in a Gallup Poll indicated approval, and it had become quite apparent that the disapproval was mainly accounted for by those who opposed continuing escalation. Late in March 1968, shortly before President Johnson announced his withdrawal from the presidential race and the limitation of bombing of North Vietnam, the proportion approving his handling of the war had gone down to 26 per cent.

[3] These data provide excellent illustrations of the effects of the wording of questions on the distribution of responses in opinion polls. "Withdrawal" is obviously a bad word, particularly if the implication of defeat is clearly drawn. Thus, 81 per cent of the respondents indicated that they would disapprove "if President Johnson were to announce tomorrow that we were going to withdraw from Vietnam and let the Communists take over." Disapproval dropped to 56 per cent when the alternative of "gradually withdrawing our troops and letting the South Vietnamese work out their own problems" was presented. When the word "withdrawal" is taken out and "free elections" are brought in, then a Communist victory becomes much less objectionable to the American public. Only 34 per cent in the Stanford–NORC Poll disapproved of "holding free elections in South Vietnam even if the Vietcong might win."

also found that the majority had reservations about continuing the war when faced with some of its possible economic or social costs, such as increased taxes or a reduced Medicare program, and some of the possible ways in which it might be enlarged, such as bombing the cities of North Vietnam or all-out mobilization of American men in the armed forces. Finally, the study showed very clearly that, contrary to previous press reports and Administration belief, those opposed to the President's handling of the war were more likely to be "doves" than "hawks," to favor de-escalation rather than escalation.

This study provides an excellent illustration of the potential contributions of social research to the policy process. Unfortunately, its findings were misunderstood and largely ignored by our policy-makers. It took another two years before the mood of the population, which was clearly revealed in the Stanford–NORC data, became apparent to the President and his advisers.

The reasons for the American public's misgivings about the war in Vietnam are no doubt varied and complex. Americans are probably not persuaded that the costs of the war are justified by its dubious returns. One source, however, of the general public's reaction, it seems to me, is a distaste for what we are doing in Vietnam—a moral repulsion which, though less articulate, is not too different from that experienced by the intellectuals. To quote Roger Hagan (1964) once more:

> Americans have never been enthusiastic, in our era, about meddling and complex "commitments" (the policy establishment's favorite masking term) to dubious allies and generalissimos. They have to be sold and re-sold on paper alliances like SEATO which are primarily American security operations. This is a decent suspicion. If it makes it hard for the Administration to aid Tito, it also makes it hard to stay in Vietnam, and millions of dollars have to be spent continually whitewashing Chiang to keep him even minimally acceptable. . . . What seems clear is that Americans lack an imperial impulse. The actions which constitute our seeming "imperialism" are not products of popular will, and so much the better for popular will (p. 87).

If Hagan is correct in this assessment, then the dissenters from the Vietnam war succeeded in calling into action some of the best elements in the American value system.

Non-cooperation with immoral policies. When an individual sees a policy as being not merely unwise but in violation of basic moral values, then he must seriously consider forms of dissent that go beyond debate and criticism. He must search for ways of dissociating himself from that policy, of refusing cooperation with it. In doing so, he not only reduces his personal complicity with the policy, but also enters a forceful plea for a fundamental reassessment of means and ends in national policies. He communicates that, in his view, existing policies—in the means they employ, or the ends they pursue, or the relationship between them—are so antithetical to the values of a decent society that it becomes incumbent upon the committed citizen to oppose the state, rather than support it, in the execution of these policies. Even if the ranks of non-cooperators remain small, the witness they bear to the violated values becomes part of the background for the government's actions. If the non-cooperators become sufficiently noticeable, because of their numbers, their social position, or the segments of the population they represent, then the government may well be confronted with a difficult choice. It may have to rely on the coercion rather than the voluntary support of important sectors of the society in order to continue its current policies, or else it may have to undertake a fundamental reassessment of these policies.

There is no way in which an individual can completely avoid complicity in immoral policies, as long as he remains within the society. He can, of course, withdraw from the society by emigrating, or going underground, or joining a self-sufficient community—actions that are appropriate if he regards the existing system as incapable of repair. But short of withdrawal from the society, non-cooperation can only be selective. Each individual must choose for himself the acts of non-cooperation that are most meaningful for him, in terms of their immediate relevance to the policies from which he seeks to dissociate himself, the general impact they are likely to have, and the price he is prepared to pay for his non-cooperation. Where precisely an individual draws the line is less important than the fact that he does draw a line, that he sets limits beyond which the state cannot take his cooperation for granted. Such selective non-cooperation is particularly appropriate for those who accept the basic values of the system but believe that existing policies violate these very values. By with-holding their cooperation they are, thus, insisting that these poli-cies be tested against the underlying values of the society.

Many forms of non-cooperation are completely legal, for example, conscientious objection to military service (for those who qualify under the existing law) or refusal to engage in weap-ons production or to sign loyalty oaths. When the law itself, however, requires complicity in immoral policies, the only rele-vant way of dissociating one's self from these policies may consist in selective acts of civil disobedience. I use the term "civil dis-obedience"—which is widely misunderstood and misrepresented —to refer to a deliberate, open, and announced violation of a law or a rule because it is seen as immoral, unjust, or in other ways inconsistent with some basic values of the society, and hence as illegitimate and no longer binding on the citizen.

Civil disobedience is a form of dissent peculiar to a demo-cratic society, in which authority is justified and limited by the consent of the governed and used in the pursuit of policies that represent the wishes, purposes, and aspirations of the population. Insofar as these conditions are met, the actions of the government are legitimate, and they are entitled to and obtain the voluntary support of the population. Civil disobedience is justified—and in fact obligatory in terms of the highest principles of citizenship— when legitimate processes break down in a system that is otherwise basically democratic. There are two interrelated components in such a breakdown of legitimate processes which, when they occur jointly, set the stage for civil disobedience:

(1) The government takes or condones actions that are in-consistent with certain important values on which the society and its political system are built, and that thus violate the basic as-sumptions on which the government's legitimacy rests. For ex-ample, as I pointed out in Chapter Nine, the prevailing policies, laws, and practices of American society vis-à-vis its Negro citizens have been unjust in that they have discriminated against one segment of the population and allowed advantages to some groups at the expense of and through the suppression of others.

(2) There are no adequate legal procedures available for individuals and groups to avoid complicity in these illegitimate actions of their government and to work effectively for change in

the policies, laws, and practices that they find abhorrent. In the struggle for racial equality, for example, effective legal procedures were unavailable because of the exclusion of Negroes from the political process and because of the imbeddedness of discriminatory practices in the nation's legal and social structures.

The war in Vietnam, in my opinion, provides an equally valid justification for civil disobedience. It is inconsistent with certain fundamental values of American society and is, in fact, abhorrent to wide segments of the population. Many of us see it as a violation of international law and morality, as an act of aggression against a small and weak people, as arrogant suppression of the forces of social change in the developing world, and as a resort to brutal means in the pursuit of questionable ends. Furthermore, we see the war as inconsistent with the vital interests of our society in that it alienates us from the rest of the world, risks the outbreak of total war, and causes both the exacerbation and neglect of our domestic crises. The Administration's actions in Vietnam are illegitimate, then, because they violate the values that we feel this nation has stood for and ought to stand for.

In an even more fundamental sense, it can be said that the actions of our government in Vietnam are illegitimate because they require citizens to violate their basic sense of human decency. When the price of loyalty is sacrifice of the citizen's sense of morality and justice, then the very foundations of the government's legitimacy have been destroyed and the citizen must dissociate himself from its policies.

Further, legal procedures for promoting change in the government's Vietnam policies have, to all intents and purposes, been unavailable, although they have begun to open up to some degree with Eugene McCarthy's challenge for the Democratic nomination. So far, the Administration has been inaccessible to the various elements in society that traditionally help to shape foreign policy. It has constantly ignored and discredited criticism from Congress, and from informed and articulate segments of the population. These actions may have been within constitutional limits, but legitimacy does not depend on mere adherence to the letter of the law. There is a presumpton that certain informal processes operate in the development of policy and that various elements of the society are able to gain a hearing and to exert some degree of influence. These informal processes have broken down, thus further adding to the illegitimacy of the Administration's Vietnam policy and to the justification for civil disobedience.

Civil disobedience is directed at a law or policy, not because it is detrimental to one's private, subgroup interests, but because it violates certain fundamental and universal values. A citizen engages in civil disobedience only when he is morally repelled by the law or policy and when its objectionable features touch on the core of his identity. He assumes that the values prompting him to engage in civil disobedience are widely shared in the society, even though they may be latent at the moment, and that they will become awakened in a majority of the population once they are dramatically called to their attention.

Civil disobedience does not represent a dissociation from society, but is, rather, an act of profound commitment to it. It is a *civil* act, that is, the act of a citizen manifesting his citizenship, not the act of an outsider. It is an act of *disobedience,* that is, a deliberate and often symbolic or even ritualistic violation of a specific rule, rather than a rejection of the system as a whole. The term "disobedience," in fact, has meaning only if one assumes that, in general, the system is entitled to obedience. Unlike revolution, which denies the legitimacy of the very system itself, civil disobedience merely denies the legitimacy of certain specific laws, policies, or practices of a specific administration, within the framework of the existing system. Those who engage in civil disobedience are usually more deeply committed to the values and procedures on which the system is built than those who always obey without question. They regard certain actions as illegitimate precisely because they see them as inconsistent with these values and procedures. By engaging in civil disobedience they are working toward a restoration of the system's legitimacy and integrity, and expressing a faith in the society's capacity to be true to its own values.

Far from threatening general respect for law and order, civil disobedience gives new meaning and vitality to law and order in the society. A system of laws and regulations is worthless if it can be maintained only by corecion. It must be accepted by the population as just, as consistent with basic values of the society, and as reflecting the aspirations of the population. In other words, it must be seen as legitimate and not merely arbitrary. Laws and regulations lose their legitimacy in the eyes of the population and come to be seen as mere instruments of state coercion unless there is an opportunity to challenge them, to throw them into question, and to test their congruence with constitutional provisions and broader principles. To mount an effective challenge, it is sometimes necessary to step outside these laws, particularly in times of great social change in which radically new problems have arisen, widely accepted values have become transformed, and traditional processes of informal influence on decision-makers have lost their efficacy.

In such times, there is more frequent resort to the well-established legal tradition of breaking a law in order to provide an occasion for a new judicial review of its constitutionality. This tradition is, in essence, a form of civil disobedience, linked to a very specific legal purpose. Civil disobedience in its broader sense fulfills a similar function in that it calls for a testing of government policies and practices against the basic values and procedures of the society from which they have deviated. It thus helps to revitalize these values and procedures by encouraging new interpretations, new ground rules, and new processes of informal influence in the light of changing circumstances. It represents, in short, an attempt to maintain the legitimacy of the system and to re-establish the basis of law and order in the voluntary support of the population rather than in the coercive power of the state.

To fulfill these functions effectively, civil disobedience must be based, as I have pointed out, on moral repulsion rather than mere personal dislike of a law or policy. The line between these two cannot be sharply drawn and, thus, the justifiability of civil disobedience in any given case must remain, in part, a matter of subjective choice. Nevertheless, there are some broad criteria for choosing the occasion and form of civil disobedience that can readily distinguish it from "taking the law into your own hands." These include strict adherence to nonviolence, readiness to accept punishment, as close a connection as possible between the action and the object of protest, and minimal alienation of the wider community.

(1) Nonviolent action, as I stressed in Chapter Nine, is more likely to mobilize the latent moral values of the majority,

on which the ultimate success of civil disobedience depends; and to keep the focus on the illegitimacy of the object of the protest rather than of the form of protest used. Moreover, a violent or highly punitive reaction by the authorities to a nonviolent protest helps to dramatize their reliance on coercive power, while a similar reaction to a violent protest will generally be seen as a legitimate exercise of the police function.

(2) Participants in civil disobedience violate rules deliberately and openly and must be prepared for jail or other legal consequences. This does not mean, however, that punishment is *necessary* to make the act of civil disobedience complete. Indeed, one of the outcomes of a successful campaign may be the repeal of a law whose legitimacy was challenged by the act of disobedience.

(3) Civil disobedience is most meaningful when the law or rule that it violates is the very object against which the protest is directed, such as the segregation laws in the civil rights struggle. Instances of protest against the Vietnam war that clearly meet this criterion are such actions as draft resistance and the support of draft resisters,[4] non-cooperation in war-related activities by members of the armed forces, refusal to pay war taxes, and delivery of medical supplies to North Vietnam, in all of which protesters disobey laws that require their complicity in the war. In other words, it is the evil law itself, the law that keeps the war machinery running, that is being disobeyed. There are times, however, when the act of civil disobedience has a less obvious relationship to the object of protest, for example when it involves a violation of rules against unlawful assembly. Civil disobedience

---

[4] Within the framework of civil disobedience that I have presented, efforts to expand the limits of conscientious objection are particularly relevant. I refer here to a commitment to a position of conscientious objection, whether or not it is based on religious grounds in the narrow sense of the term, and whether it is based on moral opposition to all war or to a particular war (that is, "selective" conscientious objection), a commitment coupled with a willingness, if necessary, to refuse induction and go to jail. This type of resistance has the virtue of denying support to the war while trying to establish a new conception of legitimacy, which does not force the individual to abandon his conscience to the demands of the state.

in such cases may serve to dramatize protest against existing policies, or to require a re-examination of these policies by making their execution more difficult. I would regard such uses of civil disobedience as justified when regular processes of debate have been effectively cut off, when less dramatic forms of protest have gone unheeded, and when opportunities for more direct forms of civil disobedience are unavailable.

(4) Civil disobedience inevitably alienates some segments of the population. In choosing the occasion and form of civil disobedience, however, it is relevant to consider, along with other factors, the probable reactions of others, and to keep their alienation to a minimum. The urgency of an issue may make it necessary to risk widespread social disapproval, at least for the short run. In the final analysis, however, it must be remembered that civil disobedience is a form of persuasion, whose success depends on awakening latent moral forces in the society.

The resort to civil disobedience must be highly selective and cautious. It should be contemplated only under such special circumstances and with an eye to such limiting criteria as those that I have discussed. My assumption is that ours is a democratic society, whose basic institutions and procedures—despite their serious flaws and despite the need for radical change—must be preserved and protected. Clearly, the frequent and undisciplined resort to disobedience poses severe threats to these institutions and procedures. It is at least equally clear, however, that democratic institutions and procedures cannot survive if they are harnessed in arbitrary fashion to the pursuit of illegitimate ends and if, in the face of such violations, the citizenry blindly yields to the demands of the authorities. Democratic processes become meaningless and corrupt if citizens never challenge official policies in terms of their consistency with basic societal and human values, if they never consider civil disobedience as an option of last resort. In a healthy democratic society, there is a time to obey and a time to disobey, a time to say yes and a time to say no, a time to speak in words and a time to speak in actions.

References

Ad Hoc Committee on the Triple Revolution. The triple revolution. *Liberation*, 1964, *9* (2), 9–15.

ASCH, S. E. Effects of group pressure upon the modification and distortion of judgments. In H. Proshansky and B. Seidenberg (Eds.), *Basic studies in social psychology*. New York: Holt, 1965. Pp. 393–401.

BAUMRIND, D. Some thoughts on ethics of research: After reading Milgram's "Behavioral study of obedience." *American Psychologist*, 1964, *19*, 421–423.

BEECHER, H. K. Documenting the abuses. *Saturday Review*, July 2, 1966, 45–46.

BERGIN, A. E. The effect of dissonant persuasive communications upon changes in a self-referring attitude. *Journal of Personality*, 1962, *30*, 423–438.

BERKUN, M. M., BIALEK, H. M., KERN, R. P., and YAGI, K. Experimental studies of psychological stress in man. *Psychological Monographs*, 1962, *76* (15, Whole No. 534).

BERREMAN, G. D. Anemic and emetic analyses in social anthropology. *American Anthropologist*, 1966, *68*, 346–354.

BRAMEL, D. A dissonance theory approach to defensive projection. *Journal of Abnormal and Social Psychology*, 1962, *64*, 121–129.

BRAMEL, D. Selection of a target for defensive projection. *Journal of Abnormal and Social Psychology*, 1963, *66*, 318–324.

BRIM, O. G., JR. American attitudes toward intelligence tests. *American Psychologist*, 1965, *20*, 125–130.

333

BROCK, T. C., and BECKER, L. A. "Debriefing" and susceptibility to subsequent experimental manipulations. *Journal of Experimental Social Psychology,* 1966, *2,* 314–323.

CAMPBELL, D., SANDERSON, R. E., and LAVERTY, S. G. Characteristics of a conditioned response in human subjects during extinction trials following a single traumatic conditioning trial. *Journal of Abnormal and Social Psychology,* 1964, *68,* 627–639.

Committee on Science and Astronautics, U.S. House of Representatives. *The National Science Foundation—its present and future.* Washington: U.S. Government Printing Office, 1966.

CONVERSE, E., KELMAN, H. C., and VANDENBERG, E. L. (Eds.). *Alternative perspectives on Vietnam: Report on an international conference.* Ithaca, N.Y.: Inter-University Committee for Debate on Foreign Policy, 1966.

CRAWFORD, T. J. In defense of obedience research: An extension of the Kelman ethic. University of Chicago, 1966 (mimeographed).

DADDARIO, E. Q. A revised charter for the Science Foundation. *Science,* 1966, *152,* 42–45.

DEMING, B. On revolution and equilibrium. *Liberation,* 1968, *12*(11), 10–21.

DEUTSCH, M., FISHMAN, J. A., KOGAN, L., NORTH, R., and WHITEMAN, M. Guidelines for testing minority group children. *Journal of Social Issues,* 1964, *20*(2), 129–145.

DIAMOND, S. Nigeria: The end of the first republic. *Africa Today,* 1966, *13*(2), 5–9.

Dissent in wartime: ACLU sees gathering storm, calls for vigil. *Civil Liberties,* July 1967, No. 247, 6.

DYNES, R., and QUARANTELLI, E. L. What looting in civil disturbances really means. *Trans-action,* 1968, *5*(6), 9–14.

ERIKSON, K. T. A comment on disguised observation in sociology. *Social Problems,* 1967, *14,* 366–373.

FARRELL, G. P., MARKLEY, O. W., and MATULEF, N. J. (Eds.). *Special Bulletin of the National Committee on Graduate Education in Psychology,* 1967, *1*(2).

FENDRICK, D. Feedback from readers: The life and death of Project Camelot. *Trans-action,* 1966, *3*(3), 2.

FESTINGER, L., and CARLSMITH, J. M. Cognitive consequences of forced compliance. *Journal of Abnormal and Social Psychology,* 1959, *58,* 203–210.

FILLENBAUM, R. S. Prior deception and subsequent experimental performance: The "faithful" subject. *Journal of Personality and Social Psychology,* 1966, *4,* 532–537.

FINMAN, T., and MACAULAY, S. Freedom to dissent: The Vietnam protests and the words of public officials. *Wisconsin Law Review,* 1966, No. 3, 632–723.

FRANKL, V. E. *Man's search for meaning: An introduction to logotherapy.* New York: Washington Square Press, 1963.

GOODMAN, W. Doctors must experiment on humans—but what are the patient's rights? *New York Times Magazine,* July 2, 1967, 12–13, 29–33.

GORDON, J. E. Snooping and testing. *New Republic,* January 9, 1965, 28–30.

GOULDNER, A. W. The norm of reciprocity: A preliminary statement. *American Sociological Review,* 1960, *25,* 161–179.

GREENBERG, D. S. Smale: NSF shifts position. *Science,* 1967, *158,* 98. (a)

GREENBERG, D. S. Smale: NSF's records do not support the charges. *Science,* 1967, *158,* 618–619. (b)

GREENBERG, M. S. Role playing: An alternative to deception? *Journal of Personality and Social Psychology,* 1967, *7,* 152–157.

GUETZKOW, H., ALGER, C. F., BRODY, R. A., NOEL, R. C., and SNYDER, R. C. *Simulation in international relations.* Englewood Cliffs, N.J.: Prentice-Hall, 1963.

HAGAN, R. Counter-insurgency and the new foreign relations. *The Correspondent,* 1964, No. 32, 79–87.

HAMILTON, C. V. An advocate of Black Power defines it. *New York Times Magazine,* April 14, 1968, 22–23, 79–83.

HANCE, W. A., and CURTIN, P. African studies in Africa and the American scholar. *African Studies Bulletin,* 1966, *9*(1), 24–32.

HOROWITZ, I. L. The life and death of Project Camelot. *Trans-action,* 1965, *3*(1), 3–7, 44–47.

HOWARD, J. Ethical problems in the study of a semi-secret organization. Paper read at the annual meetings of the Society for the Study of Social Problems, Chicago, 1965.

HUGHES, T. L. Scholars and foreign policy: Varieties of research experience. *Background,* 1965, *9,* 199–214.

HUXLEY, A. *Brave new world.* New York: Harper, 1932.

HUXLEY, A. *Brave new world revisited.* New York: Harper, 1958.

HUXLEY, A. *Island.* New York: Harper, 1962.

HUXLEY, A. *After many a summer dies the swan.* New York: Harper (Perennial Classic edition), 1965. (Originally published by Harper in 1939.)

JAHODA, M., and COOK, S. W. Ideological compliance as a social-psychological process. In C. J. Friedrich (Ed.), *Totalitarianism.* Cambridge, Mass.: Harvard University Press, 1954. Pp. 203–222.

JANIS, I. L., and KATZ, D. The reduction of intergroup hostility: Research problems and hypotheses. *Journal of Conflict Resolution,* 1959, *3,* 85–100.

JOHNSON, K. How foolish can we get? *Social Service Review,* 1954, *28,* 446–448.

KATZ, D. Group process and social integration: A system analysis of two movements of social protest. *Journal of Social Issues*, 1967, *23*(1), 3–22.

KATZ, M. M. Ethical issues in the use of human subjects in psychopharmacologic research. *American Psychologist*, 1967, *22*, 360–363.

KELMAN, H. C. Security and Federal employment: A recent case study. *Society for the Psychological Study of Social Issues Newsletter*, February 1957, 1–4.

KELMAN, H. C. Compliance, identification and internalization: Three processes of attitude change. *Journal of Conflict Resolution*, 1958, *2*, 51–60.

KELMAN, H. C. Processes of opinion change. *Public Opinion Quarterly*, 1961, *25*, 57–78.

KELMAN, H. C. Changing attitudes through international activities. *Journal of Social Issues*, 1962, *18*(1), 68–87. (a)

KELMAN, H. C. The induction of action and attitude change. In S. Coopersmith (Ed.), *Personality research*. Copenhagen: Munksgaard, 1962. Pp. 81–110. (b)

KELMAN, H. C. Internationalizing military force. In Q. Wright, W. M. Evan, and M. Deutsch (Eds.), *Preventing World War III*. New York: Simon and Schuster, 1962. Pp. 106–122. (c)

KELMAN, H. C. The role of the group in the induction of therapeutic change. *International Journal of Group Psychotherapy*, 1963, *13*, 399–432.

KELMAN, H. C. Social-psychological approaches to the study of international relations: Definition of scope. In H. C. Kelman (Ed.), *International behavior*. New York: Holt, 1965. Pp. 3–39.

KING, M. L., JR. *Where do we go from here: Chaos or community?* New York: Harper, 1967.

LAZARSFELD, P. F., and THIELENS, W., JR. (with a field report by D. Riesman). *The academic mind*. New York: Free Press, 1958.

LEAR, J. Do we need new rules for experiments on people? *Saturday Review*, February 5, 1966, 61–70. (a)

LEAR, J. Experiments on people—the growing debate. *Saturday Review*, July 2, 1966, 41–43. (b)

LIFTON, R. J. *Thought reform and the psychology of totalism: A study of "brainwashing" in China*. New York: Norton, 1961.

LOVELL, V. R. The human use of personality tests: A dissenting view. *American Psychologist*, 1967, *22*, 383–393.

LOWE, G. E. The Camelot Affair. *Bulletin of the Atomic Scientists*, 1966, *22*(5), 44–48.

MACDONALD, D. The root is man. *Politics*, 1946, *3*, 97–115, 194–214.

MCGUIRE, W. J. Some impending reorientations in social psychology: Some thoughts provoked by Kenneth Ring. *Journal of Experimental Social Psychology*, 1967, *3*, 124–139.

MILGRAM, S. Behavioral study of obedience. *Journal of Abnormal and Social Psychology,* 1963, *67,* 371–378.

MILGRAM, S. Issues in the study of obedience: A reply to Baumrind. *American Psychologist,* 1964, *19,* 848–852.

MILGRAM, S. Some conditions of obedience and disobedience to authority. *Human Relations,* 1965, *18,* 57–76.

MILLS, T. M. A sleeper variable in small groups research: The experimenter. *Pacific Sociological Review,* 1962, *5,* 21–28.

MULDER, M., and STEMERDING, A. Threat, attraction to group, and need for strong leadership. *Human Relations,* 1963, *16,* 317–334.

National Academy of Sciences. Report of the Committee on Loyalty in Relation to Government Support of Unclassified Research. Washington, D.C., March 13, 1956.

Office of Science and Technology, Executive Office of the President. *Privacy and behavioral research.* Washington: U.S. Government Printing Office, 1967.

ORNE, M. T. On the social psychology of the psychological experiment: With particular reference to demand characteristics and their implications. *American Psychologist,* 1962, *17,* 776–783.

ORWELL, G. *1984.* New York: Harcourt, 1949.

PETTIGREW, T. F. Social evaluation theory: Convergences and applications. In D. Levine (Ed.), *Nebraska symposium on motivation, 1967.* Lincoln: University of Nebraska Press, 1967. Pp. 241–311.

RIDGEWAY, J. The snoops: Private lives and public service. *New Republic,* December 19, 1964, 13–17.

RIECKEN, H. W. A program for research on experiments in social psychology. In N. F. Washburne (Ed.), *Decisions, values and groups.* New York: Pergamon Press, 1962. Vol. 2, pp. 25–41.

RING, K. Experimental social psychology: Some sober questions about some frivolous values. *Journal of Experimental Social Psychology,* 1967, *3,* 113–123.

RING, K., WALLSTON, K., and COREY, M. Mode of debriefing as a factor affecting subjective reaction to a Milgram-type obedience experiment: An ethical inquiry. University of Connecticut, 1967 (mimeograph).

ROGERS, C. R., and SKINNER, B. F. Some issues concerning the control of human behavior. *Science,* 1956, *124,* 1057–1066.

ROGIN, M. P. *The intellectuals and McCarthy: The radical specter.* Cambridge, Mass.: Massachusetts Institute of Technology Press, 1967.

ROSENBERG, M. J., and ABELSON, R. P. An analysis of cognitive balancing. In M. J. Rosenberg, C. I. Hovland, W. J. McGuire, R. P. Abelson, and J. W. Brehm, *Attitude organization and change.* New Haven: Yale University Press, 1960. Pp. 112–163.

ROSENTHAL, R. On the social psychology of the psychological experiment: The experimenter's hypothesis as unintended determinant of experimental results. *American Scientist,* 1963, *51,* 268–283.

ROSENTHAL, R., and FODE, K. L. Psychology of the scientist: V. Three experiments in experimenter bias. *Psychological Reports,* 1963, *12,* 491–511 (Monograph Supplement 3–V12).

ROSENTHAL, R., PERSINGER, G. W., VIKAN-KLINE, L., and FODE, K. L. The effect of early data returns on data subsequently obtained by outcome-biased experimenters. *Sociometry,* 1963, *26,* 487–498.

ROSENTHAL, R., PERSINGER, G. W., VIKAN-KLINE, L., and MULRY, R. C. The role of the research assistant in the mediation of experimenter bias. *Journal of Personality,* 1963, *31,* 313–335.

RUEBHAUSEN, O. M., and BRIM, O. G., JR. Privacy and behavioral research. *Columbia Law Review,* 1965, *65,* 1184–1211.

SCHEIN, E. H. *Coercive persuasion: A socio-psychological analysis of the "brainwashing" of American civilian prisoners by the Chinese Communists.* New York: Norton, 1961.

SCHURMANN, F., SCOTT, P. D., and ZELNIK, R. *The politics of escalation in Vietnam.* New York: Fawcett, 1966.

SEELEY, J. R. Psychoanalysis: Model for social science. *Psychoanalysis and the Psychoanalytic Review,* 1960, *47*(4), 80–86. (a)

SEELEY, J. R. Social science and psychoanalysis. Unpublished paper, originally presented at Toronto Psychiatric Hospital, November 15, 1960. (b)

SHAKOW, D. Ethics for a scientific age: Moral aspects of psychoanalysis. *Psychoanalytic Review,* 1965, *52,* 335–348.

SILVERT, K. H. American academic ethics and social research abroad: The lesson of Project Camelot. *Background,* 1965, *9,* 215–236.

SKINNER, B. F. *Walden Two.* New York: Macmillan, 1948.

SMITH, M. B. Conflicting values affecting behavioral research with children. *American Psychologist,* 1967, *22,* 377–382.

Society for the Psychological Study of Social Issues. Statement on the New York City Youth Board's report, "An experiment in predicting juvenile delinquency." *Society for the Psychological Study of Social Issues Newsletter,* April 1960, 1–2.

STEWART, W. H. An invitation to open dialogue. *Saturday Review,* July 2, 1966, 43–44.

STRICKER, L. J., MESSICK, S., and JACKSON, D. N. Suspicion of deception: Implications for conformity research. *Journal of Personality and Social Psychology,* 1967, *5,* 379–389.

Surgeon General's directives on human experimentation. *American Psychologist,* 1967, *22,* 350–355.

SWANN, M. Nonviolence: New directions needed. *WIN,* 1968, *4*(7), 6–7.

SYKES, G. M. Ethical issues in the behavioral sciences: Conference proceedings—Summary. University of Denver, 1966 (mimeographed).

TAJFEL, H. International cooperation in social psychology: Some problems and possibilities. *Bulletin of the British Psychological Society,* 1966, *19*(62), 29–36.

Testimony before House Special Subcommittee on Invasion of Privacy of the Committee on Government Operations, September 23, 1965. *American Psychologist,* 1966, *21,* 404–422.

TILLY, C. Communication to the editor. *The American Sociologist,* 1966, *1,* 84.

TOCQUEVILLE, A. DE. *Democracy in America.* (Edited by P. Bradley.) New York: Vintage Books, 1954.

U.S. House of Representatives. *A bill to amend the National Science Foundation Act of 1950.* H. R. 13696, 89th Congress, 2d Session, March 16, 1966.

U.S. House of Representatives. *A bill to establish a National Social Science Foundation.* H. R. 15459, 89th Congress, 2d Session, June 6, 1966.

U.S. Senate. *A bill to provide for the establishment of the National Foundation for the Social Sciences.* S. 3896, 89th Congress, 2d Session, October 11, 1966.

VALLANCE, T. R. Project Camelot: An interim postlude. *American Psychologist,* 1966, *21,* 441–444.

VERBA, S., BRODY, R. A., PARKER, E. B., NIE, N. H., POLSBY, N. W., EKMAN, P., and BLACK, G. S. Public opinion and the war in Vietnam. *American Political Science Review,* 1967, *61,* 317–333.

VINACKE, W. E. Deceiving experimental subjects. *American Psychologist,* 1954, *9,* 155.

WALSTER, E., BERSCHEID, E., ABRAHAMS, D., and ARONSON, V. Effectiveness of debriefing following deception experiments. *Journal of Personality and Social Psychology,* 1967, *6,* 371–380.

WILLIS, R. H., and WILLIS, Y. A. Role playing vs. deception: An experimental comparison. *Journal of Personality and Social Psychology,* in press.

WOLF, E. P. Some questions about community self-surveys: When amateurs conduct research. *Human Organization,* 1964, *23,* 85–89.

WOLFENSTEIN, M. The emergence of fun morality. *Journal of Social Issues,* 1951, *7*(4), 15–25.

WRIGHT, N., JR. *Black Power and urban unrest: Creative possibilities.* New York: Hawthorn, 1967.

Index